# Translation in Language Teaching
and Assessment

# Translation in Language Teaching and Assessment

Edited by

Dina Tsagari and Georgios Floros

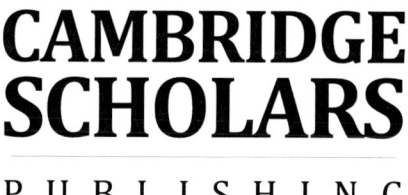

Translation in Language Teaching and Assessment,
Edited by Dina Tsagari and Georgios Floros

This book first published 2013

Cambridge Scholars Publishing

12 Back Chapman Street, Newcastle upon Tyne, NE6 2XX, UK

British Library Cataloguing in Publication Data
A catalogue record for this book is available from the British Library

Copyright © 2013 by Dina Tsagari, Georgios Floros and contributors

All rights for this book reserved. No part of this book may be reproduced, stored in a retrieval system, or transmitted, in any form or by any means, electronic, mechanical, photocopying, recording or otherwise, without the prior permission of the copyright owner.

ISBN (10): 1-4438-5044-6, ISBN (13): 978-1-4438-5044-5

# TABLE OF CONTENTS

PREFACE ..................................................................................... vii
*Dina Tsagari and Georgios Floros*

PART I: TRANSLATION IN LANGUAGE TEACHING

CHAPTER ONE ................................................................................ 3
Incorporating Translation into the Language Classroom and its Potential Impacts upon L2 Learners
*Tzu-yi Lee*

CHAPTER TWO ............................................................................. 23
Teaching Grammar through Translation
*Melita Koletnik Korošec*

CHAPTER THREE .......................................................................... 41
Audio Description as a Tool to Improve Lexical and Phraseological Competence in Foreign Language Learning
*Ana Ibáñez Moreno and Anna Vermeulen*

CHAPTER FOUR ............................................................................ 65
Translation Techniques in the Spanish for Heritage Learners' Classroom: Promoting Lexical Development
*Flavia Belpoliti and Amira Plascencia-Vela*

CHAPTER FIVE .............................................................................. 93
An Optimality Translation Proposal for the Foreign Language Class
*Christine Calfoglou*

CHAPTER SIX .............................................................................. 115
The Engaging Nature of Translation: A Nexus Analysis of Student-Teacher Interaction
*Marie Källkvist*

CHAPTER SEVEN ............................................................................. 135
Resurrecting Translation in SLT: A Focus on Young Learners
*Silva Bratož and Alenka Kocbek*

CHAPTER EIGHT .............................................................................. 155
From *Intercultural Speaker* to *Intercultural Writer*: Towards a New
Understanding of Translation in Foreign Language Teaching
*Raphaëlle Beecroft*

CHAPTER NINE ................................................................................ 173
The Didactic Use of Translation in Foreign Language Teaching:
A Practical Example
*Anna Kokkinidou and Kyriaki Spanou*

PART II: TRANSLATION AND LANGUAGE ASSESSMENT

CHAPTER TEN .................................................................................. 193
Test Adaptation and Translation: The Language Dimension
*Samira ElAtia*

CHAPTER ELEVEN ............................................................................ 215
Using Translation as a Test Accommodation with Culturally
and Linguistically Diverse Learners
*Sultan Turkan, Maria Elena Oliveri and Julio Cabrera*

CHAPTER TWELVE............................................................................ 235
Assessing Second/Foreign Language Competence using Translation:
The Case of the College English Test in China
*Youyi Sun and Liying Cheng*

CONTRIBUTORS ............................................................................... 253

# Preface

## Dina Tsagari and Georgios Floros

For a very long time and across various educational contexts and countries, translation was one of the most important tools for teaching and assessing language competence. Ever since the emergence of what became known as the *communicative turn* and the adoption of the communicative approach to language teaching, translation has gradually lost importance both as a teaching and as an assessment tool. This decline was mainly due to a) fallacious perceptions of the notion of translatability on the part of language pedagogy or a conflation of the use of L1 with translation, b) the equally fallacious interpretations of the translation task as the common attempt of finding lexical and structural correspondences among L1 and L2 (grammar-translation), and c) an inadequate—if not totally missing—attempt on the part of Translation Studies to examine ways of informing other domains of language-related activity in a manner similar to the way translation studies has consistently been informed by other disciplines. In other words, these circumstances were indexical of a relative lack of epistemological traffic among Language Learning and Translation Studies as disciplines in their own right. Nevertheless, the situation seems to start being reversed lately. Developments within Translation Studies seem to have led to a more confident profile of the discipline and Language Teaching and Assessment seems to be rediscovering translation as a tool for its purposes.

In this optimistic context, the volume attempts to a) record the resurgent interest of language learning in translation as well as the various contemporary ways in which translation is used in language teaching and assessment, b) explore new ways of consolidating the relationship between language learning and translation, by offering insights into future possibilities of using translation in language teaching and assessment, and c) examine possibilities and limitations of the interplay between the two disciplines in the light of current developments touching upon the ethical dimensions of such an interaction. The initial intention of this volume was to examine whether the call for reinstating translation as a component of language teaching (cf. Cook 2010) and assessment has indeed borne fruit and in which ways.

The volume accommodates high-quality original submissions that address a variety of issues from a theoretical as well as from an empirical point of view. Contributors to the volume are academics, researchers and professionals in the fields of Translation Studies and Language Teaching and Assessment as well as postgraduate students (PhD level) who have completed or are about to complete their doctoral studies in the area of teaching and assessing languages through translation. Covering a variety of languages (English, Chinese, Dutch, German, Greek, and Spanish) and areas of the world (the USA, Canada, Taiwan R.O.C., and European countries such as Belgium, Germany, Greece, Slovenia and Sweden) as well as various professional and instructional settings (e.g. school sector and graduate, undergraduate and certificate programs), the volume raises important questions in an area currently under scrutiny, but also attempts to show the beginning of perhaps a new era of conscious epistemological traffic between the two aforementioned disciplines—as an answer to the previously mentioned, long existing lack thereof—as well as between different parts of the world.

The volume is divided in two parts. Part I contains chapters focusing on new perspectives on how translation can be used for the teaching of core language skills (such as reading, grammar and lexis) as well as innovative general approaches to researching and using translation as a language teaching tool. Part II presents chapters focusing on the use of translation in the field of assessment, which we consider an additional innovative aspect of this volume.

Part I opens up with Tzu-yi Lee's contribution (Chapter 1), which presents findings of an experimental study designed to explore the use of translation in the reading EFL classroom. The author considers the potential impact of translation exercises on L2 learners' reading proficiency and offers pedagogical implications for both translation and EFL teachers for future curriculum design. In the next chapter (Chapter 2), Melita Koletnik Korošec addresses the role of translation in the acquisition of selected grammatical categories and reports findings of an experimental study that looks at the role of translation in linguistic competence acquisition and its influence on the development of translation competence in university students of translation. The author argues that translation activities and the judicious use of students' L1 in foreign language classrooms can be supportive of explicit language learning in the context of colleges and universities.

The next two chapters in the volume focus on the use of translation in the teaching of lexis. For example, Ana Ibáñez Moreno and Anna Vermeulen (Chapter 3) explore the use of Audio Description (AD) as a tool to improve lexical and phraseological competence in the language classroom. Through the use of a series of tools and didactic techniques that were implemented in the classroom, the authors conclude that, as a didactic tool in the foreign language classroom, AD contributes not only to the development of linguistic, but also of sociocultural competence, an essential part of language learning. In the same vein, Flavia Belpoliti and Amira Plascencia-Vela (Chapter 4) explore translation techniques to promote the development and growth of the lexical domain of Heritage Learners of Spanish by the means of implementing translation techniques as part of the language pedagogy used at university level. The results of this study show that translation-as-pedagogy has a positive effect in the language classroom, and allows for the expansion of the mediation abilities. The authors propose strategies that have a direct impact on improving lexical awareness and help learners explore language in a deeper way.

In the following five chapters, translation is presented both as a research and a teaching tool. In the first of these chapters, Christine Calfoglou (Chapter 5) focuses on the L1–L2 language pair and word order issues of Greek and English where learners draw on their L1 potential in a number of ways. The study proposes an experimental approach that could be made applicable to any pair of languages within a varied range of language phenomena, along the lines of Optimality Theory, shedding precious light on the learners' interlanguage. In the following chapter Marie Källkvist (Chapter 6), addressing the issue of how translation facilitates L2 learning, presents results from a qualitative study conducted in three EFL classrooms at a Swedish university. This longitudinal qualitative study framed by the Interaction Hypothesis and by task-based language learning and teaching shows in detail the student-teacher interaction that develops when translation tasks are used in the classroom discussing the value and room for translation in learning contexts. The author recommends that audio or video-recordings of the interaction taking place between students can provide interesting data about student-student interaction during the process of translating while quantitative and in-depth qualitative studies of student attitudes can also enrich our understanding of when to use translation for the purposes of L2 learning and build a firm theoretical and empirical basis that will enable the development of teaching practices that are evidence-based.

In a different educational context, Silva Bratož and Alenka Kocbek (Chapter 7) use translation in second language teaching by focusing on young learners with a view to encouraging learner autonomy and raising learner's awareness of the cross-cultural and linguistic differences between the first and second language. Several types of translation and contrastive activities are examined to demonstrate the different ways in which translation can effectively be used in early-level foreign language instruction. In the same light, Raphaëlle Beecroft's contribution (Chapter 8) aims at highlighting the didactic potential of the notion of translation as a holistic, communicative and (inter)cultural process for the secondary EFL classroom, the act of translation as a functional act of communication and the translator as an expert between source and target texts, situations and cultures. The chapter is aimed at teaching researchers and practitioners wishing to establish a productive dialogue between Translation Studies and Foreign Language Teaching by offering methodological recommendations on how to create and structure tasks integrating methods deployed in the subfield of translation didactics, e.g. the scenes-and-frames model and Think-Aloud-Protocols. In the last chapter of Part I (Chapter 9), Anna Kokkinidou and Kyriaki Spanou present trainee teachers' perceptions and practices regarding the use of translation in the teaching of Greek as a foreign or second language. The results of the study indicate that the majority of the teachers consider translation as an aspect of vital importance for foreign language learning, especially in terms of vocabulary acquisition. The paper concludes by presenting elements to be considered in the process of embedding translation in foreign language learning, i.e. before, during and after the translation activity.

Part II, devoted to the relationship of translation and language assessment, opens up with Samira ElAtia's contribution (Chapter 10). The author, responding to the practice of using tests outside their initial context, emphasizes the importance of the language dimension in test adaptation and translation (TAT) in the last decade and urges for more critical research on the subject. To this end, she considers issues relating to validity, reliability and fairness of assessment instruments. The chapter concludes by highlighting the interface between language assessment and TAT and the danger emanating from not addressing the different language facets in test development relying on test adaptation and translation. Discussing issues related to translation and language assessment, Sultan Turkan, Maria Elena Oliveri and Julio Cabrera (Chapter 11) discuss issues associated with using translation as a test accommodation in content assessments administered to culturally and linguistically diverse learners, specifically English learners (ELs) in the context of schooling in the United States. The issues raised in this chapter are related to improving the design, development, and validity of inferences made from assessments translated into a language other than English. The authors stress that if accommodations minimize construct-irrelevant variance associated with language learners' limited language proficiency, this proves that translation as an accommodation might successfully increase access to tested content and result in increased test fairness and equity for language learners. Youyi Sun and Liying Cheng work (Chapter 12) closes Part II. Their study investigates students' perceptions of the demands of the translation task in the College English Test in China and examines the relationships between students' performance on the translation task and their performances on listening, reading, cloze and writing tasks in this test. Findings of the study provide evidence for the validity of using translation task type to measure students' language competence and raise questions with regard to the measurement of the translational skills and strategies as defined in Translation Studies.

In sum, the contributions to this volume discuss various and innovative ways and contexts of using translation in the language teaching process. We therefore believe that there is not only substance to the claims that translation has an important role in language teaching, but also promising prospects for further elaboration. In fact, it seems that the *communicative turn* in Language Teaching, contrary to the excluding tendencies of the past, has now created a welcoming context for translation. We remain hopeful that the chapters of this volume will contribute to a narrowing of the gap between Language Teaching and Translation studies, and that, at the same time, they will offer an effective answer to students' needs in our increasingly globalised multicultural world. For this, we most sincerely thank our authors for sharing their expertise and experience in translation studies and foreign language instruction, theory and practice. We also hope that this volume will be useful to translation scholars, language practitioners, researchers, examination boards as well as graduate students with an interest in the field.

# Works Cited

Cook, Guy. 2010. *Translation in Language Teaching*. Oxford: Oxford University Press.

# PART I:

# TRANSLATION IN LANGUAGE TEACHING

# CHAPTER ONE

## INCORPORATING TRANSLATION INTO THE LANGUAGE CLASSROOM AND ITS POTENTIAL IMPACTS UPON L2 LEARNERS

## TZU-YI LEE

### 1. Introduction

Although English teachers often neglect or reject incorporating translation into language classrooms because of its close association with the grammar translation method, certain researchers (Whyatt 2009; Weydt 2009; O'Muireartaigh 2009) have proven that it is promising to apply translation tasks to improve L2 learner proficiency in language control and reading skills. Translation has mostly been recognized and used as a cognitive strategy in reading (O'Malley and Chamot 1990, 3), and considered a convenient method to verify comprehension of the source text (Vinay and Darbelnet 1995, 124). Although abundant literature exists in the professional translation field, studies on using translation as a reading assessment task remain scant and only two were found. Hence, it is much necessary to investigate the relationship between translation and reading comprehension. Among the relevant studies, Buck (1992) examined the reliability and validity of a translation-reading test in two studies. The satisfactory reports of both studies showed that translation tests had acceptable construct validity without nearly any method effect. However, translation as assessment should be used with extreme care to avoid any undesirable washback effect, referring to the degree to which the use of a test influences language teachers and learners to do things they would do to promote language learning (Messick 1996, 241), in classroom practice. In another study, Chang (2006) applied both the immediate written recall task and a translation task to explore the effect of memory on reader recall, and found that the translation task provided considerably more comprehension evidence than did the immediate written recall task. The translation task in Chang's study was based on word-by-word grading, which is understandable as language translation assessment, because Chang elicited the best reader comprehension from the original. In contrast to language translation assessment (Ito 2004; Chang 2006), we use professional translation assessment, an assessment method applied to translation courses. The assessment, different from the one language teachers usually use to score student translations, focuses on both accuracy and students' L1 expression which is important for the researcher in analyzing students' reading comprehension. It is expected that the use of professional assessment could provide useful teaching implications for language teachers. But the use of professional assessment is not the only aim of the study. More importantly, we attempt to investigate whether the use of translation could have any effects on student language learning, particularly on their reading comprehension competence.

## 2. Experiment

### 2.1 Research questions

We investigate whether the use of translation influences L2 learner reading comprehension, and address two research questions:
1. Does the use of translation after reading enhance student comprehension?
2. Is there any connection between student translation performance and their reading comprehension, particularly for EFL students with different backgrounds?

### 2.2 Participants

Participants were 35 undergraduate students enrolled in a Chinese/English translation course at a university in Northern Taiwan, including sophomores, juniors, and seniors. Although they had learned L2 (English) for more than 7 years, this was their first time to take a translation course. In this experiment, the students were divided into two groups, English majors, and non-English majors. Their different backgrounds were an important variable in this study.

## 2.3 Experiment procedure

Our experiment was conducted with the two student groups answering the two research questions. The experiment procedure was as follows: A reading passage in English was presented to the two student groups. After reading the article, the students were asked to translate two paragraphs of the reading passage into Chinese before answering five multiple-choice reading-comprehension questions. Among these five comprehension questions, three were related directly to the translated paragraphs, whereas the other two were not. The researcher investigated these five comprehension questions separately, depending on the relevance to the translation practices. This enabled us to determine whether translation could help students choose the correct answers to the comprehension questions. Combined with the analysis of their translations, we could indicate any misunderstanding or misinterpretation during the reading process, leading to wrong answers to the comprehension questions. Table 1 presents a summary of the experiment procedure.

| Group | Experiment Treatment | No. of students |
|---|---|---|
| **English Major** | Reading→Translation→Reading Comprehension Test | 24/26 (T1/T2) |
| **Non-English Major** | Reading→Translation→Reading Comprehension Test | 11 (T1/T2) |

Table 1. Overview of groups of students and of the experiment

The process was repeated the following week to increase the validity and the reliability of the experiment.

## 2.4 Translation assessment criteria

We used professional translation assessment to grade the student translations. After reading, students were requested to translate two paragraphs of the original text into Chinese. Their translation was scored based on the principles of a 6/4 scale (6 grades for "accuracy" and 4 grades for "expression") developed by Lai (2008), which has been applied in the national assessment criteria of translators and interpreters in Taiwan. Tables 2 and 3 provide the criteria used to assess the translation quality for accuracy and expression. For accuracy, a concept is coded as correct and points are awarded when the translated text is semantically equivalent or identical, or synonymous to the original. For expression, the translated sentences must be "readable" and "understandable." Points were awarded on a sentence-by-sentence basis. Scoring compares and contrasts student translation performance to their reading comprehension assessment conducted later. The two paragraphs translated in this experiment consisted of 10 sentences for a total score of 100.

| Score | Criteria |
|---|---|
| 6 | Messages in translation almost match the original with no errors |
| 5 | Messages in translation almost match the original, but with one minor error |
| 4 | Messages in translation different from the original, with two (or above) minor errors |
| 3 | Messages in translation different from the original, with one major error and three (or above) minor errors |
| 2 | Messages in translation vary significantly from the original, with two major errors or only pile-up descriptions |
| 1 | Messages in translation totally different from the original or with a lot missing in translation |

**Table 2. Translation Accuracy**

| Score | Criteria |
|---|---|
| 4 | Translation is clear and understandable with appropriate usages, register, collation, and punctuation |
| 3 | Translation is generally clear and understandable, but with one or two errors in usage and expression, typos, or redundant word |
| 2 | Translation is barely understandable, but with syntactical errors and inappropriate usage and expression |
| 1 | Translation is ungrammatical and difficult to understand, with many omissions |

**Table 3. Translation Expression**

## 3. Translation analysis and reading comprehension questions

The texts for translation and reading comprehension tests in this study were extracted from *Reading Fusion II* (Bennett 2010), a textbook series designed to help students improve their reading, vocabulary, listening, speaking, writing, and grammar skills. Each book contains various critical themes, including the environment, health, and technology. In these two experiments, we picked the topics of establishing love relationships and becoming young adults, which are expected to be more relevant to university students' personal lives. Conversely, they may stimulate more students' attention, and their relevance could help students gain background information.

For the text analysis, the study adopts professional translation assessment on a 6/4 scale with six grades for "accuracy" and four grades for "expression." During each experiment, the students are first asked to read an entire passage consisting of seven paragraphs for about approximately 15-20 mins, and then to translate two paragraphs, the first two of the passage, into Chinese. After the translation, five reading comprehension questions (Appendices A and B) are distributed to students, of which three are directly relevant to the two paragraphs that were translated, and the other two are related to the paragraphs they read but did not translate. For the three comprehension questions related to the two paragraphs they translated, two are inference-based and one is text-based. Thus, it is especially critical to determine how students of various backgrounds translated the two paragraphs and how they comprehended their translation, leading to a potential impact on their answering the reading comprehension questions. If we investigate and analyze students' translations, they may elucidate how they understand the paragraphs, and we can suggest teaching implications to enhance their reading comprehension. Therefore, the students' translation examples that correspond to the three comprehension questions they answer following the translation are particularly suited for discussion. For the convenience of analysis, the two paragraphs of the two passages in each experiment can be assessed in ten sentences. Students of different backgrounds are marked as English majors (EM) and non-English majors (NEM) in this study.

### 3.1 Test 1: Example 1

With respect to passage 1, we selected three sentences for discussion that contain the critical meaning of the passage, as well as those sentences the students translated incorrectly or misinterpreted. If the students misunderstood these sentences, we presumed that their answers for the comprehension questions could be influenced. The first sentence was extracted from the first paragraph of the passage: *[s]cientific interest in romantic love has turned up fascinating discoveries about the physiology of love, including the mapping out of several processes of physical attraction.* The underlined sentence parts were misinterpreted for either accuracy or expression, as shown in the back translations (BT) provided.

> (EM1) 科學研究上<u>浪漫綺麗的愛已被發現轉換心靈層次上的</u>，這含括了<u>一些心靈層面的接觸</u>。
> (BT: *Scientific research on romantic love has been found to be turned into the psychological level, this including some mental contacts*)
> 
> (EM2) 大部分的科學家<u>將自身對於浪漫愛情的興趣轉變成驚人的發現在心靈上</u>。
> 那包含了[…]許多<u>生理上吸引</u>的過程。
> (BT: *Most scientists turned their interests in romantic love into surprising discoveries in mental aspects. That includes a process of physical attraction*)
> 
> (NEM1) 科學家對愛情產生興趣，並對生理上的愛有更迷人的發現，包括<u>在幾次生理刺激後所提供的信息</u>。
> (BT: *Scientists are interested in love and have surprising discoveries in physiological love, including messages provided by physical impulses*)
> 
> (NEM2) 科學對浪漫愛情的興趣，促使了愛情生理學上的驚人發現。
> 包含<u>它點出了</u>[…]受到外表吸引的<u>一些</u>過程。
> (BT: *Scientific interests in romantic love prompt surprising discoveries in the physiology of love. Including it grades out some processes of […] being attracted by appearance*)

Two examples by the English majors and two by the non-English majors (see above) were selected for discussion. At first, it was easy to see that the English majors made mistakes when translating the first part of the sentence, whereas non-English majors had problems in translating the second part of the sentence. The two English majors' translations were similar to the students' misinterpretation. The lexical item *turned up* in the original confused them, leading to different interpretations. The two versions included the misinterpretation of *turned up* as *turned into*, which is an accuracy error. Furthermore, the second part of the translation in EMS1 was diverted from the original and did not make sense. Thus, this sentence only received 4 out of 10 points. Conversely, the second translated version skipped a subject, which was marked as [...] in the back translation. This error led to reduced scores for accuracy and expression.

As for the two versions by the non-English majors, the first part of the sentence had no errors regarding translation accuracy and expression. However, all four students did not understand the meaning of the term *mapping out* in the second part of the sentence, causing translation errors in accuracy. In addition, in the second translation by non-English majors, the second part was broken with a period and the sentence was left unfinished. Therefore, two points were deducted for expression. The students tended to make translation errors mostly because of misunderstandings or term confusion. In other words, they had difficulty understanding unfamiliar terms, which could influence their answers if they encountered text-based reading comprehension questions. However, non-English majors may not be as good at expressing themselves in their first language. More cases are needed to prove this assumption.

## 3.2 Test 1: Example 2

The second sentence was selected from the second paragraph of the first passage, which was interpreted and understood differently among the students, especially the second part of the sentence. The sentence was: *[the] [p]articipants were asked how much they'd spend on a date, with the results linking in a higher amount to the red-dress photo.*

(EM1) 要男人做選擇比較想和哪一個去約會,結果大多數的人都選擇穿紅色洋裝的那一張。
(BT: *Men were asked to choose which one they want to date, and most of them chose the photo wearing the red dress*)

(NEM1) 受試者被問到他們需要花多少時間約會,結果大多數和紅洋裝照有關。
(BT: *Participants were asked how much time they need to date, and most of them are related to red dress*)

(NEM2) 參與者被詢問他們願意在約會花多少錢,結果是穿著紅色洋裝的照片有比較高的金額。
(BT: *Participants were asked how much money they are willing to spend on a date, it turned out that photo wearing a red dress has a higher amount*)

Contrary to the translation errors regarding accuracy in the previous case, in this case we selected examples where students could not express the original correctly, even if they understood the original meaning. Based on the abovementioned translated versions, we determined that neither the English nor the non-English majors could express the original, and that their translations showed that men wanted to date *the photo in a red dress*, whereas it should have been *the woman in a red dress* that men preferred dating. However, if we compare their translation to the third reading comprehension question, which was inference-based, there were only few incorrect answers. Thus, it was safe to assume that the students understood the original but they paid more attention to rendering the original than to formulating an understandable utterance in L1, even though it was their first language. It could also be possible that insufficient ability regarding students' L1 can influence their learning of L2 because they are unable to express what they read correctly in L1. Therefore, it is crucial for L2 instructors to analyze students' translations in comparison to their reading comprehension questions to better understand how their background influences their L2 performance, rather than only training students to provide correct answers.

It is worth mentioning that some students tended to relate the phrase *how much they'd spend* to time rather than to money. Thus, their translation grades were reduced because of accuracy errors.

### 3.3 Test 1: Example 3

The last sentence in this passage was not tested in the comprehension questions following the translation. However, we were able to investigate the translations regarding how the students comprehended English at the sentential level. The original read: *[t]he findings correlate with other studies, as well as the prominence of color on holidays such as Valentine's Day.*

(EM1) 這項發現與其它的研究結果相呼應,包括了為什麼大家對於情人節的印象色是紅色。
(BT: *This finding corresponds to other research results, including the reason why the impression people have for Valentine's Day is red*)

(NEM1) 這項發現關聯到其他研究,以及節慶像是情人節引人注目的顏色。
(BT: *This finding is related to other research, and holidays such as the color attracting us on Valentine's Day*)

In this case, the students performed well on the first part of the sentence and correctly interpreted the term *correlate with*, which was a text-based reading comprehension question. However, it seems that they had difficulty understanding the second part. Most shifted the use of *Valentine's Day* to the front of their translated sentences, mitigating the focus of the phrase *the prominence of the color*. Thus, two points were deducted from a total of ten points. Conversely, the non-English majors' versions did not make sense, particularly the second part of the sentence, and two points were deducted for translation expression. Non-English majors may have more difficulty expressing themselves in their first language than English majors, although their L2 proficiency was fair. L2 instructors of English majors can use this finding to direct students to further English structures at the sentential level, such as topical chains and theme-rheme structures to determine emphases in the original. Furthermore, L2 instructors of non-English majors can enhance their students' L1 reading and expression to improve their L2 learning.

## 3.4 Test 2: Example 1

The second passage concerned a group of people—"kidults"—whose minds were like those of children although they were adults. Among the translations by the English and the non-English majors, some students followed the original literally when they were unable to understand the meaning because they believed this was a safe translation method. However, this strategy mostly led to versions that were hard to understand. The following sentence can be used as an example: *[o]bservers grade to positive and negative ramifications of the trend, which is all about having fun and avoiding, at all costs, the "R" word: Responsibility.*

(EM1) 研究家指出,在這種玩樂和逃避趨勢之下,所延生出來的正、反面衍生物,無論如何,只有一個"R":責任。
(BT: *Researchers grade out that in the trend of having fun and avoiding giving positive and negative ramifications, no matter what it is, is "R": responsibility*)

(NEM1) 這潮流明顯有正面和反面的兩派說法,都是關於「找樂子」和「逃避」的區別,而這些全都是關乎到「責任」。
(BT: *This trend obvious has positive and negative viewpoints, all about "having fun" and "avoiding," and all this about "responsibility"*)

The above two versions closely followed the original, but did not present the original meaning clearly and did not make sense in Chinese. A translation such as this cannot obtain a high grade for expression, although students were accurate in providing meanings that corresponded to the original. Furthermore, when we investigated their performance on the reading comprehension questions, we found that the students mostly provided incorrect answers to the inference-based questions about this sentence. Therefore, analyzing their translations can give L2 instructors ideas regarding why students cannot answer inference-based questions correctly.

## 3.5 Test 2: Example 2

For the following two examples, we selected two sentences to examine how students interpreted certain terms differently when they misunderstood the original. The first sentence read: *[c]onsumerism plays a key role in the trend, as kidults lack of financial obligations frees up money for electronic goods, cars, and clothes*. The following examples were selected for discussion:

(EM1) "大孩子"缺乏經濟上的責任，他們得到電子產品，車子和衣服都花不到自己的錢。
(BT: *"Big kids" lacks in economic responsibility. They don't have to spend their own money to have electronic products, cars, and clothes*)

(EM2) 這些「小孩大人」沒有經濟基礎，卻有充裕的金錢可以購買電子產品，車子和衣服。
(BT: *These "kidults" do not have the economic foundation, but have sufficient money to buy electronic products, cars, and clothes*)

(NEM1) 當童心未泯的人缺乏了對財務上的責任，[...]隨意的使用金錢在電子產品，汽車，和衣服上，
(BT: (*When people with a young heart lack in financial obligation, [...] use money freely on electronic products, cars, and clothes*)

(NEM2) 他們背負較少的財務責任，因此促使他們可任意購買電子產品、汽車以及服飾等，
(BT: *They carry fewer financial obligations, so that they can buy electronic products, cars, and clothes as much as they like*)

In this case, we examined how the students understood the lexical item *free up*. In the first two versions, the students comprehended the term differently, and they translated the item as *don't have to spend their own money* and *have sufficient money*. Thus, two points were deducted for this term in these two versions. In contrast, the following two versions were closer to the original, but the two non-English majors were unable to represent how the kidults *freed up* their money, euphemizing, instead, the extent. Thus, the students provided versions such as *use money freely* or *buy things as much as they like*. Therefore, in this case, the non-English majors lost 2 points for expression because they did not provide precise expressions that corresponded to the original.

### 3.6 Test 2: Example 3

The second sentence for discussion was the last in the passage and featured the lexical item *instead*. The original read: *[i]ndeed, there's a constant marketing stream encouraging people to think less and, instead, enjoy life to the brim.*

(EM1) 確實,鼓勵人們少思考是一直不變的潮流趨勢,但反而享受生活是很充實的。
(BT: *Indeed, to encourage people to think less is an unchanged trend, but contrarily enjoying life is fulfilling*)

(NEM1)的確,固定的行銷趨勢鼓勵人思考少一點,而不是盡可能的享受生活。
(BT: *Indeed, a fixed marketing trend encourages people to think less, but not enjoy life as much as possible*)

In this case, although both the English and the non-English majors understood what the phrase *to the brim* meant and provided correct answers to the text-based reading comprehension question, their translations revealed that their understanding of the phrase was based on stereotypes. Because students in Taiwan learn *instead* as a transition with negative implications, the two versions translated the word as *contrarily* with a negative expression immediately following the term. By analyzing their translations, L2 instructors can determine potential problems in learning L2, as well as students' problematic habits in comprehending difficult vocabulary and terms.

## 4. Results and discussion

After each test, the researcher collected both student translations and their reading comprehension answers, and assigned scores. The results of the study are shown in Table 4 further below.

According to Table 4, translation helps students comprehend the original. Translating could, therefore, be efficient and useful assessment applied in the classroom to monitor student reading comprehension capability. Each of the four columns of the table presents student groups (either English majors (EMs) or Non-English Majors (NEMs)) and the number of tests they took. For each column, **Positive** suggests that students submitted more correct answers to the three reading comprehension questions directly related to the paragraphs they translated. **Negative** represents that students gave more incorrect answers to questions corresponding to the paragraphs they translated (see Appendices C and D). With respect to English majors, more than 80% of students gave correct answers to reading comprehension questions related to their translation in Test 1, whereas more than 60% were correct in answering corresponding reading comprehension questions after translation in Test 2. Nearly 90% of the non-English majors obtained a full score in the three reading comprehension questions after translation in Test 1, and more than 50% of them indicated correct answers to the corresponding comprehension questions. The resulting answers to the first research question in this study indicated that both English and non-English majors could benefit from translation practice in their L2 reading comprehension. Student performance in reading comprehension also improved following the translation activity, according to the results. The use of translation before taking the reading comprehension tests urged students to read closely the paragraphs they translated while simultaneously attempting to understand every term and sentence to proceed with their translation. Instead of quickly browsing the text, commonly applied to reading comprehension tests, translation after detailed reading gave students the opportunity to further understand the original and submit more correct answers to the corresponding questions.

|  | Ems (26) in T1 | Ems (24) in T2 | NEMs (11) in T1 | NEMs (11) in T2 |
|---|---|---|---|---|
| **Positive** | 86.4% | 64.7% | 88.9% | 55.6% |
| **Negative** | 13.6% | 35.3% | 11.1% | 44.4% |

**Table 4. Overview of results**

However, as translation led to enhanced performance in the reading comprehension test in Test 1, its benefit was reduced in Test 2 for both English and non-English majors, possibly because of the choice of reading passages. These two reading passages are the approximate level of TOEIC 550 (or IELTS 4) for L2 learners. Student performance in both translation and reading comprehension in Test 2 suggests that the reading passage in Test 2 is considerably more difficult for both groups of students, with an average score in translation of 75 (English majors) and 78 (non-English majors), compared to 77 and 81 for Test 1. Therefore, the use of translation cannot guarantee full understanding of the original but good translation grades indicate high comprehension of the original, resulting in more answers that were correct. The drastically lower percentage could also imply that the translation benefit in difficult texts could be reduced, particularly for non-English majors. Additional studies are required to prove this hypothesis.

However, both English and non-English majors have a tendency to make mistakes in answering the questions. English majors tended to submit wrong answers to text-based questions, such as the meanings of certain words or sentences, whereas non-English majors tended to make mistakes on inference-based questions. English majors found it difficult to guess the exact word or sentence based on context, a difficulty that is evidenced in their translation whenever any inappropriate meaning in Chinese appeared. Five out of the eleven non-English majors could not provide a correct answer on a generalized idea of a paragraph, not because they had difficulty in understanding the whole paragraph but because they tried to interpret the paragraph in their own manner and answer the question based on their own understanding, not that of the author. Therefore, non-English majors had better reading comprehension, as reflected in their translation scores, compared to that of English majors.

When asked about their reflection on these two practices in the experiment, both English and non-English majors indicated they found it odd to simultaneously perform translation and the reading comprehension test. Few students believed that translation helped improve their reading comprehension and were reluctant to conduct the reading comprehension test after translation. They said they were "very tired" after each translation activity and that the reading comprehension tests were an "extra burden" to or even a "torture" for them. Their complaints are actually understandable because students are seldom required to perform these activities. However, the results suggest that translation practice improved their reading comprehension.

The use of professional translation assessment allows the researcher-instructor to judge student translations on accuracy and expression. Translation requires language competence in at least two languages, thus students must provide accurate and expressive translation in Chinese after a full understanding of an L2 reading passage. This assessment method indicates student performance in accuracy, understanding of the original, expression, and language competence in using their mother tongue to represent the original meaning. Professional translation assessment also provides the opportunity to avoid simply focusing on word-by-word equivalence, similar to that applied by Chang (2006) and Ito (2004) in their studies, but to study how students can use their mother tongue to represent the original passages.

These experiment results highlight English and translation pedagogy and the potential effect that translating offers to L2 language learners. The results suggest that translation is helpful in reading comprehension tests because it requires students to understand more details in the paragraphs they are translating and to simultaneously apply their mother tongue. L2 instructors can take advantage of this study to design their curriculum for students with lower-reading comprehension competence. By incorporating translation into the language classroom, L2 instructors can detect and foresee which question(s) their students may make mistakes on based on their translation, which was an important indicator in this experiment. L2 instructors could design their own comprehension questions, depending on the reading comprehension questions students tend to fail. Based on the two student groups in this study, English majors are more vulnerable to questions concerning details of reading passages. Thus, L2 instructors could design similar comprehension questions to provide them with more practice and build their reading comprehension competence. Most non-English majors in this study failed questions regarding the main idea of reading passages. Hence, L2 instructors could omit questions concerning reading details and supplement them with more questions regarding general ideas of each paragraph. The assessment of translations can enhance the L2 instructor's awareness of students' reading competence regardless of whether students are English or non-English majors, and help instructors design curricula adapted to their students.

These study results could also be applied to translation pedagogy. Translation instructors could apply the same experiment at the beginning of the semester to a new group of students with various or similar backgrounds to contribute in understanding the students' initial reading comprehension competence. They could then provide students with translation practice and training corresponding to their L2 level. Translation instructors can further discuss student translation accuracy and expression to improve their linguistic competence based on their experiment. Translation instructors could even regularly conduct the experiment in the classroom to check if their students, whether they are English or non-English majors, improve in reading comprehension by means of analyzing translation accuracy and expression.

## 5. Conclusion

The study set out to investigate whether the use of translation could improve students' reading comprehension in a case study. Different from the commonly-applied traditional word-by-word grading in translation performance, this study adopted professional translation assessment to look at students' accuracy and expression in translation. It was found that translation did help students in reading comprehension, based on their performance on answering reading comprehension questions. In addition, translation somehow urged students—whether English majors or non-English majors—to read thoroughly so as to improve their understanding of the reading passages. The study offers pedagogical implications for both translation and EFL teachers for future curriculum design.

## Works cited

Bennett, Andrew E. 2010. *Reading Fusion 2*. Taiwan: Crane Publishing.
—. 2010. *Reading Fusion 2: Teacher's Manual & Test Bank CD*. Taiwan: Crane Publishing.
Buck, Gary. 1992. "Translation as a Language Testing Procedure: Does it Work?" *Language Testing* 9(2):123–148.
Chang, Yuh-Fang. 2006. "The Use of the Immediate Recall Task as a Measure of Second Language Reading Comprehension." *Language Testing* 23(4):520–543.
Ito, Akihiro. 2004. "Two Types of Translation Tests: Their Reliability and Validity." *System* 32(3):395–405.
O'Malley, J. Michael, and Anna U. Chamot. 1990. *Learning Strategies in Second Language Acquisition*. Cambridge: Cambridge University Press.
O'Muireartaigh, Rossa. 2009. "Terminology as an Aid to Enhancing Reading Skills." In *Translation in Second Language Learning and Teaching*, edited by Arnd Witte, Theo Harden, and Alessandra Ramos de Oliveira Harden, 215–226. New York: Peter Lang.
Lai, Tzu-yun. 2008. "Comparisons of four translation assessment scales." *Compilation and Translation Review* 1(1):71–92.
Messick, Samuel. 1996. "Validity and Washback in Language Testing." *Language Testing* 13(3):241–256.
Vinay, Jean P., and Jean Darbelnet. 1995. *Comparative Stylistics of French and English: a Methodology for Translation*. Translated by Juan C. Sager, and M. J. Hamel. Amsterdam: Benjamins.

Weydt, Harald. 2009. "Reading Books with Translations: Getting over the Reading Barrier." In *Translation in Second Language Learning and Teaching*, edited by Arnd Witte, Theo Harden, and Alessandra Ramos de Oliveira Harden, 291–308. New York: Peter Lang.

Whyatt, Boguslawa. 2009. "Translating as a Way of Improving Language Control in the Mind of an L2 Learner: Assets, Requirements and Challenges of Translation Tasks." In *Translation in Second Language Learning and Teaching*, edited by Arnd Witte, Theo Harden and Alessandra Ramos de Oliveira Harden, 181–202. New York: Peter Lang.

# Appendix A

It has been said that "love makes the world go round". That may be truer than we realize. Scientific interest in romantic love has turned up fascinating discoveries about the physiology of love, including the mapping out of several processes of physical attraction. The sweaty palms and quickened heartbeats of lovers have been linked to the production of specific hormones and neurotransmitters. Thus, when we talk about two people "having chemistry", it's not just a figure of speech.

*Reading comprehension questions:*

1. What is the main idea?
A. Well-known figures of speech often have a basis in scientific fact.
B. We've learned about the physiological processes involved with romantic love.
C. Hormones and neutrotransmitters perform important neurological functions.
D. Chemistry can teach us about many things, but love remains a mystery.

Another popular saying is "beauty is in the eye of the beholder." Concepts of beauty certainly very among cultures and individuals, but what fascinates scientists are the mental activities behind the eyes. One study at the University of Rochester focused on clothing color. Men were shown a photo of a woman wearing a red dress, as well as a photo of the same woman in a blue dress. Participants were asked how much they'd spend on a date, with results linking a higher amount to the red dress photo. The findings correlate with other studies, as well as the prominence of the color on holidays like Valentine's Day.

2. In the preceding paragraph, what does "correlate with" mean?
A. correct for
B. corrode from
C. cordon off
D. correspond to

3. What was revealed by the University of Rochester Study?
A. Clothing color may be a predictor of attractiveness
B. On average, people spend less on dates than they used to
C. The prominence of red in Valentine's Day gifts is hard to explain
D. Women are willing to spend more on high-quality dresses

Within 1-3 years, as people settle into a more stable relationship, these chemicals return to normal levels. Yet that isn't the end of love's impacts. People in long-term relationships show elevated levels of oxytocin, a hormone associated with forming nurturing bonds and maintaining trust. Another brain chemical, serotonin (which is associated with calmness), is also higher during this period. MRI scans have revealed that even after 20 years of marriage, people show increased activity in regions associated with these substances.

4. What is true about serotonin for people in long-term relationships?
A. The chemical shows a different pattern from oxytocin levels.
B. It helps people maintain trust in their partners.
C. Serotonin levels are elevated for such people.
D. Levels peak after people have been together for two decades.

5. What can be inferred about people who have been married for 30 years?
A. They have relatively high levels of oxytocin and serotonin.
B. They easily form nurturing bonds with everyone they meet.
C. They experience increased activity in most regions of the brain.
D. They are calmer than people who have been married for 20 years.

(From *Reading Fusion 2 Teacher's Manual & Test Bank CD*: 135-136)

## Appendix B

In 1983, Cyndi Lauper reached the top of charts with her hit song "Girls Just Want to Have Fun." These days, the same could be said for millions of men and women in their 20s, 30s, and even 40s. These so-called "Kidults" dress and behave like children. Refusing to grow up, they often live with their parents, play video games, and watch cartoons. Observers point to positive and negative ramifications of the trend, which is all about having fun and avoiding, at all costs, the "R" word: Responsibility.

*Reading comprehension questions:*

1. What is the main idea?
A. Kidults, who have many responsibilities, must learn to live under heavy pressure.
B. All social trends have positive and negative ramifications.
C. It's not uncommon for adults to have childlike interests and personalities
D. In general, people live with their parents to save money.

Consumerism plays a key role in the trend, as kidults lack of financial obligations frees up money for electronic goods, cars, and clothes. Over the last decade, marketers have cashed into on the opportunity, with companies making toys and collectibles specifically for adults. Recently, in St. Petersburg, Russia, a television channel called 2X2 was created for the young-at-heart. Featuring cartoons like *The Simpsons,* the channel tells viewers to "Switch off your brain. Switch 2X2." Indeed, there's constant marketing stream encouraging person to think less and, instead, enjoy life to the brim. Christopher Noxon, author of *Rejuvenile*, bluntly sums things up: "It has become unfashionable to be mature."

2. In the preceding paragraph, who does "to the brim" mean?
A. in a conservative manner
B. to an acceptable degree
C. as expected by one's peers
D. as much as possible

3. What is implied about companies that market products to kidults?
A. They want consumers to make thoughtful, responsible purchases.
B. They make most of their money from selling electronic goods.
C. They are given free advertising slots by TV stations like 2x2.
D. They encourage their customers to spend without thinking.

The question is, will they take advantage of the opportunity? There's a risk that the longer people put off growing up, the harder it will eventually be. By focusing on material goods, entertainment, and short-term pursuits, kidults may ignore their intellectual and emotional development. James Cote, a sociologist, has noted that people are not being pressured to mature. That can lead to trouble forming adult relationships and social skills. There's also the danger that kidults, accustomed to having their meals cooked and clothes washed for them, may never learn to take care of themselves.

4. What is the risk of focusing primarily on short-term interests?
A. It may lead to one's being pressured to mature.
B. It makes it impossible to form adult relationships.
C. It could impact one's personal development.
D. It might cause a person to ignore his or her parents.

5. What may lead to kidults having trouble looking after themselves?
A. Being used to others preparing their food and doing their laundry.
B. Never taking the time to improve their social skills.
C. Spending all their time caring for younger siblings or elderly parents.
D. Forming dangerous habits learned from other kidults.

(From *Reading Fusion 2 Teacher's Manual & Test Bank CD*: 107-108)

## Appendix C

| | T1 [Translation score-Comprehension Question Error No. (Total 3, passage translated) - Comprehension Question Error No. (Total 2, passage non-translated)] | T2 [Translation score-Comprehension Question Error No. (Total 3, passage translated) - Comprehension Question Error No. (Total 2, passage non-translated)] |
|---|---|---|
| **English Majors (Total No. 26 in T1; 24 in T2)** | 1. 76-0-2<br>2. 62-1-0<br>3. 66-0-2<br>4. 90-0-0<br>5. 80-0-2<br>6. 82-0-2<br>7. 90-0-0<br>8. 90-1-0<br>9. 68-0-1<br>10. 70-2-1<br>11. 84-0-1<br>12. 58-0-2<br>13. 72-0-1<br>14. 76-1-2<br>15. 82-0-1<br>16. 76-2-2<br>17. 72-1-2<br>18. 86-0-1<br>19. 86-0-1<br>20. 82-1-2<br>21. 76-1-2<br>22. 62-0-1<br>23. 82-0-0<br>24. 80-0-2<br>25. 76-1-2<br>26. 76-0-1 | 1. 74-0-1<br>2. 74-2-1<br>3. 72-0-0<br>4. 72-2-0<br>5. 70-1-2<br>6. 94-0-1<br>7. 58-0-1<br>8. 78-1-0<br>9. 84-0-0<br>10. 74-0-1<br>11. 78-0-0<br>12. 80-2-2<br>13. 70-2-0<br>14. 60-2-0<br>15. 64-1-1<br>16. 78-0-1<br>17. 70-1-1<br>18. 84-0-0<br>19. 86-2-1<br>20. 84-0-0<br>21. 60-3-2<br>22. 78-0-1<br>23. 86-0-0<br>24. 80-0-1 |

## Appendix D

| | T1 [Translation score-Comprehension Question Error No. (Total 3, passage translated) - Comprehension Question Error No. (Total 2, passage non-translated)] | T2 [Translation score-Comprehension Question Error No. (Total 3, passage translated) - Comprehension Question Error No. (Total 2, passage non-translated)] |
|---|---|---|
| **Non-English Majors (Total No. 11 in T1 and T2)** | 1. 84-0-0<br>2. 82-0-2<br>3. 74-0-0<br>4. 86-1-1<br>5. 74-1-1<br>6. 74-1-1<br>7. 84-0-1<br>8. 82-0-1<br>9. 88-1-0<br>10. 88-0-2<br>11. 78-0-1 | 1. 72-0-1<br>2. 82-1-0<br>3. 70-1-0<br>4. 80-0-0<br>5. 86-1-0<br>6. 84-1-1<br>7. 72-1-0<br>8. 78-0-0<br>9. 76-0-1<br>10. 74-0-1<br>11. 84-1-1 |

# CHAPTER TWO

# TEACHING GRAMMAR THROUGH TRANSLATION

# MELITA KOLETNIK KOROŠEC

## 1. Introduction

Translation has forever occupied a somewhat radical and controversial role in foreign language teaching (FLT): it was considered either essential, e.g. within the frame of the grammar-translation method, or detrimental, e.g. in the light of a variety of pedagogical and didactic approaches that favoured a communicative focus and monolingual teaching. In recent years, however, an increasing number of pleas (e.g. G. Cook 2010; Howatt and Widdowson 2004; Kramsch 1993) have been made for a more balanced examination of this role and for empirical studies which would objectively assess the effects of the use of translation in real-life classroom settings. At the same time, authors began expressing renewed interest in the use of students' native language (L1) in FLT classrooms; in addition to finding no principled reasons for its avoidance, they reported on its usefulness, above all, for explanatory purposes and particularly in relation to issues pertaining to grammar (e.g. V. Cook 2001; Widdowson 2003).

This chapter endeavours to answer the calls for a re-examination of the role of translation in FLT; at the same time, it attempts to provide evidence of the assumed usefulness of the application of L1. It reports on the preliminary findings of an on-going experimental study involving undergraduate (BA) students of English translation. This experiment assesses the role of translation exercises and instruction using students' L1 for the acquisition of L2 linguistic and—more precisely—grammatical competence. The longitudinal study was conceived with the objective of assessing the correlation between the effects of the early application of translation exercises (within the scope of general language instruction) and the development of translation competence in students of translation at a later stage of their training.

The experimental study is thus an attempt to seek evidence that explicit grammar instruction involving the use of students' L1 and predicated on selected translation exercises, in and out of both languages and targeting particular aspects of grammar under instruction, has a possible positive effect on the acquisition of linguistic competence by upper-intermediate and advanced level students in academic contexts. In addition to vindicating the merits of translation-related activities and the use of L1 in the overall development of linguistic competence and learning grammar, it is anticipated that the longitudinal study shall, once the final results are known, also provide an empirically based answer to the question as to whether it is advantageous or detrimental to use translation at an early stage in language learning of students of translation.

However self-evident it may seem that in undergraduate curricula leading to a post-graduate course in translation, translation practice should be present "from day one", the reality in current Bologna-compliant study programmes is often quite the opposite. A cursory examination of a random sample of 7 of the 54 European higher-education institutions offering master's level translation programmes revealed that in the BA curricula leading to the MA course in translation, initial hands-on translation classes usually do not start until the $3^{rd}$ or $4^{th}$ semester—i.e. the second year—or even later. This is largely because the development of various elements of linguistic competence in the languages under tuition (L1 and L2) is given priority over development of translation skills.

## 2. Disciplinary considerations and motives for the study

For much of the $20^{th}$ century, translation suffered the reputation of being an ill-suited aid in foreign language teaching and methodology. For the most part, this poor reputation was derived from the pre-eminent position of monolingual and communicatively-oriented approaches to teaching foreign languages, within which the use of L1 and translation understandably found no application or were even considered harmful, promoting—among other vices—interferences between L1 and L2, as well as negative transfer from L1, thus hindering successful learning. Since much has already been written about the grounds for the denunciation of translation in language teaching (see, for example, G. Cook 2010; Leonardi 2010; Malmkjaer 1998), it suffices to say that the reasons underpinning its rejection have not always been pedagogic or linguistic; indeed, the global spread of international language schools and the worldwide marketing of course materials and textbooks by such major publishers as Oxford University Press and Macmillan have provided sufficient economic and political motive to ensure the prevalence of a hegemonic monolingual model.

In addition to effectively excluding translation, the purely communicative approaches to foreign language teaching have also neglected grammar instruction. While some resorted to instructing grammar in an implicit manner and in context, e.g. as part of the *"focus-on-form"* syllabus (Long 1991)[1], others, supporting the idea that grammar can or could (only) be acquired naturally from meaningful input (Krashen 1985)[2], evidently excluded grammar in order not to alienate students from the language they were learning. When the criticisms of communicative methods began to be addressed in the late 20$^{th}$ century, particularly in relation to (in)accuracy in the learner's language (e.g. Ellis 1993), the debate about grammar instruction and, in this context, whether to instruct grammar implicitly as an integral topic within a (primarily) communicative curriculum or explicitly as an extracted focus, flared up anew.

The discussion as to whether grammar should be explained to students, or whether they should be allowed to learn it "without awareness that it is being learned"[3], is still ongoing. Indeed, a considerable amount of research, laboratory and classroom studies have been conducted (for a review see, for example, DeKeyser 2005) and the balance of evidence suggests

> [...] a positive role for some kind of attention to form [i.e. grammar] either through the explicit teaching of grammar [...] or at least through more indirect means such as input enhancement.[4]

---

[1] The *focus-on-form* paradigm suggested by Michael Long in his 1988 paper *Focus on form: A design feature in language teaching methodology*, presented at a conference in Italy and later published as a book, was Long's answer to the established pedagogy with a more traditional *focus-on-forms* which rested heavily on the deliberate teaching of grammar. Since, he argued, teaching grammar in isolation does not support the development of the ability to use the language communicatively, attention to form should only be paid in context and when it is needed.

[2] Stephen Krashen's (1985) theory of the natural acquisition of language, which gathered many followers, put forward the idea that the explicit learning of linguistic rules was of no use, since the order of acquisition was given naturally and independent of instruction.

[3] DeKeyser's definition of implicit learning is being used (DeKeyser 2005) for the purposes herein.

[4] DeKeyser 2005, 321.

To take a brief detour: in language teaching, the notion of *grammar* most often involves reference to grammar in the conventional or structural sense, while drawing upon the descriptive tradition. This structural understanding of grammar is based on the underlying assumption that the grammar of a language consists of a number of "structures" which are described as completely as possible in terms of morphology and syntax as in *A University Grammar of English* (Greenbaum and Quirk 1973). In addition, such an understanding of grammar also involves the classification of individual grammatical item types (parts of speech) based on their function and their use in patterns or structures, as exemplified by the most widely-recognised grammar books, e.g. *English Grammar in Use* (Murphy 2004) or *A Practical English Grammar* (Thomson and Martinet 1993). This same concept of grammar was also used for the purposes of this study.

To return to implicit and explicit teaching of grammar, the literature (for example G. Cook 2010; V. Cook 2001) identifies two reasons or justifications, where the need for explicit grammar instruction is particularly evident: first, if the aim of teaching is to convey academic knowledge about the language, i.e. if grammatical explanation is a way of teaching facts about language not the use of language itself; and second, if the structures of L1 and L2 are dissimilar and do not readily lend themselves to being well understood by students, even in context, i.e. if L1 can be used contrastively to point out problem areas of grammar, etc.

At the university level and within linguistically-oriented study programmes—this is also true for more specialized programmes, e.g. translation studies—foreign language teaching as an academic subject should be based, but not exclusively so, on the premise that students consciously understand the grammatical structures being taught, and furthermore that they are consciously made aware of the (non)existence of links between L1 and L2. As a next step, they should convert the explicit rules which have been learnt consciously into the unconscious processes of comprehension and language production. Even though students are not directly taught how to use the language, the endeavour is to create linguistic competence and a "basis for language use when the student requires it" (V. Cook 2001, 201–205). Furthermore, such a method presents an intellectual challenge and motivates students to analytically engage with the language, which is also a skill that can easily be transferred to other domains of instruction.

For explanatory purposes, and particularly in relation to issues pertaining to grammar, explicit instruction can efficiently be coupled with the use of students' native language (L1). For instance, Scheffler and

Cinciala (2011) have shown that explicit grammar instruction in L1 (e.g. translating grammar rules into L1) can contribute to the development of explicit L2 knowledge in secondary school learners, whilst their observations have been corroborated by actual reports emanating from the language classroom and language teachers' forums[5]. Furthermore, my own observations vindicate this perspective, as do those of some of my teacher colleagues who perceive translation and the judicious use[6] of L1 in language instruction as a real-life activity that occurs both naturally and inevitably. However, it is true that the use of L1 remains a controversial issue in foreign language teaching, and that there exist situations where the application of L1 in the foreign language classroom is inappropriate or inefficient. The use of a students' L1 is indeed unsuitable for multi–lingual or multi–cultural classrooms, as well as in situations where teachers do not speak the L1 of their students.

Let us now turn to the role of translation in foreign language teaching. This was primarily, and for the most part theoretically, addressed by translation scholars. In reply to the decades-old criticism that translation in ELT is dull and demotivating, G. Cook (2010, xv), among others, argues to the contrary, namely that "translating should be a major aim and means of language learning" which, in relation to teaching grammar, can help clarify certain complex grammatical points (González Davies 2001). Moreover, translation can also be particularly useful when the targeted structures in L1 and L2 are radically different. In this case, the two languages can be contrasted through translation, and learners are induced to realise that ideas and concepts can be expressed differently (Leonardi 2010, 26). Despite the overall negative sentiment towards translation in foreign language teaching, ELT research has contributed to it. For instance, among others, Swan (2007, 295) stated that the "existence of cross-language equivalents can further substantially reduce teaching need

---

[5] After visiting and searching through several forums aimed at teachers, it can be safely assumed that teachers' opinion on that issue is very much equally divided among the advocates and opponents of the use of L1. As most representative in this respect I suggest visiting the British Council / BBC forum on Using L1 in the ESL Classroom (2009) at http://www.teachingenglish.org.uk/forum-topic/using-l1-esl-classroom, or the TESL-EJ Forum for teachers of English as a Second or Foreign Language (2002) at http://tesl-ej.org/ej20/f1.html.

[6] With particular reference to the role which activities based on translation can play in fluency development in L2, Atkinson (1987, 245) suggests the following applications of L1 as "judicious use": eliciting language, checking comprehension, giving instructions, talking about language, comparing the systems of L1 and L2, translating, using compensatory strategies, and saving time.

in some areas", John Williams (cited by Malmkjaer 1998, 1) that "tasks that promote 'multi-lingual' competence (for example translation and interpreting) are valuable for language learners", and Hedge (2003, 147) that when teaching grammar, translation can, at certain stages, "clearly be a helpful strategy".

Another aspect that motivated this study was the observation that the use of translation in language teaching remains the norm in universities (Malmkjaer 2004). In advanced language teaching at the tertiary level or in an academic context, translation is often combined with explicit grammar instruction utilizing meta-linguistic knowledge and explanation. As reported by Roehr,

> [...] tertiary-level learners are often exposed to explicit teaching and learning in the context of virtually all aspects of the L2 that permit systematic description and explanation.[7]

In view of the assumption that such teaching and learning is beneficial, Roehr's study involving advanced university-level English L1 learners of German L2 draws a positive parallel between L2 proficiency and L1 language-analytic ability.

As reported by G. Cook (2010, 90–91), empirical research and experimental studies on the role of translation in language acquisition remain scant. Källkvist (2010) investigated the effect of L1-L2 translation versus no translation, and arrived at some interesting conclusions. In her research, advanced learners, who had engaged in form-focused exercises that did not involve the use of translation, performed better in L2 written tasks, while learners who taught grammar through translation had a superior performance in translation assignments. In conclusion, and in line with previous research, Källkvist calls for the judicious use of translation and a combination of both types of exercise; this implies greater exposure to targeted structures, and stimulation of students' minds "in two ways, one of which involves comparison with the L1" (2010, 199). She also makes a plea for more empirical research into the effect of translation exercises, preferably by including a larger number of informants and/or through the study of different language pairs.

The rationale for the study described herein is derived from the above observations and empirical findings. The objective was thus to elicit whether explicit grammar instruction and teacher comment in L1 (such as discussing and translating grammar rules into L1) combined with written translation exercises into L2 can positively contribute to the development

---

[7] Roehr 2006, 42.

of L2 linguistic skills in Slovene advanced learners of English in tertiary education.

## 3. Experimental Study

### 3.1 Setting and Methodology

The experimental study was carried out at the Department of Translation Studies at the University of Maribor, Slovenia, as part of the English Language Development 1/I tutorial during the first part of the winter semester of the academic year 2012/13. The study presents the first stage of a longitudinal effort focusing on the role of translation in the acquisition of linguistic competence, as well as its influence on the development of translation competence in students of translation. The final results of the study are anticipated to be published in 2014.

The experiment was conducted with a group of $1^{st}$ year students of the BA Inter-lingual Studies (English) programme, a Bologna-compliant degree offered since 2008. The general objective of the course is to consolidate, revise, and expand students' existing knowledge of English grammar at an advanced level. In addition to having introduced the students to fundamental syntactical notions, emphasis is placed on selected aspects of morphology, *inter alia* basic morphological sets, nouns and determiners, and—in this context—articles in particular. On completion of the course, students are expected to understand the rules and apply grammatical analysis, as well as use the selected sets of grammatical item types in test situations; the overriding aim, however, is for students to utilize them appropriately in future translation situations.

The students, all native speakers of Slovene, aged 19 or 20, were divided into two groups of roughly equal size (Group A=11 students, Group B=9 students) who were taught by two different teachers instructing both groups alternately to decrease idiosyncratic incidences. The students should necessarily have attended at least five of the six classes under consideration, as well as participated in classroom exercises and handed in homework assignments which targeted the particular grammatical item type under instruction.

The experimental approach involved instructing one group (Group A) through translation and resort to the students' native language, while the second group (Group B) was taught without the use of translation or the students' native language (L1). In Group A the students' L1 was used to provide additional information and explanation during explicit grammatical instruction and above all during the revision phase, i.e. when grammatical rules were (orally) translated, explained by the teacher to the students, and summarised. During the lessons and assignments provided to Group B, the use of L1 was avoided and no translation exercises were assigned.

Translation exercises were implemented as part of homework assignments, which were submitted via the virtual learning environment and discussed in class during the next contact hour, thus guaranteeing that the students had indeed prepared and/or were engaged in exercises including translation. These exercises involved translating from students' L1 into L2 individual lexical items (such as nouns and forming their plural), representative sentences (see Ex. 1 below), or shorter texts (such as fairytales), which targeted particular structures.

A combination of synthetic and authentic materials, the sentences and texts were didactically organised for this purpose from grammar textbooks and internet sources. In addition to including sentences and texts which addressed particular grammatical structures, care was also taken with Group A to incorporate examples, which informed the students of possible differences between the L1 and L2 systems (see Ex. 1 below).

[Slovene]: *Vedno si mi dajal dobre **nasvete**.*
(**abstract count noun, plural**)

[English]: *You have always given me good **advice**.*
(**abstract uncoun/mass noun, singular**)

[**Explanation**]: Some abstract nouns are used in English as singular uncountable nouns, whereas in Slovene they are used as countable nouns.

Ex. 1. Sample sentence for translation (adapted from Blaganje and Konte 1995, 53)

When discussing homework assignments and translation solutions in class, emphasis was on the targeted structures (e.g. the plural formation of nouns, uncountable nouns, the definite/indefinite article etc.) but at the same time students were made aware that in the majority of cases there is no single "correct" translation or 1:1 equivalent, and that several possible solutions and means of expression (personal/impersonal, passive/active, etc.) are possible.

Moreover, as is evident in Ex. 2, translation exercises stimulated a debate as to "translatability" in the sense of finding semantically and pragmatically, as well as idiomatically and collocationally, appropriate solutions given the limited context.

[Slovene]: *Moji starši imajo trdna politična* **prepričanja**.
(**plural noun**)

[English]: *My parents have firm political* **beliefs/convictions**.
(**formation of plural/two possibilities**)

[**Explanation**]: Some English nouns ending in –f (e.g. *sheaf, thief*) form plural irregularly (e.g. sheaves, thieves) others, including *belief,* form it regularly by adding an *–s*. The targeted word in this example was *belief,* but some students supplied *conviction(s)*. Both versions were accepted as semantically, idiomatically and collocationally correct. The issue of finding idiomatic and collocationally appropriate solutions was also touched upon.

Ex. 2. Sample sentence for translation (adapted from Blaganje and Konte 1995, 53)

## 3.2 Data Collection

According to Gottjahn's typology (Gottjahn 1978), this study is of an analytical-nomological type: it involves the collection of quantitative data (test results) through an experimental setting, and these data were then subjected to statistical analysis. Qualitative data were also sought to supplement and triangulate the results, and thus allow a more objective comparison.

The data used in the study were collected cross-sectionally in two instances: Test 1 was administered to the students at the beginning (Week 1) of the 14-week semester, and Test 2 in Week 7. A further test is to be undertaken in Week 14, i.e. at the end of the semester; the results of this, however, are not available at the time of preparation of this report. During the initial week and in addition to completing Test 1, students were also asked to provide answers to an on-line questionnaire.

The questionnaire was aimed at determining the students' linguistic background. It encompassed 18 questions addressing, among other things, the period of time they had been learning English formally within the state system, i.e. in primary and secondary school, and extra-curricularly, e.g. in a language school or similar institution in Slovenia or abroad. They were also asked if they themselves or their teachers had ever deployed translation as part of instruction, and in what way. Interestingly, in each group some students (two students from Group A, and three from Group B) answered this question in the affirmative. According to their answers, they have been learning English for as few as 4 and as many as 12 years prior to enrolling in the University, a factor which, however, did not have an immediate effect on the level of their linguistic ability, which was measured by the second test. The student with the least years of learning English institutionally performed just as well as the majority of the students participating in the test (reaching C1 on the CEFR scale).

In order to assess their initial general linguistic competence, students were invited to take the Oxford Online Placement Test (Test 1), testing their language and vocabulary through situated interactions. The test has two sections: *Use of English,* measuring knowledge of grammatical forms in relation to the semantic and pragmatic meaning; and *Listening,* measuring the student's listening ability. The *Use of English* section of the test incorporates tasks assessing the linguistic competence of a student by providing measures of their knowledge of i) grammatical forms, ii) semantic meaning, iii) grammatical form and meaning, and iv) pragmatic (i.e. implied) meaning. Although knowledge of grammatical forms constitutes the very object of the study, the test did not permit the individualisation of scores according to separate tasks, but only according to sections.

The Oxford Online Placement Test reports scores on a scale of 0 to 120, as well as in relation to the Common European Framework of Reference (CEFR)[8]. Every 20 points scored correspond to a CERF level on a scale ranging from A1 (basic user / breakthrough or beginner) to C2 (proficient user / mastery or proficiency). To ensure an even distribution, both groups had two underperforming members, who reached the CEFR levels of B1 (independent user / threshold or intermediate) and/or B2 (independent user / vantage or upper intermediate), as well as two outperforming students who attained the topmost score of C2. The remainder of the students had linguistic abilities corresponding to CEFR level C1.

The second test (Test 2) was undertaken by students during Week 7 of the semester. It consisted of 9 exercises focusing on the subject-matter dealt with in class, and addressing in particular the morphosyntactic categories of nouns and determiners. The top score was 90 points and the maximum possible score for each individual exercise was 10 points. The exercises included cloze test exercises, where students were asked to fill in the blanks for which some or no context was provided. No test exercises involved translation. The individual test items corresponded to a large extent to cases which were dealt with in class or as part of homework

---

[8] Common European Framework of Reference for Languages (CEFR) [online]. Available at: http://www.coe.int/t/dg4/linguistic/Source/Framework_EN.pdf.

assignments. It can therefore be assumed that if the students participated in class and did their homework, no further study input would be needed to score at least 56%, which was set as the pass mark for the test. And, indeed, no student from either of the groups failed this exam.

The decision to apply also Test 2 was based on the intention to elicit only the knowledge of those grammatical item types under instruction, as well as to ascertain which group outperformed the other. In this context, Test 1 was used as a general benchmark against which the relative performance of students in Test 2 was mapped. Since both tests addressed the knowledge of grammatical forms it was felt that such a decision was methodologically justified; it does not, however, allow an unqualified comparison of absolute values.

While the teachers did not have any influence on the structure of Test 1, they devised Test 2 themselves in order to elicit specific knowledge of the targeted grammatical forms. In the design of Test 2, *Ofqual*[9] assessment criteria and techniques were taken into account in order to "minimise bias" and to provide assessments that "are valid, reliable, comparable and manageable".[10] Data from both tests were subjected to statistical analysis, which was undertaken using SPSS software. An independent *t*-test was performed to determine whether there was a statistically significant difference in the performance of the groups in the final test broken down by individual tasks, while the *t*-test and the Mann-Whitney test for two independent variables were used to determine whether the performance of any group in Test 2, assessed in relation to Test 1 performance, differed significantly from the performance of the other group.

Due to the relatively small size of the sample a further statistical analysis (Cohen's *d*) was undertaken to determine the effect size on the studied phenomena, utilizing an online calculator[11]. Unlike the previously mentioned significance tests, Cohen's test measures the magnitude of treatment effect, independent of the sample size, and thus provides a statement about the strength of the relationship between the two selected variables.

---

[9] *Ofqual* stands for: Office of Qualifications and Examinations Regulation. See website at: http://ofqual.gov.uk/
[10] Ibid.
[11] *Effect Size Calculator*, copyright by Nicolas J. Cepeda (2008), available online at: http://cognitiveflexibility.org/effectsize.

## 4. Evaluation

Linguistic competence was measured by way of both tests, while no attempt was made to assess a student's explicit grammatical meta-knowledge or translation competence. The objective of Test 1 was to establish, at the beginning of instruction, the level of general linguistic ability in pragmatic situations and, at the same time, an initial value against which a student's competence could be compared at a later stage - presumably at the end of the academic year after two semesters of this protocol or later. Test 1 results were also used to assign students to individual groups to ensure a levelled initial performance.

Test 2 was devised to assess the students' formal knowledge of the targeted grammatical structures and also—to some extent—the application of such knowledge in authentic situations. Given the disparate nature of the two tests, no comparison between their results in absolute value terms can be drawn. As it was impossible to establish a normal distribution for either group, i.e. the mean value of both groups differed, a Mann-Whitney U test was therefore applied but no statistical significance could be established in relation to absolute performance of both groups ($p=0.603$, i.e. $p>0.05$).

|  | Total n=20 | | Group A n=11 | | Group B n=9 | | t | p |
|---|---|---|---|---|---|---|---|---|
|  | M | SD | M | SD | M | SD |  |  |
| **Test 1** | 83.2 | 13.7 | 82.1 | 13.4 | 84.5 | 14.8 | -0.385 | 0.705 |
| **Test 2** | 76.2 | 9.0 | 76.4 | 8.0 | 75.8 | 10.6 | 0.146 | 0.886 |
| **Gain** | -7.0 | 13.7 | -5.7 | 16.3 | -8.7 | 10.3 |  | 0.603[12] |

M: mean  SD: standard deviation
t: *t*-test for independent samples  p: statistical significance

**Table 1. Statistical analysis of Test 1 vs. Test 2 results (in %)**

In order to establish the magnitude of the treatment effect Cohen's standardized mean difference (*d*) was calculated using the post-test (Test 2) mean together with the pooled standard deviation values of the two groups. The following values are given as indicative of the tests: small

---

[12] Mann-Whitney test for samples where the variable deviates from a normal distribution.

effect size, $d$ = 0.2 to 0.3; medium effect size, $d$ = ca. 0.5; and large effect size, d = 0.8 to infinity. The calculated effect size was 0.067, indicating a non-significant effect. Nevertheless, if we compare the performance in percentage terms, it is evident that Group A students in Test 2 more closely matched their performance in Test 1 (Gain: -5.7) than did those in Group B (Gain: -8.7) across the two tests (see Table 1). It is also manifest that Group B outperformed Group A in Test 1, but performed more poorly in Test 2.

Table 2 presents the results of Test 2 broken down into individual exercises in relation to the mean value for both groups. Since some exercises were considered irrelevant to this study, only exercises 4, 5, 6, 7, and 8 were statistically evaluated. Exercise 4 tested the use of indefinite pronouns in determiner (attributive) functions; Exercise 5 tested the use of articles with proper nouns; Exercise 6 tested the use of articles with specific unidentified or identified references and/or a generic reference; Exercise 7 investigated the use of articles in an authentic context, while Exercise 8 tested the formation of plural nouns.

Exercises 4-6 and 8 were formulated by teachers, i.e. non-native speakers of English, targeting the tested grammatical item types in isolation; Exercise 7, however, was a part of a short internet news item whose author is deemed to be a native speaker, with articles blanked out; students were instructed to fill in the gaps (insert articles) as appropriate.

|  | Group A n=11 | | Group B n=9 | | t | p |
|---|---|---|---|---|---|---|
|  | M | SD | M | SD | | |
| **Exercise 4** | 9.1 | 0.9 | 9.0 | 1.1 | 0.3 | 0.70 |
| **Exercise 5** | 7.3 | 1.8 | 7.2 | 1.3 | 0.1 | 0.85 |
| **Exercise 6** | 7.8 | 1.1 | 7.8 | 1.3 | -0.0 | 0.96 |
| **Exercise 7** | 8.3 | 1.8 | 8.7 | 0.8 | -0.6 | 0.53 |
| **Exercise 8** | 7.6 | 1.3 | 7.1 | 0.9 | 0.8 | 0.40 |

Note: Maximum possible score for each individual exercise was 10 points.

M: mean  SD: standard deviation
t: $t$-test for independent samples  p: statistical significance

**Table 2. Statistical analysis of Test 2 results**

Again, no statistically significant differences between the groups' results could be established. Group A, which had received bilingual explicit grammatical instruction and translation exercises, however, seems to have achieved somewhat better, although the results are statistically insignificant as in all relevant exercises, except for Exercise 7, and the results for Exercise 6 are identical. As the research design is not robust, the results remain to be supported by further tests.

Consequently, the results presented in Table 2 seem to point towards a trend that the use of students' L1 combined with translation exercises into L2 could be helpful in the development of linguistic skills when formal knowledge is demanded; at the same time, however, no evidence has been provided that they contribute to student performance in those tasks which do not immediately relate to the classroom or homework, i.e. learned situations.

## 5. Discussion

The presented preliminary and tentative experimental results combined with previous reports on investigations into the effectiveness of translation and L1 in foreign language classrooms seem to indicate that both practices are supportive of the development of linguistic skills of language learners; however, no statistically significant differences between the achievements of experimental groups could be established utilizing the conventional statistical methods. Also, several limitations should necessarily be taken into consideration.

First, let us address the limitations frequently associated with research into implicit and explicit learning (DeKeyser 2005, for example, provides more detailed information on this issue). The initial problem is finding measures that reveal exactly how much has been learned. At the same time the actual amount of learning taking place is relatively limited, and this particularly holds true for this short study. Consequently, all flaws and shortcomings are likely to exert a rather profound impact on the final results. It is therefore essential that the tests reliably "probe the kind of knowledge that underlies performance" (DeKeyser 2005, 319), which, it is hoped, has been successfully achieved.

The second relevant issue is the selection of the testing timeframe. According to Reed and Johnson (1998), there is no explicit criterion for deciding on an appropriate period of time across which to test. On the whole, researchers seem to agree that short-cycle experiments favour explicit learning since they provide immediate results, while at the same time they are biased against implicit learning which takes longer to manifest and attain full effect. All are in agreement that thus far no perfect testing procedure has been developed to probe into the effectiveness and efficiency of explicit and/or implicit learning; therefore, we must content ourselves with eliciting knowledge under conditions that are more or less conducive.

Despite the careful preparation and implementation of this research, some inevitable limitations as to its validity also exist beyond the immediate testing subject and methodology. Firstly, there is the rather limited scope of the sample; however, in order to maintain comparable parameters within the two groups, almost one-half of the participants had to be eliminated from the evaluation due to various variables (they had either not attended the required number of classes or submitted the homework assignments; some students opted out of one of the tests, etc.). Since the experiment remains on-going, it is hoped that as many variables as possible can be adjusted, and that a larger sample can be secured in the future. It is also hoped that this research and analysis can be proceeded with, and that there will be a follow-up at the beginning of the coming academic year. Indeed, involvement of a second group of students would undoubtedly contribute weight to the study as regards both its representativeness and any conclusions which may be drawn.

Another limitation, the consequence of objective reasons, is the somewhat short duration of the experiment and the preliminary nature of the results. However, as has been highlighted already, the experiment is on-going and due to end at the close of the 2012/13 academic year. The final results of the longitudinal research into the role of translation in the acquisition of linguistic competence, as well as its influence on the development of translation competence in students of translation, are anticipated to be available in 2014.

## 6. Conclusions

For much of the 20th century, translation suffered the reputation for being an ill suited aid in foreign language teaching and learning English. At the same time, the use of students' native language in FLT classrooms was also considered useless and detrimental to the development of linguistic abilities, owing mostly to the pre-eminent position of monolingual and communicatively-oriented approaches. As the pleas for a more balanced examination of both aspects of foreign language teaching multiplied at the beginning of the 21st century, so did the need for objectively conceived and empirically based studies in this domain.

Addressing the issues of implicit and explicit grammar teaching and learning, together with the disparate requirements addressed in language instruction at different levels of education, the study provides limited evidence in support of the judicious use of translation and of L1 in foreign language instruction. The benefits of explicit language teaching in L1 seem most likely when formal knowledge is required from students in classroom-like situations. This said, however, the issue as to whether this contributes to student performance in those tasks which do not immediately relate to the classroom—i.e. learned situations—remains open to further investigation.

In conclusion, the evidence presented, however limited and statistically insignificant, seems to point to the belief that translation activities and the judicious use of students' L1 in foreign language classrooms seem to be supportive of explicit language learning in the context of colleges and universities. Having combined the preliminary experimental results with reports of previous investigations into the effectiveness explicit language instruction, and the use of L1 in the FLT, I therefore believe that there is substance to the claims that translation has a role in language teaching, and that it is of particular educational value at an advanced level. Furthermore, I remain hopeful that these findings will contribute to a narrowing of the gap between language teaching and translation, as well as at the same time offer an effective answer to student needs in our increasingly globalised multicultural world.

## Works Cited

Atkinson, David. 1987. "The Mother Tongue in the Classroom: A Neglected Resource?" *ELT Journal* 41(4):241–247.

Blaganje, Dana, and Ivan Konte. 1995. *Modern English Grammar.* Ljubljana: DZS.

Cook, Guy. 2010. *Translation in Language Teaching: An Argument for Reassessment.* Oxford: Oxford University Press.

Cook, Vivian. 2001. *Second Language Learning and Language Teaching.* London: Arnold.

DeKeyser, Robert. 2005. "Implicit and Explicit Learning." In *The Handbook of Second Language Acquisition,* edited by Catherine J. Doughty, and Michael H. Long, 313–348. London: Blackwell.

Ellis, Rod. 1993. *The Study of Second Language Acquisition.* Oxford: Oxford University Press.

Hedge, Tricia. 2003. *Teaching and Learning in the Language Classroom.* Oxford: Oxford University Press.

Howatt, Anthony P. R., and Henry G. Widdowson. 2004. *A History of English Language Teaching*. Oxford: Oxford University Press.
González Davies, Maria. 2001. "Translation in Foreign Language Learning: Bridging the Gap." Paper presented at the APAC-ELT Convention, Barcelona, Spain.
Gottjahn, Rüdiger. 1987. "On the Methodological Basis of Introspective Methods." In *Introspection in Second Language Research*, edited by Claus Faerch, and Gabriele Kasper, 54–78. Clevedon: Multilingual Matters.
Greenbaum, Sidney, and Randolph Quirk. 1990. *A Student's Grammar of the English Language*. Harlow, Essex: Longman.
Källkvist, Marie. 2010. "L1-L2 Translation vs. No Translation." In *The Longitudinal Study of Advanced L2 Capacities*, edited by Lourdes Ortega and Heidi Byrnes, 182–202. New York & London: Routledge.
Kramsch, Claire. 1993. *Context and Culture in Language Teaching*. Oxford: Oxford University Press.
Krashen, Stephen. 1985. *The Input Hypothesis: Issues and Implications*. New York: Longman.
Leonardi, Vanessa. 2010. *The Role of Pedagogic Translation in Second Language Acquisition. From Theory to Practice*. Bern & Berlin: Peter Lang.
Long, Michael. 1988. "Focus on Form: A Design Feature in Language Teaching Methodology." Presentation given at the National Foreign Language Centre European Central Foundation Conference on Empirical Research on Second Language Learning in Institutional Settings. Bellagio, Italy.
—. 1991. "Focus on Form: A Design Feature in Language Teaching Methodology." In *Foreign Language Research in Cross-cultural Perspective*, edited by Kees de Bot, Ralph Ginsberg and Claire Kramsch, 39–53. Amsterdam: Benjamins.
Malmkjaer, Kirsten, ed. 1998. *Translation and Language Teaching, Language Teaching and Translation*. Manchester: St. Jerome.
Malmkjaer, Kirsten. 2004. *Translation in Undergraduate Degree Programmes*. Amsterdam: Benjamins.
Murphy, Raymond. 2004. *English Grammar in Use*. Cambridge: Cambridge University Press.
Office of Qualifications and Examinations Regulation (Ofqual). Accessed June 18, 201. http://comment.ofqual.gov.uk/
Reed, Johnatan M., and Peder J. Johnson. 1998. "Implicit Learning: Methodological Issues and Evidence of Unique Characteristics." In

*Handbook of Implicit Learning,* edited by M. A. Stadler and P. A. Frensch, 261–294. Thousand Oaks, CA: Sage.

Roehr, Karen. 2006. "Metalinguistic Knowledge and Language-analytic Ability in University-level L2 Learners." *Essex Research Reports in Linguistics* 51:41–71.

Scheffler, Pawel, and Marcin Cinciala. 2011. "Explicit Grammar Rules and L2 Acquisition." *ELT Journal* 65(1):13–23.

Swan, Michael. 2007. "Why Is It All Such a Muddle, and What Is the Poor Teacher to Do." In *Exploring Focus on Form in Language Teaching,* edited by Miroslaw Pawlak, 285–289. Special issue of *Studies of Pedagogy and Fine Art.* Kalisz-Poznan: Faculty of Pedagogy and Fine Arts.

Thomson, A. J., and A. V. Martinet. 1993. *A Practical English Grammar.* Oxford: Oxford University Press.

Widdowson, Henry G. 2003. *Defining Issues in English Language Teaching.* Oxford: Oxford University Press.

# CHAPTER THREE

## AUDIO DESCRIPTION AS A TOOL TO IMPROVE LEXICAL AND PHRASEOLOGICAL COMPETENCE IN FOREIGN LANGUAGE LEARNING

## ANA IBÁÑEZ MORENO AND ANNA VERMEULEN

### 1. Introduction[1]

Audio description is a culture-based translation activity of inter-semiotic nature that consists in turning the visual content of an event into language. Sometimes, audio description offers additional information on cultural references to audiences who do not share the background of the source text (Orero and Warton 2007; Braga Riera 2008). In cinema, television, theatre, opera and museums, AD aims to present the world of images to blind and visually impaired audiences. Using the time spam between dialogues, the *audio descriptor* discretely provides the necessary information to compensate for the lack of visual capture on the part of the recipient. This enables the visually impaired recipient to perceive the message as a harmonic whole, and thus follow the plot.

Over the last few decades, cinema has become an interesting educational instrument: it has been shown to have a positive influence on

---

[1] The research presented in this chapter has been written in the wide context of the SO-CALL-ME project, funded by the Spanish Ministry of Science and Innovation (ref.no.: FFI2011-29829). Our acknowledgements are also due to Emmie Collinge, for reviewing the aspects related to our writing in the English language. the SO-CALL-ME project, funded by the Spanish Ministry of Science and Innovation (ref. no.: FFI2011-29829). Our acknowledgements are also due to Emmie Collinge for reviewing the aspects related to our writing in the English language.

the learners' motivation and therefore on their development of communicative strategies, especially with regard to listening (Weyers 1999). More recently, various studies have proven that the different modalities of audiovisual translation (AVT) offer an excellent opportunity to promote foreign language (FL) learning, especially intra- and interlingual subtitling (Vanderplanck 1988; d' Ydewalle 2002; King 2002; Vermeulen 2003; Danan 2004; Talaván Zanón 2006, 2010; Díaz Cintas and Fernández Cruz 2008; Pavesi and Perego 2008), and—to a lesser extent—dubbing (Chiu 2012). In this work we explore the possibilities of another type of AVT as a didactic resource in FL teaching: audio description (AD).

Within translation studies there is a growing interest in AD (Benecke 2004; Jiménez Hurtado 2007a, 2007b, 2008; Vermeulen 2008b; Basich Peralta *et al.* 2009; Remael, Orero and Carroll 2012). These studies highlight the audio descriptor's competences as a translator. In this sense, Basich Peralta *et al.* (2009) suggest that translators have to develop a number of specific competences in order to carry out the task of audio describing: they have to be good observers, capable of formulating what they see in a concise and accurate way, using specific and precise language and register that complies with the context and framework in which the action takes place. Cambeiro and Quereda (2007) consider AD as a tool to foster the learning of the translation process. However, the didactic application of AD to the FL classroom, and more specifically, to Spanish as a FL, has not been explored. One of the very few works that address this type of AVT in the FL classroom is Clouet (2005), who proposes the use of AD as a didactic tool to promote writing skills in English as a FL. In the same vein, we aim to shed some light on the possibilities of integrating AD within the classroom of Spanish as a FL. Accurate language and idiomatic formulations are essential for the recipients of AD to understand the plot. This makes this kind of AVT a very useful didactic tool to work with at higher language levels.

The main research question here is whether applying AD in the FL classroom, in this case to the teaching of Spanish as a FL, is adequate to foster competence in Spanish among Dutch speaking Belgian students. Our focus will be on whether AD is a good resource to increase lexical and phraseological competences. A secondary question relating to the type of materials used is also formulated: Does the content of the audiovisual material selected for practicing AD exert an influence on learners' outcomes?

In order to answer these questions we will analyse the results obtained from the ARDELE project[2] that was carried out in 2012, at the Faculty of Applied Linguistics of the University College of Ghent (Belgium), with third-year Dutch-speaking students of Spanish (level B2). Following the task-based approach, we designed a didactic unit based on the AD of scenes from the Spanish movie *Sin Ti* (Masllorens 2006). This didactic unit provided motivating and useful activities to practice the four language skills. Focusing on the learning of lexical and phraseological units, this chapter shows a series of didactic techniques that were used in the classroom, as well as the results obtained from their implementation.

## 2. Context: audio description

AD is a type of translation that overcomes physical and cognitive barriers to ensure that any AV product is accessible, be it in the cinema, television, Internet, live performances (i.e. opera, theater), audio guides (in museums), etc. Following Jakobson (1959), this is an example of intersemiotic translation, since images are translated into words. A useful definition of AD is provided by Hyks:

> Audio description is a precise and succinct aural translation of the visual aspects of the live or filmed performance, exhibition or sporting event for the benefits of visually impaired and blind people. The description is interwoven into the silent intervals between dialogue, sound effect or commentary.[3]

The audio descriptor meticulously describes what he/she sees, selecting, retrieving, structuring and reformulating the relevant information from the visual content, without explaining. He/she describes the scenery (place and time), the physical attributes (age, ethnical group, appearance, outfit, facial expressions, body language etc.) and sometimes the emotional state of characters, as well as their actions (perception and movements).

A basic element in AD is the AD script (ADS): the text that will be included as an oral commentary within the silent intervals of the AV document. This oral comment has to describe what appears on screen with a ratio of 180 words per minute. Given that the audio descriptor has very little time—the intervals between dialogues—and that he/she cannot

---

[2] ARDELE stands for *Audiodescripción como Recurso Didáctico en la Enseñanza del Español como Lengua Extranjera* (*Audio description as a Didactic Tool in the Teaching of Spanish as a Foreign Language*).
[3] Hyks 2005, 6.

interrupt the plot or contaminate the acoustic elements of the AV document (sounds that visually impaired people can perfectly distinguish, such as a telephone, a piano, typewriting), the descriptions must be precise, using very specific and accurate single words and multiword units to evoke the space, the time, objects, characters and actions.

## 3. Theoretical framework

With the implementation of AD in the classroom we expected the students to increase their lexical competences and to foster idiomaticity (Sinclair 1995), as well as to increase their insight into their own language learning process. In FL learning, it is essential for students to understand the importance of chunks (Lewis 1993) or phraseological units (Sinclair 1995) in order for them to produce a fluent and idiomatic FL. Thus, lexis is essential as a component that, unlike the traditional vocabulary, gives priority to multi-word, prefabricated chunks and fits with contextual models of language (cf. Sinclair's contextual approach, as in Herbst 2011). Such models give phraseology a more central role in language.

In order to accomplish our objectives we designed specific tasks that were aimed at enabling students to reach a C1 level, as defined by the European Council (2001, 24–28, see *Independent user*). These tasks treat issues such as the use and learning of lexically accurate terms, collocations, expressions, idioms, and valences that sound natural to native speakers. We also aimed to enhance students' awareness of the FL via meta-linguistic reflection. The concept of *task* adopted here is in line with the task-based learning paradigm (Long 1985; Willis 1996; Ellis 2003; Littlewood 2004), in which this study is framed. A task is normally defined as a communicative activity whose goal is to achieve a specific learning objective. A communicative task aims at fostering competence in the FL by means of communication. Another important feature is the inclusion of processes or activities that take place in the real world, such as filling in a form or having a job interview. They also need to have a clearly defined communicative result. Littlewood (2004) redefines the closed and dual concept of activities in the classroom—exercises versus tasks. Both roles—form and content respectively—are complementary and necessary to achieve successful learning results. Lai Kun (2010) and other researchers ascertain that function and form are inseparable, and they allow for the development of different aspects of the FL. In accordance with this view, we introduced activities based on reality. These reflect Ellis' (2003) concept of *tasks*, in the sense that they depart from *authentic* material and are based on *authentic* situations, with a part of formal learning (*pedagogically-based learning*, Long 1985). Crucially, our tasks reflect specialized activities such as those performed by professional translators. Therefore, we can confidently state that we applied task-based learning to the teaching and learning of Spanish as a FL, where Spanish was used both as a means of communication and as a working tool in the specialized field of AVT, and more specifically, AD.

## 4. Methodology

The following section will outline in detail the methodology we used for eliciting data for the purposes of our study.

## 4.1 Sample

In total, 52 adult students, both male and female, were involved in the process. The participants were aged between 20 and 22 at the time of this research. All of the participants were Belgian students, native speakers of Dutch[4], and they were studying Spanish as one of their specialization languages in the Bachelor Degree in Applied Language Studies of the University College of Ghent. The students had already been learning Spanish in an intensive way (eight hours per week) for two years and a half. They had already obtained a B2 level of Spanish in terms of the *Common European Framework of Reference for Languages*. At this level, a user already handles the four linguistic skills and

> Can understand the main ideas of complex text on both concrete and abstract topics, including technical discussions in his/her field of specialization. Can interact with a degree of fluency and spontaneity that makes regular interaction with native speakers quite possible without strain for either party. Can produce clear, detailed text on a wide range of subjects and explain a viewpoint on a topical issue giving the advantages and independent disadvantages of various options.[5]

Based on this definition, lexical and phraseological competences are necessary in order to achieve a higher level by means of learning and practicing the correct collocations, phrases, idioms, and words that native speakers would use.

---

[4] The three official languages of Belgium are Dutch, French and German. In the Flemish region the predominant language is Dutch, whereas in the Wallonian region it is French.
[5] European Council 2001, 24.

The lectures were delivered in three parallel session groups, arranged according to the students' language combination. For practical reasons, we respected this formal setting. The first group was composed of 14 students who studied English and Spanish. The second group was composed of 29 students who studied French and Spanish. The third group was composed of a mix of students (9 in total) who studied English or German and Spanish.

## 4.2 Design

Each student was required to audio describe a clip from the Spanish film *Sin Ti* (Masllorens 2006). The plot is simple: Lucia is a happily married mother of two, and a successful painter. After slipping in the shower she loses her sight. Once blind, she goes through a crisis as she realizes that her life had been based on fake light. As she learns how to live without seeing the external world, she also learns how to see herself and her inner world. This plot necessarily implies that the visual part is very important. Also, it is an ideal film for a first contact with AD, as there is not a lot of dialogue. The three clips chosen for the project had a duration of less than four minutes: clip 1 shows Lucía in hospital just after the accident (3 minutes and 13 seconds); in clip 2 Lucía, already blind, first tries to put on some make-up, and later helps her husband to prepare a meal in the kitchen (3 minutes and 40 seconds); finally, in clip 3 Casimiro—a friend Lucía met in the residence school for blind people—commits suicide by throwing himself in front of a bus (3 minutes and 54 seconds).

We manipulated one independent variable (IV): the clips used in class. We looked at its effect on one dependent variable (DV): lexical and phraseological competence. Thus the treatment involved manipulating this IV to see its effects on the DV. It was carried out by means of the material used: each group had to audio describe a different clip: group 1 dealt with clip 1, group 2 worked with clip 2, and group 3 audio described clip 3. The aim was to see whether the narrative contents of an AV document have an impact on the results of the learners' outcomes. That is, to examine the effects of different types of clips on learning lexical and phraseological units, and on motivating the students.

## 4.3 Instruments

The tools used to compile the data for this study were: a) controlled observation, b) two assignments per student, and c) a final questionnaire created with *Google documents* application, which they had to fill in online at the end of the project.

As for the two assignments, the data were compiled during and after the lessons. Each student prepared two ADs from the same clip: one during the first lesson, and a second one at the end of the didactic unit, after the third lesson. Therefore, they had the opportunity to make a second version of their AD once they had analysed, corrected and discussed their own texts and their classmates' texts, and compared them with the ADS on the DVD. By then, they had learned the basics of AD techniques.

The final questionnaire included different types of questions, which provided data collection of various kinds and formats. Its paper version (which was later published electronically via *Google documents*) is provided in the Appendix. There were 26 closed questions, to which students assigned a score of 1 to 5 (from 1: *I am not satisfied/Nothing* to 5: *I totally agree/I have learned a lot*). These 26 questions were divided into different categories, outlined below in Fig.1:

1. I have applied my Spanish skills.
2. How would you rate your improvement on the different areas of linguistic knowledge that you have worked with?
3. Are you happy with the project as regards your learning about AD?
4. Are you happy with the project as regards collaborative learning?
5. In general, has the project met your expectations?

Fig. 1. Sections within the final questionnaire

All of the sections included different subsections regarding grammar, lexis (both single words and multi-word units), written or oral skills, reception or production skills, sociocultural competence, etc. Our focus in this chapter will be on the results obtained from those questions that enable us to assess whether AD is a successful tool to improve or promote lexical and phraseological competence. These questions were 2b (*My vocabulary has increased*), 3a (*Thanks to AD I have learned useful vocabulary and practical expressions in Spanish*), and 3f (*AD made me realize how important and complex it is to use accurate and exact language*). Additionally, the questionnaire included ten open questions, which were introduced with the heading *Linguistic contents and inter-semiotic translation*. These ten sentences were selected based on the most recurrent mistakes found in the students' ADs. Students had to follow a series of instructions: 1) correcting the errors in the sentences given (taken from their own texts), 2) highlighting the mistake/s, and 3) proposing a correct version of the sentence.

## 4.4 Procedures

In this section we describe the different steps we followed to compile the necessary data. It was carried out over the course of one month, in which students worked on the AD of their respective clips.

### 4.4.1 Preparation phase

This phase had an overall duration of one hour. It took place during the first lesson (lessons are referred to as sessions from now on) on AD. In that hour, we introduced the students to the tasks they were going to do and provided them with the synopsis of the film *Sin ti*. Afterward, we taught them the basics of AD. Some key indications were given (Fig. 2):

a. Use only present tenses.
b. Describe only sounds that visually impaired people cannot understand.
c. Do not use expressions such as "we see…"
d. Describe what you see, not what you think you see.
e. Be concise.

Fig. 2. Indications given to students to make their AD

The use of present tenses (a) is an obvious rule in AD. It implies that AD as a didactic tool in the FL classroom has limitations, such as the fact that past tenses cannot to be practiced, at least not as a primary exercise. As for the rules given in (b), (c) and (d), their aim was to ensure that students were aware of their role as speakers and of the possible power and influence people have when communicating. These rules make explicit the fact that the recipient is visually but not cognitively impaired. We do not need to describe what we—and also the visually-impaired viewer—hear, too. With regard to rule (e), students were not—at this stage—given a limitation of words to use (180 words per minute), although we did draw their attention to the limited time of the dialogue intervals. A real task, such as audio describing, was thus modulated and adjusted to the class. A real task was opted due to the fact that our main goal was to elicit students' language competence by means of producing written texts out of what they have seen, and this limitation would have hindered their production. In the second phase, however, this limitation was enforced: it was mentioned and they had to take it into account.

### 4.4.2 Production phase

This phase lasted three hours. It was divided into two stages: The first stage involved working individually in the second hour of session 1. Each student had to describe what appeared on the screen in their corresponding clip, by writing a text on a word document to be handed in by e-mail to us at the end of the session. The second stage consisted of two hours of group work in class and took place during session 2. Instead of getting their own texts back in the class (printed by us), students had to review another classmate's work. After highlighting the main errors in these texts, students had to comment on the different versions, compare them, and finally choose the most adequate one and justify their choice. They worked in pairs or in groups of three for this session. Particular attention was paid to the necessity of choosing precise and accurate words and phraseological units, taking into account the Spanish audience and the limited time available to accurately describe what happens on the screen.

### 4.4.3 Review and final reflection phase

This phase lasted approximately four hours, sequenced into three stages: The first stage took place in session 3, which lasted two hours. The students spent two hours analysing their own linguistic errors. They received their own ADs with the corrections made both by a classmate and by us. We had extracted the most common mistakes and put them in an extra handout. After looking at their linguistic errors and correcting them together, another group discussion followed in which the main goal was to analyse the main differences between the students' ADs and the official ADS made by a native speaker. There was a specific focus on two aspects: a) the way of formulating sentences, and b) the way of interpreting the world. The lexical and phraseological units were broadly analysed and discussed. In the second stage, with an average duration of one to two hours, the students were asked to do the same AD again and send it back to us. Finally, in the last stage they had to fill out a final questionnaire at home, for which they spent around one hour to do this.

## 5. Results and analysis

On the basis of the data obtained from the controlled observation of the tasks that were implemented, we can state that the students positively improved their writing production skills. They swapped their roles (from being audio descriptors to being reviewers) through tasks aimed at improving their awareness of their own learning process. The tasks carried out in class required all students to participate in oral comprehension and production. In the final phase, lexical and phraseological competences were promoted. The students' ADs revealed that although they possessed a B2 level and a large amount of Spanish language items, their resulting texts tended to look like a rough literal translation from Dutch. This is why special attention was given to specific lexical items, collocations, valence patterns, the use of pronominal verbs, the use of periphrasis, the Spanish preference for synonymic variation and even diatopic variation.

As for the description of images, the project showed that the way in which the utterances were formulated led to many different interpretations. One of the cases that was discussed in the final session describes how the protagonist, after becoming blind, tries to put some make-up on. On the DVD we hear the version of the ADS: *Acerca las yemas de sus dedos a los ojos; muy cerca, casiro zándoselas pestañas* (*She raises her fingertips to her eyes; very close, almost brushing her eyelashes*). However, the students wrote sentences such as the ones provided in Ex. 1 below:

a. *Muy tranquilamente toca la cara para averiguar cómo hay que pintarse.*
(*Very quietly, she touches her face in order to know how one should put on make-up.*)

b. *Muy prudentementetoca la cara. Lo hace muy tristemente.*
(*Very prudently she touches her face. She does it very sadly.*)

Ex. 1. Two students' ADs of one scene of the film

Following the instructions of good practice of AD, the ADS on the DVD does not include adverbs or expressions that show subjectivity, it just describes what the character does very succinctly. The students, however, included adverbs such as *quietly*, *prudently*, and even *sadly*. Discussing this example, as well as other scenes and different versions of the same scene, students realised how what we see and what we interpret is directly connected to what we express and communicate. The task based on the principles of AD proved to be very useful to them in observing the importance of selecting the adequate lexical or phraseological units, and also in eliciting the students' awareness that lexical and phraseological competence are of prime importance.

## 5.1 Results obtained from the open questions

In this section, numerical data are presented, obtained from the students' responses to the open questions of the questionnaire (the test that focused on lexical and phraseological choices). All of the percentages shown below have to be considered as absolute—52, the total number of students, being the absolute or reference quantity. Thus, every label in each table is independent from one another, since the occurrences are recorded not per student but per correction provided. If we sum up all the numbers in table 1, for example, we see that the students proposed a total of 69 corrections. If we take into account that 52 students participated in the project, it is clear that each student provided an average of one or two corrections per sentence, because some sentences have more than one mistake, although here we focus only on those related to lexical and phraseological items.

For the purposes of this research, we only comment here on questions iii, iv, and ix, due to their content which is related to lexical items and phraseological units. As regards sentence iii shown in Fig. 3 below, the main objective was to check if students could see that the periphrasis—given in italics—could be substituted by a specific word: *interfono*, *telefonillo*, or *porter automático* [entricom]:

> Se dirige ala puerta para pedir asistencia a través de un aparato que está al lado de la puerta.
> (She approaches the door to ask for help through a device that is next to the door.)

Fig. 3. Open question iii of the final questionnaire

In the ADS on the DVD the part in italics is omitted. Driven by this, 15 students suggested that this part of the sentence is not relevant, providing a correction that has to do with AD techniques. Out of these 15, five students omitted the last part of the sentence and suggested leaving just *Se dirige a pedir ayuda* (*She goes to ask for help*), thus solving the problem of having to correct what interests us here, the periphrastic form. As regards this, 15 students changed this periphrasis into a specific word or phrase in Spanish: *interfono* (12 students) and *porter automático* (3 students). Additionally, 13 students changed the word *asistencia* (*assistance*), a correct word but not frequently collocated with the verb *pedir* (*to ask for*) (zero occurrences in CREA, *Corpus de Referencia del Español Actual* (*Reference Corpus of Modern Spanish*)), by near synonyms: *ayuda* (132 occur. in CREA) or *socorro* (12 occur.).

Prepositions are a source of problems due to interferences by the mother tongue (Ibáñez Moreno and De Wilde 2009). In this case, the prepositional construction *a través de* was corrected by 8 students: one student used *por*, another one used *con*, four used *mediante*, and three used *por medio de*. Besides this, 5 students suggested changing *a* to *hacia*. Since *a* and *hacia* are equally correct, it is a case of hypercorrection. A summary of the corrections made by the students can be seen in Table 1 below:

| Responses | N° of students |
|---|---|
| *Uses an AD technique (omission)* | 15 (29%) |
| *Provides an inaccurate or incomplete solution* | 14 (27%) |
| *Provides an accurate solution for the word asistencia* | 13 (25%) |
| *Provides an accurate change of the preposition* | 13 (25%) |
| *Substitutes the periphrasis for a specific word* | 14 (27%) |

**Table 1. Percentage of students' answers to question iii**

These percentages reveal a rather low success rate in the corrections. This is probably due to the fact that when there are several errors to pay attention to, students tend to focus on just one or, at the most, on two of them.

In sentence iv, the main objective was the lexical error *encuadres* (*frames*), which should have been modified into *fotos* or *fotografías* (*pictures*) (Fig. 4):

> En la habitación hay dos encuadres. En una foto salen los hijos de Lucía y en otra posan Lucía y Toni.
> (In the room there are two frames. In one picture you see Lucia's children and in the other Lucía and Toni are posing.)

Fig. 4. Open question iv of the final questionnaire

This sentence proved to be easier for students, since there was only one mistake in it to correct, the word *encuadres* (*frames*), which does not mean *fotografías* (*pictures*) in Spanish. In Spanish the same word is used for pictures that are put in a frame as well as for those that are not. In this case, 34 students (65%) suggested changing *encuadres* for *fotos* or *fotografías*. Besides this, 11 students suggested omitting or shortening the sentence, thus applying an AD technique. Additionally, 13 students remarked that the sentence was ordered wrongly, or that the verbs *posar* or *salir* were not correct. However, these two are not mistakes, so they are included in the table below under the label *Provides an inaccurate or incomplete solution*. Finally, 10 students provided accurate solutions to improve the overall expression of the sentence, although they did not mention the mistake of the word *encuadres*. Thus, their answers are located under the label *Provides a solution but not related to the problem*. All these results are summarized in Table 2 below:

| Responses | N° of students |
|---|---|
| *Uses an AD technique (omission)* | 11 (21%) |
| *Provides an inaccurate or incomplete solution* | 13 (25%) |
| *Provides an accurate solution* | 34 (65%) |
| *Provides a solution but not related to the problem* | 10 (19%) |

**Table 2. Percentage of students' answers to question iv**

Finally, in sentence ix the mistaken word was *parquet*, whose meaning refers to a wooden floor in interior spaces, which was used instead of *acera*, *vía peatonal* or *bordillo* (*pavement*) by many students (Fig. 5):

Casimiro sigue andando. Sus pies llegan al final del parquet.
(Casimiro keeps on walking. His feet reach the end of the parquet flooring.)

Fig. 5. Open question ix of the final questionnaire.

Out of the 31 students who recognized this error, 26 students selected the word *acera*, three pointed at the word *bordillo*, one chose the general word *calle* (*street*) and one chose the nominal phrase *vía peatonal*. Apart from this, 21 students commented that there was a mistake in the use of the possessive form *sus pies*, stating that *los pies* should have been used instead. This is a further case of hypercorrection, because in this case the use of the possessive form is not incorrect. As a result of interference of their native language, Dutch, in which the possessive is always used when referring to parts of a person's body, students tend to overuse the possessives in combination with body parts (Vermeulen 2008a). In the class of ELE, they are frequently warned against this overuse, which tends to lead them to hypercorrection. Additionally, under the label *The student does not provide the correct answer*, 8 students provided solutions that were not necessary, thereby not solving the problem, such as suggesting *caminando* instead of *andando*, and 5 students did not answer the question. Finally, two students proposed correct solutions related to AD strategies, such as the lack of need to mention Casimiro since, according to them, the audience is aware that he is the person walking. All these data are summarized in Table 3 below:

| Responses | Nº of students |
|---|---|
| *Uses an AD technique (omission)* | 2 (6%) |
| *Provides an inaccurate or incomplete solution* | 12 (23%) |
| *Provides an accurate solution* | 31 (60%) |
| *Provides a solution but not related to the problem* | 22 (43%) |

**Table 3. Percentage of students' answers to question ix**

In general, we can say that a majority of students identified the main lexical and phraseological errors, particularly with simple sentences that included one error. Sentence iii proved to be more difficult for them, since it included more than one error. This could be due to the fact that what they had to correct was not an individual word, but a periphrasis, which is grammatically correct, even if it sounds unnatural due to its lack of lexical accuracy.

## 5.2 Results obtained from the closed questions

In this section, we go over the results obtained from the answers to the closed questions concerning this study. In question 2b *My vocabulary has increased*, in total 19 students (37%) answered with a 3 (*Enough, I am satisfied*), 23 students (44%) chose option 4 (*I am happy with what I have learned*), and four students (8%) selected 5 (*A lot*), the maximum rank. One student chose 1, which indicated *Very little or nothing*. This is 2% of the total. Also, three students selected answer 2 (*A bit, but not enough*). This is 6% of students. Thus, if we consider answers 1 and 2 as negative, we have four students out of 52 that were not satisfied with their learning outcomes, which amounts to 8% of the subjects. Considering answers 3, 4 and 5 as positive, we have 48 students out of 52 (92%) that where happy with the results. This can be considered a success due to the fact that 27 (52%) students chose 4 or 5 as their answers, which means that they were very satisfied with their outcome.

As for question 3a, *Thanks to AD I have learned useful vocabulary and practical expressions,* if we compare these results to the ones of question 2b, we observe a slight increase in the number of students that were not quite satisfied (eight students, 15%).15% is a small percentage, but it does show that there may be aspects of AD that need improvement if we are to apply it to the FL classroom. The positive results, however, show that, in general, AD is well accepted by students as a didactic tool: 42 students (76%) chose 3 (*Enough, I am satisfied*), 4 (*I am happy with what I have learned*), or 5 (*A lot*), out of which 22 (42%)—almost half of them—were very satisfied.

Finally, the positive results obtained from question 3f *AD has served me to realize how important and complex it is to use accurate and exact language* clearly show that AD is very helpful to raise learners' insight into their own learning process. There were no negative answers. Thus, 100% of the students thought that AD had helped them become aware of the importance of lexical competence as part of communicative competence, and, even more, 75% of them were very positive about this project.

To sum up the results, the majority of answers is rated 4 (67 hits) on a scale of 1 to 5, where 4 (with 67 hits) and 5 (with 21 hits) can be considered positive, and 1 (with 2 hits) and 2 (with 10 hits) negative. The average score is thus 4.2 on a scale of 1 to 5.

# 6. Discussion and final conclusions

The answer to our main research question on whether the application of AD in the FL classroom is an adequate tool to foster lexical and phraseological competences is definitively affirmative. The students felt that they had applied their Spanish skills. Consequently, they gave high scores to their improvement of those different areas of linguistic knowledge they worked with. In general, the project met their expectations.

The results from the open questions (the test) show that AD is a good resource to increase lexical and phraseological competences, a major difficulty at advanced levels (Nesselhauf 2005). In two out of the three sentences (iv and ix), more than 60% of the students were able to correct the errors from the clip they worked with. When they were confronted with a sentence from another clip, they tended not to find the accurate solution. In one of the sentences (iii) the result was disappointing. This is perhaps due to the fact that there were several mistakes to identify and students only looked for one or two.

Overall, these results show that the selection of the AV material has an impact on the students' learning outcomes as regards lexical competence. This is supported by the fact that in all three sentences there was a percentage of 25 to 27% of students who did not know the answer. In most cases, students provided incorrect answers when the sentence they had to correct did not belong to the clip they had audio described. This shows that the teaching of lexicon is context-specific. Also, the type of AV material to be used in the FL classroom for AD purposes has to be selected in terms of language specificity, difficulty, and the objectives that we want our learners to achieve.

As for the results obtained from the answers to the closed questions, they show that students perceived AD as a useful tool that requires competency in all areas of language use. From the results of the questionnaire we can conclude that AD is a good tool to foster lexical and phraseological competence and to make students aware of the importance of this competence as an essential part of communicative competence.

Tasks based on AD allow students to observe the importance of selecting the most accurate lexical items and colloquial expressions. This is because in AD it is of primary importance to select precise words to describe specific scenes so that the recipients can receive the message in the most accurate and natural way possible. In conclusion, and in response to our main research question, we can argue that AD is an adequate didactic tool in the FL classroom because it contributes to the development of lexical and phraseological competence, which enhances idiomaticity (Sinclair 1995, 833).

There are many other elements that deserve further research, particularly regarding the potential of AD as a tool to promote intercultural and sociocultural competences. Students' ADs manifested the fact that we tend to identify what we see with what we interpret. This project helped to raise awareness of how powerful communication is. Language users are not objective. Our expressions and the way in which we communicate directly reflect our perceptions of reality, not reality itself. It is fascinating to notice the influence that communication can have. Another aspect that we will leave for future research is the correlation between AD applied in the FL classroom and an increase in student motivation. The use of AD-based tasks seems to be highly motivating for students because of its social value: AD is useful not only to communicate something but also to present the world of images to blind and visually impaired audiences, and thus facilitate and promote accessibility to AV products.

## Works cited

Basich Peralta, Kora Evangelina, Ana Gabriela Guajardo Martínez, and Miguel Ángel Lemus. 2009. "Desarrollo de habilidades de audio descripción como parte del desarrollo de competencias en la formación de traductores." *Revista Virtual Plurilingua* 5(1):1–12.
Benecke, Bernd. 2004. "Audio-Description." *Meta* 49(1):79–80.
Braga Riera, Jorge. 2008. "Modelos y tendencias investigadoras en el ámbito de los estudios de traducción." *Revista del CES Felipe II* 9:1–13.
Cambeiro Andrade, Eva, and María Quereda Herrera. 2007. "La audio descripción como herramienta didáctica para el aprendizaje del proceso de traducción." In *Traducción y accesibilidad. Subtitulación para sordos y audio descripción para ciegos: Nuevas modalidades de traducción audiovisual,* edited by Catalina Jiménez Hurtado, 273–287. Frankfurt: Peter Lang.
Chiu, Yi Hui. 2012. "Can Film Dubbing Projects Facilitate EFL Learners' Acquisition of English Pronunciation?" *British Journal of Educational Technology* 43(1):24–27.
Clouet, Richard. 2005. "Estrategia y propuestas para promover y practicar la escritura creativa en una clase de inglés para traductores." In *Actas del IX Simposio Internacional de la Sociedad Española de Didáctica de la Lengua y la Literatura*: 319–326.
Danan, Martine. 2004. "Captioning and Subtitling: Undervalued Language Learning Strategies." *Meta* 49(1):67–77.
Díaz Cintas, Jorge, and Marco Fernández Cruz. 2008. "Using Subtitled Video Material in Foreign Language Instruction." In *The Didactics of Audiovisual Translation,* edited by Jorge Díaz Cintas, 201–214. Amsterdam: Benjamins.
D' Ydewalle, Gery. 2002. "Foreign-language Acquisition by Watching Subtitled Television Programs." *Journal of Foreign Language Education and Research* 12:59–77.
Ellis, Rod. 2003. *Task-based Language Learning and Teaching.* Oxford: Oxford University Press.
European Council. 2001. *Common European Framework of Reference for Languages: Learning, Teaching, and Assessment.* Cambridge: Cambridge University Press and the Council of Europe.

Herbst, Tomas. 2011. *The Phraseological View of Language. A Tribute to John Sinclair*. Berlin & Boston: Mouton De Gruyter.
Hyks, Verónica. 2005. "Audio Description and Translation. Two Related but Different Skills." *Translating Today* 4:6–8.
Ibáñez, Moreno, Ana, and July De Wilde. 2009. "Tipos de errores en el habla de alumnos flamencos en el aprendizaje de E/LE." *Mosaico* 23:19–23.
Jakobson, Roman. 1959. "On Linguistic Aspects of Translation." In *On Translation*, edited by Reuben Brower, 6–8. Cambridge, MA: Harvard University Press.
Jiménez Hurtado, Catalina. 2007a. "Una gramática local del guión audiodescrito. Desde la semántica a la pragmática de un nuevo tipo de traducción." In *Traducción y accesibilidad*, edited by Catalina Jiménez Hurtado, 55–80. Frankfurt: Peter Lang.
—. 2007b. "De imágenes a palabras: la audio descripción como una nueva modalidad de traducción y de representación del conocimiento." In *Quo Vadis Translatology?*, edited by Gerd Wotjak, 143–159. Berlin: Frank & Timme.
—. 2008. *Traducción y accesibilidad: Subtitulación para sordos y audio descripción para ciegos: nuevas modalidades de traducción audiovisual*. Frankfurt: Peter Lang.
King, Jane. 2002. "Using DVD Feature Film in the EFL Classroom." *ELT Newsletter* 88. Accessed December 5, 2012:
http://www.eltnewsletter.com/back/February2002/art882002.htm
Lai Kun, Choi. 2010. "Authenticity in ELT Task-Design: A Case Study of an ESP Project-Based Learning Module." PhD diss., University of Leicester. Accessed November 6, 2012:
https://lra.le.ac.uk/handle/2381/9065/
Lewis, Michael. 1993. *The Lexical Approach: The State of ELT and a Way Forward*. Hove: Language Teaching Publications.
Littlewood, William. 2004. "The Task-based Approach: Some Questions and Suggestions." *ELT Journal* 58(4):319–326.
Long, Michael, H. 1985. "A Role for Instruction in Second Language Acquisition: Task-based Language Teaching." In *Modelling and Assessing Second Language Acquisition*, edited by Kenneth Hylstenstam and Manfred Pienemann, 77–99. Clevedon: Multilingual Matters.
Masllorens, Raimon, director. 2006. *Sin ti*. Barcelona: Lavinia Production, Bausan Films, Catalonia Television.
Nesselhauf, Nadja. 2005. *Collocations in a Learner Corpus*. Amsterdam & Philadelphia: Benjamins.

Orero, Pilar, and Steve Warton. 2007. "The Audio Description of the Spanish Phenomenon: Torrente 3." *The Journal of Specialized Translation* 7:164–178.

Pavesi, María, and Elisa Perego. 2008. "Tailor-made Interlingual Subtitling as a Means to Enhance Second Language Acquisition." In *The Didactics of Audiovisual Translation*, edited by Jorge Díaz Cintas, 57–97. Amsterdam: Benjamins.

Real Academia Española de la Lengua. "CREA. Corpus de referencia del español actual." Accessed March 2, 2013: http://corpus.rae.es/creanet.html/

Remael, Aline, Pilar Orero, and Mary Carroll. 2012. *Audiovisual Translation and Media Accessibility at the Crossroads. Media for all 3*. Amsterdam & New York: Rodopi.

Sinclair, John, ed. 1995. *Collins Cobuild English Dictionary*. Glasgow: Harper Collins.

Talaván Zanón, Noa. 2006. "Using Subtitles to Enhance Foreign Language Learning." *Porta Linguarum: Revista internacional de didáctica de las lenguas extranjeras* 6:41–52.

—. 2010. "Audiovisual Translation and Foreign Language Learning: The Case of Subtitling." In *Ways and Modes of Human Communication*, edited by Raquel Caballero Rodríguez and Maria José Pinar Sanz, 1313–1332. Cuenca: Castilla-La Mancha University Press.

Vanderplanck, Robert. 1988. "The Value of Teletext Subtitles in Language Learning." *ELT Journal* 42:272–281.

Vermeulen, Anna. 2003. "La traducción audiovisual en la enseñanza de idiomas." In *Actas del II Congreso de Español para Fines Específicos*, 159–168. Amsterdam: Instituto Cervantes Press.

—. 2008a. *A VER... Deel 1: Spaanse woordsoorten. Handboek met oefeningen*. Ghent: Academia Press.

—. 2008b. "AD: een nieuwe uitdaging voor tekstschrijvers en vertalers." *De Taalkundige, Le Linguiste* 57(2):18–23.

Weyers, Joseph R. 1999. The Effect of Authentic Video on Communicative Competence. *The Modern Language Journal* 83(3):339–353.

Willis, Jane. 1996. *A Framework for Task-based Learning*. Harlow, Essex: Addison Wesley-Longman.

# Appendix

## Final questionnaire (paper format)

**CUESTIONARIO FINAL- PROYECTO ARDELE**

NOMBRE Y APELLIDOS:
Clip(s) que has audiodescrito:

*Por favor, selecciona la respuesta que mejor defina tu opinión acerca del proyecto ARDELE:*

(1. Muy poco o nada; 2: un poco, pero no lo suficiente; 3: bastante, estoy satisfecho/a; 4: estoy contento/a con lo que he practicado/aprendido; 5: mucho, ha sido una buena manera de practicar/aprender/mejorar el español)

1. He trabajado mis destrezas en español:

|  | 1 | 2 | 3 | 4 | 5 |
|---|---|---|---|---|---|
| a. Comprensión oral en lengua española |  |  |  |  |  |
| b. Comprensión escrita en lengua española |  |  |  |  |  |
| c. Expresión escrita en lengua española |  |  |  |  |  |
| d. Expresión oral en lengua española |  |  |  |  |  |
| e. Competencia intercultural (formas diferentes según la cultura de origen de comunicarnos) |  |  |  |  |  |

2. ¿Cómo describirías las siguientes áreas de tu aprendizaje lingüístico una vez realizadas las tareas propuestas durante este proyecto?:

|  | 1 | 2 | 3 | 4 | 5 |
|---|---|---|---|---|---|
| a. Mi gramática ha mejorado |  |  |  |  |  |
| b. Mi vocabulario ha aumentado |  |  |  |  |  |
| c. Mi nivel de expresión escrita ha mejorado |  |  |  |  |  |
| d. Mi nivel de expresión oral ha mejorado |  |  |  |  |  |
| e. Mi seguridad en el uso de la lengua española ha mejorado |  |  |  |  |  |

# Audio Description as a Tool to Improve Lexical Competence

3. ¿Estás satisfecho/a con los siguientes aspectos del proyecto en cuanto al proceso de aprendizaje en el mismo en relación a la audiodescripción?:

| | 1 | 2 | 3 | 4 | 5 |
|---|---|---|---|---|---|
| a. Gracias a la audiodescripción he aprendido vocabulario en español útil y expresiones prácticas | | | | | |
| b. El uso de materiales audiovisuales auténticos relacionados con la audiodescripción me ha resultado beneficioso para desarrollar mis habilidades de traducción | | | | | |
| c. El uso de materiales audiovisuales auténticos relacionados con la audiodescripción me ha resultado beneficioso para desarrollar mi competencia del español | | | | | |
| d. La audiodescripción me ha servido para reflexionar sobre mi propio aprendizaje | | | | | |
| e. La audiodescripción me ha ayudado a reflexionar sobre cómo nuestra manera de ver el mundo influye en cómo nos comunicamos | | | | | |
| f. La audiodescripción me ha servido para observar la importancia y dificultad de emplear el lenguaje justo y adecuado | | | | | |
| g. La audiodescripción me ha servido para observar la importancia que tiene la labor de hacer todo tipo de material accesible para personas con discapacidad visual empleando el lenguaje de forma que se tenga en cuenta al receptor | | | | | |
| h. He tenido que ser creativo/a y eso me ha sido útil en mi proceso de aprendizaje | | | | | |

4. ¿Estás satisfecho/a con los siguientes aspectos del proyecto en cuanto al *trabajo colaborativo* del mismo?:

| | 1 | 2 | 3 | 4 | 5 |
|---|---|---|---|---|---|
| a. Revisar y dar críticas constructivas sobre el trabajo de mis compañeros me ha ayudado a mejorar en mi propio aprendizaje | | | | | |
| b. Recibir críticas y comentarios constructivos sobre mi trabajo por parte de mis compañeros me ha ayudado a mejorar en mi aprendizaje | | | | | |
| c. El trabajo colaborativo me ha hecho reflexionar sobre mi propio aprendizaje | | | | | |
| d. Pienso que este tipo de trabajo colaborativo es motivador, ya que contribuye a que todos trabajemos juntos por mejorar | | | | | |

## Contenidos lingüísticos y de traducción intersemiótica (AD):

Por favor, identifica el tipo de error de las siguientes expresiones, y propón una alternativa correcta. Ejemplo: "Se ve alrededor de sí": "Mira a su alrededor. [Explicación lingüística: MIRAR en lugar de VER, uso incorrecto del reflexivo SE y uso incorrecto de los posesivos al combinarlos con una preposición, alrededor";

Nota adicional respecto a la AD y sus técnicas: dado que Lucía se haquedado ciega, es un tanto inapropiado señalar que "mira" a su alrededor. Se podría haber usado el verbo: "palpa", o "tantea", etc.].

i. Vemos a Lucía que ha bajado la escalera y que se orienta con sus brazos tendidas y anda hacia la cocina

ii. Lucía está en la ducha y lava su cabellera.

iii. Se dirige a la puerta para pedir asistencia a través de un aparato que está al lado de la puerta

iv. En la habitación hay dos encuadres. En una foto salen los hijos de Lucía y en otra posan Lucía y Toni

v. Toca de nuevo la cara con los dos manos para restregar el maquillaje

vi. Ella también da un susto y tira una bota con verduras al suelo.

vii. Su marido la sigue, se vuelve al muro y se asienta contra el muro.

viii. Vemos una autopista y un autobús rojo que se acerca.

ix. Casimiro sigue andando. Sus pies llegan al final del parquet.

x. Pasa por el espejo y se diriga hacia la cocina donde coge un vaso en el tablero.

## Observaciones generales finales

Por favor, selecciona la respuesta que mejor defina tu opinión acerca del proyecto ARDELE:

(1. Muy poco o nada; 2: un poco, pero no lo suficiente; 3: bastante, estoy satisfecho/a; 4: estoy contento/a con el resultado; 5: mucho, este proyecto me ha servido de gran ayuda)

5. ¿En general, se han cumplido tus expectativas?

|  | 1 | 2 | 3 | 4 | 5 |
|---|---|---|---|---|---|
| a. Con el trabajo de audiodescribir |  |  |  |  |  |
| b. Con mis destrezas lingüísticas |  |  |  |  |  |
| c. Con mis destrezas de traducción |  |  |  |  |  |
| d. Con la forma en que el proyecto se ha desarrollado |  |  |  |  |  |

6. Sugerencias para un futuro proyecto:

   a. ¿Habrías preferido trabajar con otra película?

Si …… No …….

Si tu respuesta ha sido SI, elige la mejor opción de las que te sugerimos:

| | |
|---|---|
| *Volver*, de **Pedro Almodóvar (tragicomedia)** | |
| *Air Bag*, de **Juanma Bajo Ulloa (comedia)** | |
| *Torrente*, de **Santiago Segura (comedia)** | |
| *Mar adentro*, de **Alejandro Amenábar (drama)** | |
| *Alatriste*, de **Agustín Díaz Yanes (acción)** | |
| *Otra*. **Por favor señala cuál:** | |

   b. ¿Crees que audiodescribir es una tarea complicada?

   c. Observaciones general adicionales: por favor, escribe lo que consideres oportuno (si es en relación a alguno de los puntos mencionados, haz referencia al mismo). Tu opinión es muy valiosa para nosotras:

# CHAPTER FOUR

## TRANSLATION TECHNIQUES IN THE SPANISH FOR HERITAGE LEARNERS' CLASSROOM: PROMOTING LEXICAL DEVELOPMENT

## FLAVIA BELPOLITI AND AMIRA PLASCENCIA-VELA

### 1. Introduction: Heritage learners and mediation

In the past three decades, the field of Heritage Languages has consistently grown in the United States, becoming one of the most active areas of interest for research, policy and pedagogy (Hornberger and Wang 2008; Valdés 2005, 2012). However, a consensual definition of what a Heritage Language Learner is continues to be discussed; generally, the term *heritage learner* (HL) refers to those individuals who grow up listening to and/or speaking a minority language different from the official (majority) language of the community (Webb and Miller 2000; Valdés, 2001, 2005; Polinsky & Kagan 2007; Montrul 2009). In addition, HLs are differentiated from both native speakers and second language speakers, as they

> [...] have internalized two implicit linguistic knowledge systems. Whether they acquired the societal language and the heritage language simultaneously as infants or sequentially as young children or adolescents, L1/L2 users utilize their two languages on an everyday basis.[1]

The level of proficiency, however, in the societal (majority) language and the heritage one differs greatly: Variations in the length of exposure to the language, age of acquisition, formal education and other social factors contribute to a variable degree of competence. Research has shown that by

---

[1] Valdés 2005, 415.

adulthood, the heritage language becomes the weakest one in most cases (Silva-Corvalán 1994, 2001). At the same time, HLs routinely engage in linguistic *mediation*[2] (CEFR 2001; Dendrinos 2006; Dévény 2011), also known as *brokerage* (Shannon 1987), *natural translation* (Harris and Sherwood, 1978), *family interpreting* (Valdés 2001), or *para-phrasing* (Orellana *et al*. 2003). Through mediation, HLs build a linguistic bridge to allow communication between the familiar context and the larger community. Their parents or immediate relatives rely on them since early age to "broker" linguistic transactions that require management of both languages. According to Dorner and colleagues,

> [t]he different aspects of language brokering may uniquely influence, or combine to influence, developmental outcomes including levels of stress and acculturation, cognitive and linguistic skills, and academic achievement.[3]

Furthermore, they have found that Spanish/English bilingual youths are able to identify some of the methodologies used by experts when translating or interpreting. Among those are "breaking words into component parts, use and manipulation of cognates, skimming, and rereading for specific information" (Dorner *et al*. 2007, 454). These language abilities are accessible when HLs enter a heritage language classroom, having developed their own linguistic background and experience in both languages (Said-Mohand 2011, 96). Subsequently, these courses can directly tap on their bilingual skills in order to advance proficiency.

Relating this previous experience as "linguistic brokers" and their knowledge of Spanish as a heritage language, this study focuses on the lexical development achieved by a group of students who study and practice translation techniques. The main questions for the study were: a) what the impact of translation techniques as pedagogical tools is on the development of the lexical domain of HLs, b) what particular techniques HLs use when translating, and finally c) what lexical components are most affected in their production. We posed the hypothesis that translation

---

[2] Defined as all written and/or oral activities performed by a person that makes communication possible within a group of people who, for some reason, are unable to communicate with each other directly. The mediating process of translating or interpreting in an informal setting is also characterized by an unequal power relationship between the mediator and the beneficiaries of this exchange (Common European Framework of Reference (CEFR), Council of Europe 2001; Dévény 2011; Cervantes 2010).

[3] Dorner *et al*. 2007, 454.

techniques would enhance students' individual strategies for mediation while accelerate their lexical development in the heritage language.

## 2. Lexical domain of heritage learners

The growing field of Heritage Languages in the US has gained considerable space in the study of the English-Spanish contact situations. As a great number of researchers have argued (Lynch 2003; Valdés 1995, 2003, 2005; Kagan and Dillon 2008; Fairclough 2011, among others), more research is needed to measure more precisely the HLs' proficiency in both languages, and design teaching methods that better fit these learners' needs. At the same time, the past decades reflect a deeper understanding of the HLs' affective, linguistic, and pedagogical needs. This understanding has promoted the development and implementation of different approaches to the teaching of heritage languages (Said-Mohand 2011, 99–101). One area of major relevance is the pedagogy related to the lexical domain. In earlier studies, Polinsky (2000, 2007, 2008) observed a strong correlation between a speaker's knowledge of lexical items, measured against a basic word list (about 200 items), and the speaker's control of grammatical phenomena (Polinsky 2007, 376). This correlation highlights lexical knowledge as a key feature in the development of higher proficiency in the heritage language, and, consequently, heritage language pedagogy should be directed to methodologies that support and advance lexical growth.

Montrul (2009) explains that research continues to advance in the description of heritage language grammars; there is still less information on the status of the heritage language lexicon and the underlying processes that describe gain, retention or loss of the heritage language words. Her study compared second language learners with HLs measuring vocabulary knowledge and lexical processing. She found a number of factors directly affecting word processing speed and accuracy: word frequency, cognates, morphological complexity, syntactic category, and age of acquisition were the most influential aspects in lexical access. Attrition or incomplete acquisition of the heritage language directly affects the HLs' lexical domain. As a consequence, they encounter difficulties when attempting to retrieve a word in their heritage language (cf. Montrul 2009, 20). This, subsequently, promotes the use of different strategies in order to cope with the difficulties. These strategies include *coinage of new forms, borrowing from the dominant language, use of calques and false friends* or, in many cases, *rephrasing of the whole sentence* to avoid the problematic expression. These strategies have been described by García with the term *translanguaging*, as

[...] the act performed by bilinguals of accessing different linguistic features, or various modes of what are described as autonomous languages, in order to maximize communicative potential.[4]

In addition, the use of these strategies closely relates to the lexical component of the Spanish of the US, which originates from the Spanish-English contact situation. This matter has been explored by a number of researchers (with special attention to Otheguy 1993; Silva Corvalán 1994, 2001; Torres 2002; Lipski 2002). Hybrid forms, calques, and borrowings are characteristic and, in some cases, central components of the HLs' lexical knowledge. Different studies show that HLs rely on the forms they are most familiar with when searching for a word to complete a linguistic task. They also indicate that they can easily coin new forms, if needed. Proficiency in the target language, time and topic constrains, as well as contextual cues are the basis for transformations which result in different types of lexical forms (Otheguy 1993; Lipski 2002). In this study, several kinds of transformations and borrowed items were found, signaling the complex processes of language interference in the lexical domain. The analysis provides a detailed description of the different form that result from learners' manipulation and transformation of their two accessible lexical systems. Better understanding of these processes would support vocabulary teaching to promote lexical knowledge and further proficiency in the heritage language.

## 3. Translation-as-pedagogy in L2 and heritage language classrooms

One of the main differences between instruction in a second language and in a heritage language originates in the students' sociolinguistic background. A HL has been previously exposed to the language of study through his/her parents, extended family and friends. This experience greatly varies and, therefore, a heritage language class is very diverse. The Spanish in US includes diverse dialects as well as sub-varieties, which become tangible in the classroom (Said-Mohand 2011, 93). This setting is particularly challenging for instructors because each individual student presents differences in their cultural background as well as diverse levels of proficiency. This rich diversity, however, allows the implementation of pedagogical interventions that focus on variation as the cornerstone of heritage language teaching.

---

[4] García 2009, 140.

In recent years translation-as-pedagogy has become a useful teaching approach in L2 classes, ending a long period of absence (Laufer and Nation 1995; Laufer and Girsai 2008; Machida 2008; Goundareva 2011). Translation—considering most definitions and methods—involves the general process of "searching for form, recalling, and evaluating" (Goundareva 2011, 145). Moreover, translation has been proven to activate different aspects of language processing, such as awareness of correspondence and difference between L1 and L2, distinction among patterns in each language, growth of transfer ability, and enhancement of mental flexibility and memorization (González and Celaya 1992; Mallol Macau 2003; Goundareva 2011). In the lexical domain, translation appears as a consistent task in any L2 classroom. At the early stages of learning a L2, "the students approach the study linking word-for-word from the L2 to L1" (Goundareva 2011, 147). Although in the heritage language classroom students do not necessarily approach language word-for-word, they still employ different transfer strategies when looking for equivalent forms or structures. Directing instruction towards explicit techniques and processes used in translation support growth HLs linguistic abilities.

In this research we examine two particular areas of lexical transfer in the written production of a group of college-level Spanish HLs: First, the transfer of idiomatic expressions, and second, the transfer of false friends,[5] which are problematic for students. Finally, the analysis contrasts the use of low frequency words in the pre- and post-test.

The literature reveals an ambiguous use of the terms *idiomatic expression* and *idiom* (for a full discussion, see Andreou and Galantomos 2008)[6]. They are frequently referred to as "idiomatic phrase", "proverb", "formulaic expression", "cliché", "lexical phrase", and "fixed expression". Despite this diverse tagging and the consequent difficulty in classifying these lexical items, it has become clear that they are a fundamental component in advancing language proficiency toward native-like fluency. This is because speakers employ them every day (Schmitt 2000, Simpson and Mendis 2003; Prieto Grande 2004, among others). Following Simpson and Mendis' initial definition, this study considers idioms to be those groups of words combined in a fixed expression, whose meaning cannot be understood by analyzing their individual components (Simpson and Mendis 2003; Kömur and Çimen 2009). The meaning of idioms is

---

[5] Defined as: "pairs of words that appear similar, but have different meaning in some or all contexts" (Inkpen *et al.* 2005, 1).
[6] In this presentation, *idioms* and *idiomatic expressions* are all compound lexical expressions identified with Simpson and Mendis' definition (Simpson and Mendis 2003, 423.)

processed through an underlying metaphor that has been set in a certain lexical domain; idioms are built as metaphoric constructs that relate a "culturally salient source domain" (Simpson and Mendis 2003, 423) to an institutionalized (communitarian) target domain. Such expressions convey meanings that have been formalized from "what initially was an *ad hoc, novel expression*" (ibid.). In other words, "conceptual metaphor is used to refer to a connection between two semantic areas at the level of thought such as the relationship between *anger* and *fire*" (Kweldju 2005, 167).

Comprehension and use of idiomatic expressions require the ability to process the underlying conceptual metaphor. The simple presentation of idioms as common lexical items does not help learners grasp the meanings these expressions convey. For instance, the frequent English idiom *money does not grow on trees* metaphorically relates the agricultural domain *fruit growing on trees* (providing the idea of the abundant and easily reachable) with the economic domain of *money*, which is the product of effort or labor and, therefore, not easily accessible or plentiful. This underlying metaphoric connection is then transferred to other conceptual domains. This transfer allows a productive use of expressions such as *do not grow on trees* in phrases similar to *good girls do not grow on trees*, *successful entrepreneurs do not grow on trees* etc. Comprehension of the conceptual metaphor becomes an essential tool to decode and use idioms, which permeate language use in all contexts. Language learners, both L2 and HLs, need to be aware of this metaphorical process in order to understand and utilize them in real-life communication (Lakoff and Johnson 1980, Kweldju 2005, Kömur and Çimen 2009, Samani and Hashemian 2012).

A second area of interest was the analysis of *cognates*, in particular *false cognates* or *false friends*, such as *carpet* (translated as *carpeta* (*folder*) instead of *alfombra*), *parents* (translated as *parientes* (*extended family*) instead of *parents*), or *consistency* (translated as *consistencia* (*firmness*) instead of *constancia*). This set of words presents a specific challenge for HLs in the English-Spanish pair. In many cases, students have been using a false friend for a long period, instead of the equivalent expression which best translates the concept. As a result, the false friend becomes fossilized.

> False friends are especially problematic for language learners as they tend to overgeneralize and assume they know the meaning of these words, which are actually misleading.[7]

---

[7] Chacón 2006, 29.

Thus, language instructors need to work within a process of new recognition of this type of words, internalization, and proper linguistic production. According to Boumali Asma, a valuable implementation through translation involves

> [...] activities about the different meaning nuances in order to make them remember those false friends and to deal with polysemy and homonymy at the same time.[8]

As learners become more skilled in identifying false friends, they increase their competence and advance their accuracy (Martínez Agudo 1999). Based on this, a set of translation-as-pedagogy activities[9] were designed to enhance students' recognition and a conscious transfer of false cognates in their linguistic production. The exposure of heritage learners to translation-as-pedagogy strategies was also directed to engage students in activities that relate to "linguistic realities and foster positive attitudes" (Said-Mohand 2011, 93) toward their family language.

# 4. Methodology

## 4.1 Participants

The participants in this study were 60 college students enrolled in Spanish for Heritage Learners courses (Intermediate Level) in a metropolitan university in the US Southwest area. The participants had already completed an intensive semester of Beginner Level Spanish, or were placed via the institutional placement exam.[10] Most participants belonged to the second or third generation of immigrant families, and demonstrated a similar degree of proficiency in Spanish. They were enrolled in the course to fulfill their foreign language requirement,

---

[8] Asma 2010, 36.
[9] For this study, the term *translation-as-pedagogy strategies* is defined as problem-solving methodologies while translating (Molina and Hurtado Albir 2002). The term *translation technique(s)* is defined as "the result of the translation functions in relation to the corresponding unit in the source text" (Molina and Hurtado Albir 2002, 499). Finally, based on Vinay and Darbelnet (1995), Orozco (2007), Baker (1992), Molina and Hurtado Albir (2002), and Machida (2008), we present a set of translation techniques used to categorize learner's production.
[10] Participants in the study were placed based on a standardized Placement Exam that differentiates Heritage from Second-Language Learners, and distinguishes HLs in three levels: Beginners, Intermediate and Advanced learners. For a complete description of the exam, see Fairclough, Belpoliti and Bermejo (2010).

although many of them were planning to continue studying Spanish for personal or professional reasons. The following table (Table 1) describes the group composition according to gender, origin, and age.

|  |  | Participants =60 |
|---|---|---|
| Gender | Male | 19 (46%) |
|  | Female | 41 (54%) |
| Origin | Mexico | 9 (15%) |
|  | US | 50 (83%) |
|  | Honduras | 1 (2%) |
| Age |  | 28.3 (average) |

**Table 1. Participants**

With respect to their academic profile in their heritage language (Spanish), participants had between zero to three years of Spanish at high school, and 60% had completed at least one semester of Spanish at university level. Contact with monolingual speakers of Spanish was frequent for most of them; 57% indicated that they traveled once a year to a Spanish-speaking country, while 28% travelled often. Only 15% indicated that they did not visit Spanish-speaking countries.

When asked about their practice of translating from English into Spanish, and vice versa, most participants indicated that they engaged in this task often, with similar percentages for both pairs of languages, as shown in Table 2:

|  | **Rarely** | **Monthly** | **Weekly** | **Daily** |
|---|---|---|---|---|
| E/S | 14 (23%) | 6 (10%) | 19 (32%) | 21 (35%) |
| S/E | 13 (22%) | 8 (13%) | 20 (33%) | 19 (32%) |

**Table 2. Frequency of translation English/Spanish and Spanish/English**

About 60% of the participants indicated that they translate on a daily to weekly basis, while 10% translate on a monthly basis; 23% indicated that translation was a "rare" activity in their lives. These answers indicate that heritage learners are familiar with the process of translation. They naturally deploy different mechanisms to fulfill the task, which normally involves mediating meanings for a third person. Therefore, including translation theory and practice in the heritage language classroom would bolster and improve a language activity they already perform regularly, taking advantage of their bilingualism.

Participants were divided in two groups: The first group (G1=40) was trained with translation-as-pedagogy strategies while a more traditional teaching approach including grammar, writing activities, and intensive reading was implemented with the control group (G2=20). G2 also practiced translation of short paragraphs to review grammar structures and vocabulary, but did not receive direct instruction on translation work.

## 4.2 Instrument

Data was collected with a two-part instrument consisting of a sociolinguistic questionnaire, and two news excerpts in English and in Spanish. Both segments were controlled to match the students' language level, and to include lexical items of low and high frequency, idiomatic expressions, and speech figures. The two news articles were simplified to reduce the number of words (avg=230) so the translation task could be completed in the time allotted (see Appendix for details). The same texts were presented as pre-test, the first week of classes and as a post-test after the teaching strategies were implemented in a period of eight weeks. Participants completed the task with a time limit of 45 minutes, in the regular class session.

## 4.3 Setting

Four extensive lesson plans were carried out with G1. G2 did not receive this implementation and they were taught with a more traditional approach. The G1 lesson plans covered the following topics: 1) lexical resource management, 2) idioms as conceptual metaphors, idiomatic expressions and rhetorical devices, 3) recognition and use of false friends, and 4) translation analysis through the reading of newspaper articles in English and Spanish. The lessons were implemented during eight weeks and adapted to the general topics included in the general plan of the class. The main goals of this implementation were: a) to further develop the students' heritage language skills, b) to work closely with English and Spanish grammar, and lexical systems, c) to strengthen and develop lexical knowledge, and d) to develop awareness of cultural differences that influence lexical variations in Spanish. The following subsections present the individual techniques.

## 4.4 Content of applied translation-as-pedagogy strategies

### 4.4.1 Lexical resource management

An explicit discussion about vocabulary related to technology (vocabulary module in the lesson plan) was conducted as introduction to the lesson. The conversation focused on current technology and different ways to name a device in English or Spanish (e.g. *computer* can be *computadora*, *ordenador* or *máquina* depending on the Spanish variety or social context). The instructor asked the students what dictionaries or thesauri they used (main answer: online dictionaries), and introduced other dictionaries, thesauri, and specialized glossaries. Working in groups, students received a short newspaper article in Spanish to read twice. All articles covered a topic related to modern technology. Each group had 15 minutes to read the article; after the first reading, the instructor asked individual comprehension questions to ensure understanding. There was a general round of questions about each group's article to introduce different aspects of the topic. The groups then were asked to reread the article paying special attention to the words they did not understand or were not sure about their meaning. Students were asked to write down those words and look up their meaning in the different lexical resources previously introduced. Groups were asked to write some of those words on a wiki (previously prepared by the instructor) following a bilingual glossary structure. At the end of the lesson, instructor and students analyzed and discussed the glossary on the wiki page and reflected on lexical resources in order to understand the content of a text.

### 4.4.2 Idioms as conceptual metaphors

The instructor made an introduction to conceptual metaphors (e.g. *relationship between the head and a bowl = the head is a container*) and conducted a brief analysis of a common idiomatic expression in English and Spanish in order to emphasis the different domains underlying the idiom's meaning (e.g. *When I saw her I felt butterflies in my stomach / Cuando la vi sentí un nudo en el estómago [When I saw her I felt my stomach knot]*). The instructor presented a set of conceptual metaphors through a discussion activity in order to explain how the metaphoric connection is established (e.g. *La vida es un viaje/Life is a journey*). From this primary relationship, students sought related common expressions, such as: *Estoy en una encrucijada [to be at crisis point]*, or *Mi abuela llegó al final del camino [My grandmother passed away]*). Following the analysis of the conceptual metaphor the instructor explained how conceptual metaphors are found in everyday language, and are found in proverbs, fixed expressions and idioms. After the discussion, the students were assigned a three-part exercise: a) idiomatic expression matching exercise (English-Spanish), b) everyday Spanish idioms to analyze, from which they had find other examples related to the primary metaphor, and c) explanation of idiomatic expressions in Spanish to search for their counterparts in English. After completing the first task, students were able to reflect on the reasons why an idiomatic expression cannot be literally translated, as cultural domains do not directly transfer between languages. Instructor and students discussed the difficult task of translating metaphors without knowing cultural contexts.

In the second part, the students worked in groups of four. They read a new conceptual metaphor only in Spanish (e.g. *El tiempo es oro [Time is gold]/Time is money)*. They were asked to look for an equivalent in English, and look for related expressions (e.g. *No pierdas tiempo [Do not lose time]/Do not waste your time*). Instructor and students discussed afterwards the various possibilities a metaphor can project in meaning and use.

The final task was to analyze five new metaphors in Spanish; in groups, students explained them, searched for an English equivalent, if possible, and then proposed context of use for that expression in everyday discourse (e.g. *Pan comido [Eaten bread]/Easy as pie*). These finding were presented in class to be discussed by all participants. The final conclusion presented by the students was that users commonly speak using metaphors without being aware of it. They also highlighted the usefulness of working with idioms in a language class to further develop vocabulary skills.

### 4.4.3 Recognition of false friends

The instructor introduced the concept of false friends as a starting point. Instructor and students then compared form and meaning of some false friends in English and Spanish (e.g. *actual* translated as *actual* instead of *current*; *disgusto* translated as *disgust* instead of *to be upset*; or *éxito* translated as *exit* instead of *success*). Students then wrote a number of sentences using the analyzed false friends, in English and Spanish. The instructor and students discussed some of the written samples, made corrections, and reflected on the similarities and differences of false friends. The second task was to read two short articles, one in English and one in Spanish where false friends were previously underlined. After reading, students looked for the meaning of false friends – either in the articles or glossaries and dictionaries – and discussed their findings with their classmates. Then, the instructor introduced a new list of 15 false cognates (in English and Spanish); students in groups of four worked to find the meaning of these words using different lexical resources. The instructor asked groups to choose 3 pairs of false friends and write 6 sentences with them. After checking this work, the instructor provided feedback and led a final discussion on the issues these words present.

### 4.4.4 Translation analysis through newspaper articles

The instructor took two articles, equivalent in content and length, from the sports section of two newspapers (one in English and one in Spanish). The instructor manipulated the articles in order to include idiomatic expressions, false friends, and new vocabulary related to sports, according to the planned vocabulary module. The students were asked to read both articles individually in 20 minutes. After reading, students and instructor discussed the content of both texts and focused on the nature of translation of longer texts. The students formed groups to analyze the texts through a four-part exercise. In this task, the English text was considered the original text, and the one in Spanish was presented as the translated version.

Students read the translated text and looked for words or expressions they did not understand, or about whose meaning they were not sure, then they wrote down those items. If the students did not know the meaning at all, they had to look for it in the available lexical resources; if they were unsure, they could read the original text again and look at the context to grasp the meaning. If they were unsuccessful, then they would look in their lexical resources. In the second part, the students were asked to look for 5 words and their equivalents from English into Spanish. They wrote down 10 words in total (5 in English and 5 equivalents in Spanish).

In the final part, they were asked to look for metaphors in the translated text, and check if they had equivalents in the original text. They were asked to write down the metaphors and explain them. Finally, the instructor collected the groups' work, checked it after class, and handed it back the next class. Instructor and students discussed the exercise, and reflected on translation as a difficult task to perform, and on the needs and challenges the translator faces when translating a text (e.g. research in specific topics, research in words in context, etc.). They also reflected on how text analysis helped comprehension, and summarized the new vocabulary acquired in the lesson.

## 5. Analysis and discussion

To analyze and understand the effects of the pedagogical implementation, three types of lexical forms used by participants to translate news' segment from English to Spanish were selected. This repertoire allowed a detailed description of the variety of techniques HLs used in the translation process. The set of lexical forms includes three main categories. The first category was *idioms/fixed expressions*, "a group of words that occur in a more or less fixed phrase and whose overall meaning cannot be predicted by analyzing the meanings of its constituent parts" (Simpson and Mendis 2003, 423). The second category was *low-frequency words*, i.e. words "that occur very infrequently and cover only a small portion of any text" (Nation 2001, 19). From all lexical units presented in both excerpts, six words were chosen that belong to the set of less frequent words in Spanish. These are words above the 3000 cut point that limits high-frequency words (Nation 2001, 2006; Schmitt and Schmitt 2012). This study utilized CREA[11] (*Corpus de Referencia del Español Actual*) for the analysis. The last category was *false friends*, i.e. words which share phonological and morphological features but diverge in their semantic content:

> [C]ognates are words in two or more languages which share phonological and/or morphological meaning, and normally, but not necessarily are also semantically related.[12]

Lexical components of each category were selected, including items from both English and Spanish, as presented in the two news excerpts. The selection was based on completion (completion was considered the inclusion of the necessary items); if one item showed less than 50% of responses among all participants, it was excluded from the study. The following table (Table 3) lists the items selected.

---

[11]CREA is the online Spanish corpus designed by the Real Academia Española that includes more than 200 million words from written and spoken corpora.
[12]Hall 2002, 1.

| Idiomatic expressions | Milestone<br>Pivotal moment<br>Racial barriers<br>Don't grow on trees<br>Change overnight<br>Pone punto final |
|---|---|
| Low frequency words | Challenge (desafío, freq.=4869[13])<br>Bans (prohíbir, freq.= 11543)<br>Denigrate (denigrar, freq.= 141954)<br>Judoca (freq.=159350)<br>Precedente (freq.= 6859)<br>Saudíes ( freq.= 14973) |
| False friends | Carrera<br>Admitir<br>Actual<br>Constante<br>Éxito |

**Table 3. Lexical items**

Following the proposals discussed by Vinay and Darbelnet (1995), Orozco (2007), Baker (1992) and Machida (2008), the set of lexical items generated in the translation exercise reflected the following nine translation techniques (examples taken from the learners' production; number indicates the individual participant):

1. *Equivalence*: selection of an equivalent expression in the target language without meaning distortion.
   a. *Milestone*: *un hito* (10)
2. *Generalization*: the source word or expression is replaced by a hypernym or general term in the target language.
   b. *Denigrated*: *son maltratadas* (27)
3. *Paraphrasing*: the source item is translated by a definition, description or similar linguistic expansion.
   c. *Saudíes*: *women from Saudi Arabia* (13)
4. *Transposition*: changes in syntactic categories without affecting the meaning of the lexical item.
   d. *Bans$_{(verb)}$*: *la prohibición$_{(noun)}$* (12)
5. *Adaptation*: transformation of structure and meaning to convey a cultural reference. This strategy is mostly used in the translation of idioms.
   e. *Don't grow on trees*: *no caen del cielo* (22)

---

[13] The number indicates the word order in the frequency list of the CREA corpus.

6. *Borrowing*: the word is transferred directly from source to target language, with or without adaptation to the morpho-phonetical target system.
   f1. *The challenge: la challenge* (1)
   f2. *Pivotal moment: un momento pivotal* (20)
7: *Literal* or *word-by-word translation*.
   g1.*Underground: abajo del piso* (16)
   g2. *Don't grow on trees: no crecen en los árboles* (51)
8. *Choice-error*: the lexical item or expression is translated with a target language item that has no relation with the source language item:
   h1. *Racial barriers: barros de rasa* (1)
   h2. *Judoca: judge* (28)
9. *Null content/deletion*: there is no word in the final translation, missing one or more components:
   i. [...] *has been accepted in many countries: se ha aceptado* [null] (59).

Translation techniques 1 to 5 describe the most common procedures that translators normally employ in their work. As Nation (2001, 27) explains, vocabulary knowledge implies a number of aspects, comprising knowledge about the word's form, meaning, and use. In the case of bilingual speakers, this knowledge includes the ability to translate the word between systems (Nation 2001, 27). Advanced learners of a second or heritage language are able to mediate meaning by translating the source text, and make the most convenient lexical selection in the target language. Therefore, this set of five procedures is found in their production (techniques 1 to 5 above). However, less proficient learners struggle to transfer semantic content from one language to another; if that is the case, the selection they make corresponds to the techniques 6 to 9 of the list. Making such choices directly affects discourse meaning, and in some cases renders the passage unintelligible. As expected, participants with less language experience and less schooling in both languages present a higher percentage of these items in their work. Some of the options are directly related to well-studied phenomena in Spanish in the US, as are the cases of coinage, loanwords and false cognates.

In this analysis, null selection or "deletion" (Baker 1992) has been considered an independent technique. Selection of this option can be explained by a number of reasons: participants skipped some items due to stylistic choices, lack of time to review the translation, non-comprehension of the item, etc. Choosing the deletion technique is a possible option in translation (as discussed by Baker 1992, 40), which may not affect the target text. However, deletion could negatively impact the final product if there is a direct transformation of the semantic structure. In some cases, the final discourse is a simplistic, very general version that lacks details and dimension. In other cases, the effect of deletion turns the text unreadable. This study does not focus on this particular choice, but more research on deletion and its effects on translation should be pursued.

Table 4 presents the overall results of the analysis after codification. A short discussion further down compares techniques utilized in the pre- and post-test, showing main changes between G1 and G2. It also introduces examples from both languages to better explain the positive changes observed between the pre- and post-test.

|  | Pre-test | | | | Post-test | | | |
| --- | --- | --- | --- | --- | --- | --- | --- | --- |
|  | G1 | | G2 | | G1 | | G2 | |
| Equivalence | 155 | 22% | 202 | 28% | 72 | 20% | 81 | 23% |
| Generalization | 120 | 17% | 175 | 24% | 59 | 16% | 75 | 21% |
| Paraphrasing | 51 | 7% | 5 | 1% | 25 | 7% | 13 | 4% |
| Transposition | 2 | 0% | 7 | 1% | 5 | 1% | 5 | 1% |
| Adaptation | 0 | 0% | 9 | 1% | 6 | 2% | 0 | 0% |
| Borrowing | 33 | 5% | 47 | 7% | 20 | 6% | 24 | 7% |
| Literal | 50 | 7% | 57 | 8% | 34 | 9% | 28 | 8% |
| Choice-error | 34 | 5% | 59 | 8% | 24 | 7% | 37 | 10% |
| Null | 275 | 38% | 159 | 22% | 114 | 32% | 96 | 27% |
|  | *720* | *100%* | *720* | *100%* | *359* | *100%* | *359* | *100%* |

**Table 4. Pre- and post-test comparison**

Figures 1 and 2 further down show the variation in the selection of techniques between the pre- and post- test for G1 and G2. The first chart indicates percentage in the selection of accurate techniques while the second presents non-accurate and null selection.

In the pre-test, both groups managed to complete the task with similar results. The techniques 1 to 5, which do not affect negatively the final version, account for an almost equal percentage in Groups 1 and 2. G1 used 43.5% of these options to complete the task, while G2 45.7%. Techniques 6–8, which have a negative impact on the meaning of the translation, account for 19.4% in G1 and 22% in G2. In both groups, these choices involved different linguistic processes: translating the expression word by word: *underground, bajo la tierra* (14), *abajo de piso* (47); using a direct loan: *challenge, el challenge* (60), *la challenge* (38); using calques (based on similarity of morpho-phonological features): *judoca, judge* (16), *jewish* (38). An interesting case of calquing happened with the expression *racial barriers*, which was translated into Spanish using expressions such as *barros de raza* (1), literally *racial mud* and *barrios raciales* (52), literally *racial neighborhoods*.

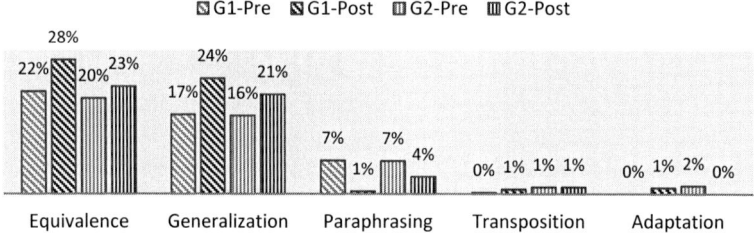

Fig. 1. Pre- and post-test comparison (accurate selection)

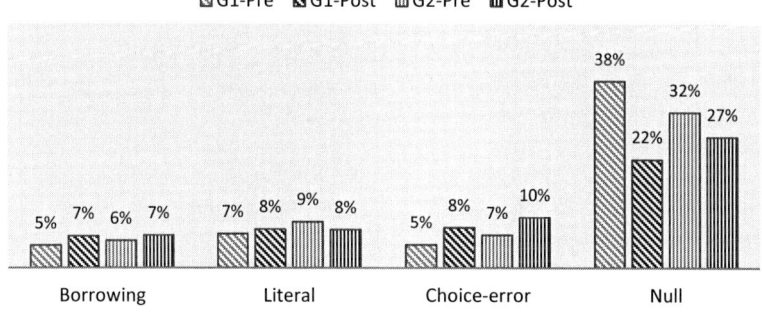

Fig. 2. Pre- and post-test comparison (non- accurate selection and null)

Another frequent technique was the translation of false friends as cognates: *actual* was translated as *actual* instead of *current, at the present*; *éxito* was translated as *entrance* and *exit* instead of *success*. Finally, null selection represented 37% of choices of Group 1, and 33% of Group 2. In several cases, the absence of a lexical item seems to relate to time management (a full paragraph was not completed) while in many others the deletion was indicated with an empty space in the text, or a line. Moreover, certain words or expressions were not translated because of paragraphing of the section, which shows the learners' ability to transform and modify items conveying the same meaning. Future research will take into account the different cases of null selection to better understand the reasons for its use.

The post-test indicates relevant changes in the learners' lexical management of Spanish and English when completing the same task. After the translation-as-pedagogy strategies were implemented, G1 was able to select better techniques, i.e. incorporating more accurate forms and avoiding options with negative effects. Techniques 1–5 accounted for almost 59% of options, including more cases of equivalence (from 21% to 28%) where an equal form or expression was chosen. For instance, the expression *change overnight* was correctly matched with the Spanish counterpart, *cambiar de la noche a la mañana* and *cambiar de un día para otro*. There were similar options with *pivotal moment*, which was translated using equivalent forms: *momento crucial* and *momento esencial*, which did not appear in the pre-test. There was a similar increase in the use of general forms (in particular, hypernyms and general synonyms) which moved from 16% to 24%. Learners were able to better tap into their knowledge of general words, which are also more frequent, to successfully translate more specific terms. In the case of the Spanish word *judoca,* the post-test of G1 presented general options, such as *judo player*, *athlete* and *player* instead of using a calque as *judge* or making a null option.

Paraphrasing—a very useful technique to translate fixed expressions and false cognates—decreased by 2.4 percent in G1: 38 items (5.3%) were translated with this technique in the pre-test compared to 21 items (2.9%) in the post-test. A possible explanation for this change could be the important increase in the use of the first two techniques, equivalence and generalization, although a more detailed comparison of each item is still needed.

With regard to adaptation (the transformation of both structure and meaning to convey a cultural reference), participants in G1 selected this technique 9 times in the post-test, incrementing usage to 1.3% of the total options. Although this seems a very small change, it represented a new option for them as the pre-test showed no selection of this particular technique. The teaching of metaphors as a guiding principle for understanding and translating idioms and fixed expressions was most probably the main factor influencing this change. It allowed students to comprehend, analyze and contrast metaphoric process in both languages. Clear examples relate to the expressions *do not grow on trees* and *underground*. In the post-test, the first was successfully translated with the equivalent Spanish expression *no caen del cielo* (*do not fall from the sky*) to express the concept of *scarcity*, while the second term was converted into Spanish using the expressions *por abajo del radar* (*under the radar*) and *por debajo de la mesa* (*under the table*) to convey the primary meaning of *clandestine*.

Selection of techniques 6–8 did not change between the pre- and post-test. In both instances, G1 kept 20% of this group of strategies. This demonstrates that many lexical choices were not modified by the learning process, and learners still relied on accessing the most familiar words without reflecting on their use. Interestingly, borrowing items were almost identical (5.7% in the pre-test against 5.6% in the post-test). This shows the resilience of certain words which are maintained through the translation process. This is the case for low-frequency words, such as the English terms *denigrated, pivotal* and *milestone*, and the Spanish words *judoca, saudí* and *constante*. Null selection or deletion showed an important reduction; most participants in G1 managed to complete the translation exercise without resorting to deletion of words or expressions; while in the pre-test there was 37% of empty selections, the post-test showed a reduction of 16%, which represents 21% usage of this technique. However, nearly 20% is high enough to be considered relevant for a more detailed analysis which goes beyond the scope of this work. The following table (Table 5) summarizes the changes between pre- and post- test.

|  | Tech. 1–5 | Tech. 6–8 | Null |
|---|---|---|---|
| **G1- total items** | | | |
| Pre-test | 43.5% | 19.4% | 37.2% |
| Post-test | 58.8% | 20.1% | 21.1% |
| **G2- total items** | | | |
| Pre-test | 45.7% | 22.0% | 32.2% |
| Post-test | 47.0% | 26.4% | 26.5% |

**Table 5. Pre and post-test changes by type of strategy**

Based on overall results, it is clear that both groups performed better the second time, both in the use of techniques 6–8 and the use of the null option. However, it is clear that the most important gains were presented in the G1 results: this group showed 15.7% increase in the use of positive techniques, with a relevant selection of equivalent and general forms to complete the translation. In addition, G1 was able to reduce the choice of null selection, which diminished by 16%. Although negative techniques did not show relevant changes (19.4% in the pre-test and 20.1% in the post- test), learners in this group managed to use more positive techniques instead of simply avoiding items by deletion. G2, on the other hand, only expanded the use of positive techniques by 1.3%, from 45.7% in the pre-test to a slightly higher 47% in the post-test. This group also reduced the use of the null option (from 32.2% to 26.5%) but this change increased the number of negative techniques: participants in the control group utilized more borrowing, direct translation and erroneous choices amounting to 26.5%. G2 students who did not learn with the translation based methodology improved only in general production (as the null choice was decreased), but did not show an impact on the overall selection of strategies.

## 6. Conclusion

Based on the social questionnaire answers, it is clear that most HLs conduct informal translations and interpretation in their daily life. For them, working as mediators with family members, colleagues or classmates, is an ordinary linguistic task done at home, at the doctor's office or at school. Thus, introducing translation-as-pedagogy in the heritage language classroom helped them to consciously increase their linguistic abilities in the minority language. Furthermore, this analysis showed significant changes from the pre-test to the post-test, demonstrating that translation-as-pedagogy became a useful component in the growth of lexical knowledge of most learners. The analysis also presented a variety of translation techniques used by the learners before and after the eight-week period of instruction, showing a positive impact when comparing the pre- and post-tests. First, there is an increase in the use of accurate (or positive) techniques in G1. The increment is more noticeable in the translation of low-frequency words, with a gain of 12% from the pre- to the post-test. In this area, G2 reported a difference of only 4%. We assume that the implementation of the pedagogical strategies broadened the lexical competence of the students, providing them access to new forms as well as analytical tools to find the most accurate term. Second, both groups showed an important improvement in the translation of false friends (12% in G1 and 13% in G2). This indicates that the improvement can be found in the general pedagogical strategies shared by the two groups, rather than a direct effect from the implementation of translation-as-pedagogy strategies. Third, G1 showed an increase of 4% in the translation accuracy rate of idiomatic expressions, while G2 reduced the accuracy of idiomatic expressions translation by 3%. This difference between the groups shows that the translation of idioms, regardless of the pedagogical input, continues to be challenging for the learners. The slight improvement in G1 can be a product of the work with conceptual metaphors. With regard to the non-accurate (or non-positive) techniques, it is interesting to notice that G1 kept the same percentages in both low-frequency words and false friends (14% and 12% respectively), while the accurate use of idioms increased by 3% in the post-test. However, G2 increased the use of the non-accurate techniques in both low-frequency and false friends usage (incrementing the use of non-positive techniques by 7% and 6.8%, respectively). This group slightly reduced accuracy in the idiom category by 3%. Considering overall results, participants in G1 increased the management and usage of accurate forms while reducing the null item option. In the case of participants in G2, they reduced the null option, too, but also reduced the use of accurate forms.

Translation-as-pedagogy has shown a positive effect on the Spanish heritage language classroom, and has allowed expansion of the mediation abilities of this group of students both as general competence and in lexical management. Strategies proposed in this study have a direct impact by improving lexical awareness in the participants of this study, and helping them gain greater insight into language. Nevertheless, as it can be seen above, there are areas where translation-as-pedagogy did not have a definite effect on the lexical domain. There is, indeed, need for more studies regarding these pedagogical interventions, in particular to analyze their long-term effects on heritage language preservation and use.

## Works cited

Andreou, Georgia, and Ioannis Galantomos. 2008. "Teaching Idioms in a Foreign Language Context: Preliminary Comments on Factors Determining Greek Idiom Instruction." *Metaphorik* 15:7–26.

Asma, Boumali. 2010. "False Friends: A Problem Encountered in Translation." MA diss., Mentouri University-Constantine.

Baker, Mona. 1992. *In Other Words: A Coursebook on Translation.* London: Sage.

Carlo, María, Diane August, Barry Mclaughling, Catherine Snow, Cherryl Dressler, David Lippman, Teresa Lively, and Claire White. 2004. "Closing the Gap: Addressing the Vocabulary Needs of English-

Language Learners in Bilingual and Mainstream Classrooms." *Reading Research Quarterly* 39(2):188–215.

Cervantes-Kelly, María. 2010. "Translation and Interpretation as a Means to Improve Bilingual High School Students' English and Spanish Academic Language Proficiency." PhD diss., University of Arizona.

Chacón Beltrán, Rubén. 2006. "Towards a Typological Classification of False Friends (Spanish-English)." *RESLA* 19:29–39.

Council of Europe, 2001. *Common European Framework of Reference for Languages. Learning, Teaching, Assessment.* Cambridge: Cambridge University Press.

Dendrinos, Bessie. 2006. "Mediation in Communication, Language Teaching and Testing." *JAL* 22:9–35.

Dévény, Ágnes. 2011. "Foreign Language Mediation Task in a Criterion-Referenced Proficiency Examination." Paper presented at the ALTE 4th International Conference, Krakow, Poland.

Dorner, Lisa, Marjorie Faulstich Orellana, and Christine P. Li-Grining. 2007. "'I Helped My Mom,' and It Helped Me: Translating the Skills of Language Brokers into Improved Standardized Test Scores." *American Journal of Education* 113(3):451–478.

Fairclough, Marta. 2011. "Testing the Lexical Recognition Task with Spanish/English Bilinguals in the United States." *Language Testing* 28(2):273–297.

Fairclough Marta, Flavia Belpoliti, and Encarna Bermejo. 2010. "Developing an Electronic Placement Exam for Heritage Learners of Spanish: Challenges and Payoffs". *Hispania* 93(2):273–291.

García, Ofelia. 2009. *Bilingual Education in the 21st Century: A Global Perspective.* Malden & Oxford: Basil/Blackwell.

Goundareva, Irina. 2011. "Effect of Translation on Vocabulary Acquisition in L2 Spanish." *Working Papers of the Linguistics Circle of the University of Victoria* 21:145–154.

González, María, and María Luz Celaya. 1992. *New Teachers in a New Education System: A Guidebook for the Reforma.* Barcelona: PPU.

Hall, Christopher. 2002. "The Automatic Cognate Form Assumption: Evidence for the Parasitic Model of Vocabulary Development." *International Review of Applied Linguistics in Language Teaching* 40(2):69–88.

Harris, Brian, and Bianca Sherwood. 1978. "Translating as an Innate Skill." In *Language, Interpretation and Communication*, edited by David Gerver, and Wallace Sinaiko, 155–170. New York: Plenum.

Hornberger, Nancy, and Xiao-lei Wang. 2008. "Who Are Our Heritage Language Learners? Identity and Biliteracy in Heritage Language

Education in the United States". In *Heritage Language Education: A New Field Emerging*, edited by Donna Brinton, Olga Kagan, and Susan Bauckus, 3–35. New York: Routledge.

Inkpen, Diana, Oana Frunza, and Grzegorz Kondrak. 2005. "Automatic Identification of Cognates and False Friends in French and English." *Proceedings of the International Conference on Recent Advances in Natural Language Processing (RANLP)*, 251–257. Accessed December 20, 2012: http://www.site.uottawa.ca/~ofrunza/Page/Papers/ranlp2005_cognates.pdf/

Kagan Olga, and Kathleen Dillon. 2008. "Issues in Heritage Language Learning in the United States." In *Encyclopedia of Language and Education*, edited by Nellke Van Deusen-Scholl, and Nancy Hornberger, 143–156. New York: Springer.

Kömur, Şévki, and Şéyda Çimen. 2009. "Using Conceptual Metaphors in Teaching Idioms in a Foreign Language Context." *Sosyal Bilimler Enstitüsü Dergisi* 23:205–222.

Kweldju, Siusana. 2005. "Lexically-based Language Teaching: Metaphor for Enhancing Learning." *Indonesian Journal of English Language Teaching* 1(2):164–177.

Lakoff, George and Mark Johnson. 1980. *Metaphors We Live By*. Chicago: University of Chicago Press.

Laufer, Batia, and Nany Girsai. 2008. "Form-focused Instruction in Second Language Vocabulary Learning: A Case for Contrastive Analysis and Translation." *Applied Linguistics* 29(4):694–716.

Laufer, Batia, and Paul Nation. 1995. "Vocabulary Size and Use: Lexical Richness in L2 Written Production." *Applied Linguistics* 16(3):307–322.

Lipski, John. 2002. "'Partial' Spanish: Strategies of Pidginization and Simplification." In *Romance Phonology and Variation*, edited by Caroline Wiltshire, and Joaquim Camps, 117–143. Amsterdam: Benjamins.

Lynch, Andrew. 2003. "Toward a Theory of Heritage Language Acquisition: Spanish in the United States." In *Milengua: Spanish as a Heritage Language in the United States. Research and Practice*, edited by Ana Roca, and M. Cecilia Colombi, 25–50. Washington: Georgetown University Press.

Machida, Sayuki. 2008. "A Step Forward to Using Translation to Teach a Foreign/Second Language." *Electronic Journal of Foreign Language Teaching* 5:140–155.

Mallol Macau, Cristina. 2003. "Teaching Foreign Languages through Translation: Considering Multiple Intelligences." PhD diss., Universitat de Vic.

Martínez Agudo, Juan de Dios. 1999. "Reflexiones psicolingüísticas sobre la naturaleza y dinámica del fenómeno de interferencia durante los procesos de aprendizaje y adquisición de una lengua extranjera." PhD diss., Universidad de Extremadura.

Molina, Lucía, and Amparo Hurtado Albir. 2002. "Translation Techniques Revisited: A Dynamic and Functionalist Approach." *Meta* 47:482–512.

Montrul, Silvina. 2009. "Lexical Knowledge and Access in Spanish Heritage Speakers". Paper presented at the 3rd Heritage Language Summer Institute, Urbana. Accessed November 8, 2012: http://nhlrc.ucla.edu/events/institute/2009/abstracts/Montrul.pdf/

Nation, Paul. 2001. *Learning Vocabulary in Another Language.* Cambridge: Cambridge University Press.

—. 2006. "How Large a Vocabulary Is Needed for Reading and Listening?" *The Canadian Modern Language Review* 63(1):59–82.

Orellana, Marjorie, Jennifer Reynolds, Lisa Dorner, and María Meza. 2003. "In Other Words: Translating or 'Para-phrasing' as a Family Literacy Practice in Immigrant Households." *The Reading Research Quarterly* 38(1):12–34.

Orozco, Mariana. 2007. *Traducción del inglés al castellano, Materiales de introducción a la traducción general directa*. Barcelona: Servei de Publicacions de la Universitat Autònoma de Barcelona.

Otheguy, Ricardo. 1993. "A Reconsideration of the Notion of Loan Translation in the Analysis of the US Spanish." In *Spanish in the US: Linguistic Contact and Diversity*, edited by Ana Roca, and John Lipski, 21–45. Berlin: Mouton de Gruyter.

Polinsky, María. 2000. "The Composite Linguistic Profile of Speakers of Russian in the US." In *The Learning and Teaching of Slavic Languages and Cultures*, edited by Olga Kagan, and Benjamin Rifkin, 437–465. Bloomington: Slavica.

—. 2007. "Reaching the End Point and Stopping Midway: Different Scenarios in the Acquisition of Russian." *Russian Linguistics* 31:157–199.

—. 2008. "Gender under Incomplete Acquisition: Heritage Speakers' Knowledge of Noun Categorization Gender under Incomplete Acquisition." *Heritage Language Journal* 6:40–71.

Polinsky, Maria, and Olga Kagan. 2007. "Heritage Languages: In the 'Wild' and in the Classroom." *Language and Linguistics Compass* 1(5):368–395.

Prieto Grande, María. 2004. "Hablando en plata: de modismos y metáforas culturales". *Actas del XV Congreso de ASELE*, 710–718.
Real Academia Española. Banco de datos CREA. *Corpus de referencia del español actual.* Accessed October 2, 2012: http://www.rae.es/
Said-Mohand, Aixa. 2011. "The Teaching of Spanish as a Heritage Language: Overview of What We Need to Know as Educators." *Porta Linguarium* 16:89–104.
Samani, Elham, and Mahmood Hashemian. 2012. "The Effect of Conceptual Metaphors on Learning Idioms by L2 Learners." *International Journal of English Linguistics* 2(1):249–256.
Shannon, Sheila. 1987. "English in el Barrio: A Sociolinguistic Study of Second Language Contact." PhD diss., Stanford University.
Schmitt, Norbert. 2000. *Vocabulary in Language Teaching*. Cambridge: Cambridge University Press.
Schmitt, Norbert, and Diane Schmitt. 2012. "A Reassessment of Frequency and Vocabulary Size in L2 Vocabulary Teaching." *Language Teaching Online*, 1–20. Cambridge: Cambridge University Press. DOI: 10.1017/S0261444812000018.
Silva-Corvalán, Carmen. 1994. *Language Contact and Change: Spanish in Los Angeles.* New York: Oxford University Press.
—. 2001. *Sociolingüística y pragmática del español.* Washington: Georgetown University Press.
Simpson, Rita, and Dushyanthi Mendis. 2003. "A Corpus-Based Study of Idioms in Academic Speech." *TESOL Quaterly* 37(3):419 440.
Torres, Lourdes. 2002. "Bilingual Discourse Markers in Puerto Rican Spanish." *Language in Society* 31:65–83.
Valdés, Guadalupe. 1995. "The Teaching of Minority Languages as 'Foreign' Languages: Pedagogical and Theoretical Challenges." *The Modern Language Journal* 79(3):299–328.
—. 2001. "Heritage Language Students: Profiles and Possibilities." In *Heritage Languages in America: Preserving a National Resource*, edited by Joy Peyton, Donald A. Ranard, and Scott McGinnis, 37–80. Washington: The Center for Applied Linguistics and Delta Systems.
—. 2003. *Expanding Definitions of Giftedness: The Case of Young Interpreters from Immigrant Countries.* Mahwah, NJ: Erlbaum.
—. 2005. "Bilingualism, Heritage Language Learners, and SLA Research: Opportunities Lost or Seized?" *Modern Language Journal* 89(3):410–426.
—. 2012. "Future Directions for the Field of Spanish as a Heritage Language." In *Spanish as a Heritage Language in the United States*,

edited by Sara Beaudrie, and Marta Fairclough, 279–289. Georgetown: Georgetown University Press.

Vinay, Jean-Paul, and Jean Darbelnet. 1995. *Comparative Stylistics of French and English: A Methodology for Translation*. Amsterdam: Benjamins.

Webb, John, and Barbara Miller. 2000. *Teaching Heritage Language Learners: Voices from the Classroom*. Yonkers: ACTFL.

# Appendix

## English version of excerpt[14]

*Muslim Women Participation in 2012 London Olympics is the start, not the goal*
For the first time, Brunei, Qatar and, most notably, Saudi Arabia are sending female athletes to the Olympics. This is truly a milestone for Muslim women in the Middle East. The traditions and beliefs of the region have kept many women from participating in sports for years, a fact that Saudi runner Sarah Attar hopes to change. Widespread participation in women's sports is something that has only recently been accepted in many countries. Almost every country has its own pivotal moment in women's sports history. Additionally, racial barriers have been broken across many sports in many different countries. In the case of the Middle East, the challenge is not only gender but also the fact that great athletes don't grow on trees. They also tend to be rather difficult to discover when you prohibit them from participating in sports; such is the case in Saudi Arabia. Saudi Arabia bans athletic activity in most girl schools and often prohibits women's athletic events. Teams do exist, but they are underground; women are publicly denigrated if they chose to participate. All this is not to say that women's athletics in the Middle East is a lost cause, but rather to point out that the battle has just begun. This situation will not change overnight, and it still requires strong support from international institutions. If these women's contributions are to extend past the category of simply a neat story, then there is still major work to be done."

---

[14] Pillow, Andrew. 2012. "Muslim Women Participation in 2012 London Olympics is the start, not the goal". *The Bleacher Report*. July 27, 2012. Accessed August 5, 2012: http://bleacherreport.com/articles/1275194-muslim-women-participation-in-2012-london-olympics-is-the-start-not-the-goal/

## Spanish version of excerpt[15]

*Por primera vez, los Juegos Olímpicos contarán con dos mujeres saudíes*
Se informó la participación de dos mujeres de Arabia Saudita en los Juegos Olímpicos de Londres 2012; esta noticia pone punto final a un tabú con orígenes en los sectores religiosos más conservadores del Cercano Oriente. El jueves pasado, el Comité Olímpico Internacional (COI) confirmó la elección de la judoca WodjanAbdulrahim y la atleta Sarah Attar, especialista en carrera de 800 metros. El diálogo entre el COI y el Comité Olímpico Saudí tiene consecuencias tangibles tanto para Arabia Saudita como para Catar y Brunéi, los otros dos países que hasta ahora no habían seleccionado ninguna mujer para los Juegos Olímpicos. "Presenciamos un momento muy positivo en las políticas de género en esta región, y vamos a estar contentos de admitir a estas dos atletas en Londres", ha señalado Jacques Rogge, el presidente actual del COI, en un comunicado de prensa. A pesar de este importante avance y de que la situación sienta un precedente novedoso, el panorama del deporte femenino y de los derechos de la mujer en Arabia Saudí todavía es difícil. En el reino árabe, las mujeres no están autorizadas para conducir ni para practicar deportes en público. La asistencia de las dos atletas saudíes en los Juegos de Londres es una señal de éxito hacia la mayor representación femenina, y se espera que ésta sea constante en el futuro.

---

[15] AFT. 2012. "Por primera vez, los Juegos Olímpicos contarán con dos mujeres saudíes". *El tiempo.com.* 14 de Julio, 2012. Accessed August 3, 2012: http://www.eltiempo.com/mundo/asia/articulo-web-new_nota_interior-12030423.html.

# CHAPTER FIVE

## AN OPTIMALITY TRANSLATION PROPOSAL FOR THE FOREIGN LANGUAGE CLASS

### CHRISTINE CALFOGLOU

### 1. Introduction

The use of translation in language teaching can be traced back to the end of the 18th century (see Howatt 1984; Howatt and Widdowson 2004) but developed its full potency after the middle of the 19th century (cf. Cook 2010, 22 for a rough timeline), as an essential component of the grammar-translation method and era. It persisted well into the 20th century, given a strong boost by contrastive analysis and its behaviourist underpinnings, which pointed to the significance of highlighting L1-L2 differences, bound, as it was believed, to give rise to erroneous L2 performance (see James 1980 for a discussion). Focussing on discrete sentence equivalence and the acquisition of forms, translation was abandoned, "outlawed" in Cook's (2010) terms, when, in the wake of the communicative revolution, language teaching shifted its interest on to meaning and native-like authenticity, only to make a modest comeback when, as is the case with all revolutions, the no-L1-in-class fervour abated.[1] This comeback was smoothly accommodated within the framework of the "Bilingual Reform" (see, among others, Butzkamm 2011; Butzkamm and Caldwell 2009), acknowledging the necessity of taking the learner's first language seriously into account in the teaching process. Still, while most language teachers will admit to having resorted to the mother tongue, mostly for lexical explanation purposes, it appears that this has been more or less random, while tracing systematic L1-L2 differences or similarities is usually assigned to the professional linguist.

---

[1] Though the use of the mother tongue and that of translation should not be treated as identical (see, among others, Cook V. 2001), the rehabilitation of the former was the 'green light' for the latter.

This chapter draws on the belief that translation not only needs not but also should not be kept out of the foreign language learning process, as its use can facilitate learning, quite independently of the use of the mother tongue in class. It is, indeed, counterintuitive to argue that translation processes are not at work in the language learner's mind, either in the form of mental translation (see, for example, Yau 2011) or in more directly visible L1>L2 or L2>L1 forms. In other words, the foreign language class is, essentially, a bilingual class.[2] Such processes can be positively exploited by the use of translation as a pedagogical tool (Källkvist 2004, 2008; Laufer and Girsai 2008). Yet, this is largely unexplored territory. I therefore propose that translation may enter the language class in a structured manner and take advantage of instances of difference or affinity between learners' L1 and L2 to predict errors and evaluate them as developmental stages in a principled way. And this can be both authentic and meaningful, in the sense that it responds to the needs of the L2 language learner and that, even if form-focussed, as in the case made in this chapter, it can shed light on dark areas and help learners engage in L2 tasks more easily.

More specifically, in the approach adopted, form-related violations are allowed to surface and, thus, transfer effects and interlanguage errors are predicted, deviant and target L2 behaviour being characterized by different constraint ranking. Errors can be treated as part of a developmental continuum between the different rankings, and constraint re-ranking can be seen as a gradual approximation of the desired L2 form. Importantly, affinities between pairs of languages can eventually take the place of a prohibitive divide focusing on points of divergence alone.

This chapter is organized as follows: Section 2 introduces the Optimality-theoretic framework upon which the proposal is based, section 3 presents the focal forms used to implement the framework as well as the methodology followed in the research conducted, and section 4 involves a presentation and a discussion of the data collected as evidence for constraint ranking and re-ranking, along the lines of the theory. The final section focuses on the pedagogic benefits of the approach advocated. It is, further, argued that translation tasks can reveal particularly interesting developmental issues and, if practiced within the proposed framework, can

---

[2] This may be related to the route followed by the L2 acquisition process generally. If, for instance, an approach such as Full Access/Transfer is adopted, the path followed would be hypothesized to be via L1 (e.g. Lakshmanan 2006), an interesting issue to explore. Such a discussion would go beyond the scope of this chapter, however.

point to elements of convergence rather than divergence alone between languages, which may help learners reconcile the two language systems.

## 2. The theoretical framework: Optimising translation outputs

The theoretical framework underlying my proposal draws on the spirit of Optimality Theory (Archangeli 1997; Prince and Smolensky 1993, 2004, 2006; Tesar and Smolensky 2000), a linguistic theory of the 90s minimizing the linguist's "equipment" in seeking to explain universality and difference in natural languages, and screening language outputs generated from a rich base, with the help of a set of ranked constraints. In more concrete terms, there is a "generator", which creates a candidate set of potential "outputs" for a given language input, out of which the evaluator selects the optimal output for a particular language. In other words, there is a universal set of constraints that are ranked on a language-particular basis.

Here's an example (based on Prince and Smolensky 2006, 125–126): The input {John, what, saw} yields the surface output *What did John see?* in English, featuring the question word in sentence-initial position, which means that the question word fronting constraint is more forceful than the S-V-O one. This is not absolute, however, since *Who saw what?* is acceptable in English while **Who what saw?* or **What who saw* aren't, which suggests that there is yet another constraint that is stronger than the question word fronting one. Thus, *Who saw what?* is the English grammatical structure

> [...] satisfying the constraints of the grammar not perfectly, but **optimally**: no alternative does better, given the relative strength of the constraints in the grammar of English.[3]

On the other hand, the output generated for the above input in Greek would also involve fronting the question word, as in *Ti ide o yanis?* (*What saw Yannis?*), which, however, would not outrank word order constraints, since O-V-S is attested in the language (under specific circumstances). Nor would this fronting conflict with the relative order of the question words, since Greek allows for a number of possibilities (even though *Pjos ide ti?* (*Who saw what?*) may again be favoured).

---

[3] Ibid., 126 (emphasis in the original).

There are two important conclusions to be drawn from the above discussion. One involves the relativistic nature of the grammar, which allows for optimal and not always perfect outputs,[4] and the second relates to the universality of the constraints. It is this universality that makes outputs comparable in some way for speakers of various languages. As we will see in the discussion that follows, these two points lend themselves most readily for the purposes of translation.

So, how would we translate this framework for our purposes? In other words, how would we make it work as a tool for the introduction of translation into the language class? If we substitute the fully developed system of L1 for the input fed into the generator, and the potential L2 translation equivalents for the candidate set of outputs it generates, then we need the constraints on the basis of which the evaluator will screen these outputs and determine their optimality.

Interestingly, one of the key constraints in Optimality Theory is FAITHFULNESS, which "tie(s) the success of an output candidate to the shape of the corresponding input" (Prince and Smolensky 2006, 128). In other words, the output should be as close to the input as possible. This is an articulation of the "do only when necessary" or "be faithful if you can" principle of the grammar (Prince and Smolensky 1993). Such a FAITHFULNESS constraint would allow us to screen the relation of the Greek L1 input *ksafnika kseprovale mja parakseni figura* (*suddenly emerged one strange figure*), for example, to its potential L2 outputs. If we postulate one such constraint in our construct, which is, indeed, tempting because of the obvious relevance of the notion of faithfulness to translation processes, we might have gone some way towards accounting for L2 learners' allegiance to L1 forms in interlanguage grammar.

Kager (1999, 343) argues that "outputs will be identical to inputs [...] except when divergence between them is forced by a high-ranking well-formedness constraint". My next constraint will therefore be well-formedness, i.e. ACCEPTABILITY, outranking FAITHFULNESS where the latter runs counter to the rule system of the target language. In the case of the example provided above, for instance, the faithful rendering would be overridden by the acceptable one *suddenly a strange figure emerged*. Now, it might be suggested that this is always bound to happen, in the sense that what we aim at is acceptability in L2 outputs but the key point is that the form violating the fewest possible constraints is opted for (see

---

[4] Unlike the Chomskyan model, according to which "If you can't say something nice, don't say anything at all", Optimality Theory advocates that "If you can't say something nice, say the best thing you can" (Pesetsky 1997, 150; see also Kager 1999).

Archangeli 1997 among others). This means that an output observing both the faithfulness and the acceptability constraint is expected to outrank an output conforming to acceptability alone. In this sense, *suddenly there emerged a strange figure*, faithful in so far as it retains the postverbal order of the L1 input, as well as acceptable, might outrank its unfaithful but acceptable preverbal subject counterpart (*a strange figure emerged*). In cases where no such alternative is available, however, the developmental path may involve a transition from high-ranking faithfulness to high-ranking acceptability. In other words, we may observe the transfer of faithful, though unacceptable, forms until these give way to the corresponding L2 structures.

The third constraint in the framework postulated is CONSISTENCY, namely the need to observe patterns, wherever this is relevant, or applying a constraint consistently. Following the example provided earlier, a sequence of L1 postverbal subject occurrences, for instance, might induce a specific kind of behaviour in L2. If, for example, a form repeats itself in a similar context in L1, the learner might be expected to treat both or all instances in identical ways. This, however, might become a high-ranking constraint and, therefore, an optimisation determinant among more advanced learners. The constraints presented are summed up in Table 1 below:

| FAITHFULNESS | *The translation output should be faithful to the source language input.* |
|---|---|
| ACCEPTABILITY | *The translation output should conform to acceptability criteria in the target language.* |
| CONSISTENCY | *Input patterns should be heeded.* |

**Table 1. Constraints operative in the framework proposed**

What makes such an Optimality-based framework most readily applicable in a translation-related context is the fact that, as noted earlier in this section, it involves a relativism which is particularly relevant to both language learner outputs and translation processes, translation requiring a systematic choice among "alternative" options. As Smolensky, Legendre and Tesar (2006, 515) put it, Optimality Theory is "inherently comparative." Of course, in the case of learner language, the end-state is much more fixed than in the case of translation generally but, still, viewing intermediate grammar choices as part of a wider repertoire helps treat errors developmentally, that is in a process-oriented perspective, as can be seen in more detail below. Exposing learners to translation tasks opening up the prospect of multiple options further reinforces this link. Violability becomes a challenge in the sense that it can accommodate several instances of deviance.

As was also suggested above, yet another important element in this approach is the universality of the constraints, which would allow predictions and evaluations to be made in not just a single pair of languages. Different languages might involve different rankings, as postulated in the theory, and this can help capture similarities and differences across language learners' behaviour in a number of contexts.[5] In the following section the methodology employed in researching learners' susceptibility to the theory is presented.

## 3. Researching translation outputs

### 3.1 Translation task 1

To test the efficacy of the theory developed in the previous section, a translation task was distributed to Greek learners of English as a Foreign Language in a model experimental lower secondary school in Athens.[6] Out of a total of 131 12–14 year-old student participants, girls and boys represented equally, 25 were asked to translate 12 sentences and the remaining 106 were asked to translate 14. Students were allowed a full teaching hour (45 min.) to cope with the demands of task completion, as it was deemed important that they be given the opportunity to reflect on each item. They were expected to work on the sentences individually and were explicitly told that this task was no test and was only meant to explore their intuition in the language, which would help the teacher (me) in the design of the course. The specific task design was selected because

---

[5] It is important to note that the present analysis follows the spirit rather than the letter of Optimality Theory. The issue of inherently conflicting constraints (cf. Prince and Smolensky 2004), for instance, is not considered.

[6] Lower secondary school students were chosen because it was thought that it would be interesting to see whether the literary input used in the experiment would produce the results expected among learners of this age. On the other hand, however, although the student population was quite varied both in terms of cognitive and in terms of foreign language competence, generalizing the data obtained more safely would require replicating the test in other school contexts, too.

through it the constraints operative on the translation of syntax could be controlled. The level of the students, as established via a diagnostic test distributed earlier in the year, ranged from A2+ to C1+, with an average of B1+, but there was ample vocabulary support provided to help them all cope with the task.

The sentences composing the task were discrete items demonstrating specific word order properties, as will be illustrated below. Among them, however, there were also a few items involving no particular challenge, which were meant to act as "distractor" sentences. Students were instructed to produce a close translation, in the sense of attempting to reproduce all parts of the sentence, without, however, being biased on the side of faithfulness, one of the constraints supposedly at work. Such close, form-focussed translation obviates the usefulness of paraphrasing and avoidance strategies generally, and "draws both the student's and the teacher's attention to the problem, and is thus the first stage towards its solution" (Cook 2010, 137).

Despite being discrete, the test sentences were meaningful, as they were literary.[7] More specifically, they were modelled after samples of mostly poetic expression in Greek, as can be seen in Ex. 1 below:[8]

Ex. 1     Βουλιάζει ο κόσμος, έρχεται σιωπή, ήρθε η νύχτα, νύχτα σκοτεινή.
          *Vuliazi o kozmos, erhete sjopi, irthe i nihta, nihta skotini*
          (*Sinks the world, comes silence, came the night, night dark*)

The purpose of including poetic items was to present learners with instances where deviance boundaries are more relaxed than in ordinary language, and, therefore, to allow deeper affinities between the two languages, L1 and L2, to emerge. This contradicts what has been standard practice in linguistic analysis, namely the use of sentences with full control of vocabulary and style to minimize the cognitive weight and allow respondents to focus on the form researched alone. Yet, it is of great value in this case, as poetry incorporates a number of non-prototypical, non-mainstream or else marked forms. Following Dillon (1980), for instance,

---

[7] The use of a formal faithfulness criterion in literary translation is a highly debated issue (see Hassan 2011 for an overview). Scott (2010, 110) suggests that "all literary translation should translate from the linguistic towards the paralinguistic, from script towards dict, that is towards spoken or performed text". Cognitive approaches invoking form-content iconicity considerations in literary translation (Calfoglou 2014; Tabakowska 2003), however, strongly argue in favour of the significance of equivalence in form; and, when it comes to language teaching, the advantages of working on form-related issues become most evident.

[8] For the full list of sentences, see Appendix A.

post-verbal subjects, very common in Greek (see Lascaratou 1989; Alexiadou 1999 among others), appear quite robustly in the poetic paradigm in a language such as English, where subjects are most distinctly pre-verbal (see discussion in Calfoglou 2004, 2010a). Therefore, I would argue that, by exposing learners to L2 tokens where otherwise marginal, native-like forms are instantiated, we enhance the idea of an L1-L2 continuum and introduce an alternative stance in relation to errors, as part of a process. We can then facilitate learners' perception of the context in which such marked instances occur in L2 and gradually help them move away from the overgeneralization of the marked forms.[9]

In proposing learner exposure to marked target language forms, I am adopting a rather different approach to markedness as viewed in Optimality Theory or L2 acquisition. Unlike the argument advanced in Optimality Theory (e.g. Prince and Smolensky 2006), whereby faithful outputs may be avoided if marked, I would support the idea that faithfulness may override markedness. In acquisition terms, contrary to what has been proposed in the literature about marked forms not being transferred (James 1998), I would argue that markedness is transferable, that is, marked forms can well form part of intermediate grammars. To give an example, post-nominal adjectives, treated as non-prototypical, that is marked, in Greek (Stavrou 1996, 1999),[10] can appear in learners' interlanguage and persist up to advanced L2 acquisition stages, as the informal study of student written output has shown:

Ex. 2     *night dark

Let us now consider the specific word order properties the translation items possessed. The types of word order tested were V-S, that is post-verbal subjects, as illustrated in example (1) earlier, N-A, that is post-nominal adjectives, as in Ex. 2, and pre- and post-nominal genitives, as in Ex. 3a and 3b:

Ex. 3a    δελφινιών ράχες
          delfinion rahes
          (dolphins-of backs)

---

[9] It might be argued that poetic language poses additional difficulties but the counterargument is that, as has been suggested by a number of poets, poetry is closer to the language of infancy and, therefore, I would argue, not so inaccessible as generally thought (cf. Calfoglou 2010a).
[10] Consider, by contrast, Fischer's (2001, 2006) arguments concerning the unmarked status of post-nominal adjectives in older English and the unmarked properties of postmodification.

Ex. 3b   *ο νους τ' ανθρώπου*
         *o nus t'anthropu*
         (*the mind of-the man*)

How do these forms fare in each of the two languages in my research paradigm? As noted earlier, post-verbal subjects are common, that is unmarked, in Greek and uncommon, that is marked, in English. In Greek, they are mostly attested in intransitive, verb-subject complexes (cf. Lascaratou 1989), which thus form the bulk of tokens in my test. There is only one instance of a transitive object-verb-subject sequence included (item 3 in Appendix A) and this will not be discussed.

In English, things are very different. Post-verbal subjects in declarative clauses can only be licensed under specific conditions, most typically when a prepositional or adverbial phrase opens the sentence, as in Ex. 4a and 4b:

Ex. 4a   *At the top of the hill stood the ghost of an old castle.*

Ex. 4b   *Far away, in the grim darkness, (there) emerged a stunningly beautiful fairy.*

The increased possibility of full-verb inversion following a prepositional phrase in English has been discussed extensively in Prado-Alonso (2008, 2011, 2013; see also Chen 2003), who also dwells systematically on the correlation of the specific form and genre, with fiction featuring an increased amount of prepositional phrase inversion by far. The semiotics of such inversion instances, especially when appearance or emergence is denoted, has also been considered (cf. Enkvist 1981, 1989; Calfoglou 2000, 2010b, 2014). Importantly, as suggested earlier in this section, such structures seem to be allowed increased license. With regard to the specific items in the translation task, and on the basis of the "be faithful if you can" principle postulated in the previous section, I hypothesized an increased incidence of post-verbal subjects, possibly subsuming instances with no preposed prepositional or other phrase, where no such order is tolerated in L2. Let me now turn to the other two forms tested.

I have already referred to some of the properties of adjectival pre- and post-modification. There has been a lot of talk about the derivational or non-derivational nature of adjectival pre-modifiers (Alexiadou, Haegeman and Stavrou 2007). Generally, however, post-nominal adjectives are associated with predication, which might be related to the fact that, like relative clauses, they define the nominal they accompany. Interestingly, in

Greek, where post-nominal adjectival modification is legitimate, it tends to be restricted by the definiteness/indefiniteness parameter. Thus, while, for instance, Ex. 5:

    Ex. 5    *νύχτα σκοτεινή*
                *nihta skotini*
                (*night dark*)

is perfectly valid, definiteness introduces the need for the definite article to precede the post-nominal adjective (Stavrou 1999, note 25):

    Ex. 6    *η νύχτα η σκοτεινή*
                *i nihta i skotini*
                (*the night the dark*)

This increased tolerance for adjectival post-modification with indefinite nouns can also be said to be at work in English, though only marginally. We could thus perhaps accept lengthy predicational adjectival modifiers, as in the following example:

    Ex. 7    *a night dark, dim and magic*

On the basis of the above, it seems interesting to test learners' observance of the faithfulness constraint in relation to forms which are much more marginally attested in L2.

Finally, as regards genitive pre- and post-modification, L1 and L2 patterns seem to converge more. In Greek, post-modification may in several cases look less marked, as we can see in Ex. 8a and 8b, where 8b, the pre-modifier case, leans more heavily on the literary side:

    Ex. 8a    *Η ομορφιά της φύσης*
                 *i omorfia tis fisis*
                 (*The beauty of-the nature*)

    Ex. 8b    *Της φύσης η ομορφιά*
                 *tis fisis i omorfia*
                 (*Of-the nature the beauty*)

In English, genitive pre- and post-modification, generally determined by the relational properties of the head-noun in connection to the genitive nominal, yields a complex image. Consider Ex. 9a, 9b and 10a, 10b below (from Haegeman and Guéron 1999, 413):

    Ex. 9a    *the top of the mountain*

Ex. 9b    *the mountain's top

Ex. 10a    the cat's tail

Ex. 10b    the tail of the cat

It would indeed be interesting to see how learners treat genitives in translating into English, and whether there is a tendency to adopt the pre-modificational Saxon genitive indiscriminately, as has been observed in a number of L2 learning contexts, even at the expense of faithfulness. This might be further triggered by the literary nature of the items to be translated, where, perhaps, the highly marked "the butterfly's wings" (Haegeman and Guéron 1999, 413) would become more palatable. Finally, it would be interesting to see what happens with items featuring a pattern—multiple post-verbal subjects or pre- or post-nominal genitives (see items 4, 6, 7 and 11 respectively), a good test for the ranking of the CONSISTENCY constraint.[11]

## 3.2 Translation task 2

The second translation task was distributed to tertiary education level students and, more specifically, to students at the English department of the University of Athens, as part of their translation course practice. The work to be done involved the following:[12] 120 students were asked to translate an extract from *Dokimes* (*Δοκιμές*) by the Greek poet Giorgos Seferis. The extract featured a sentence with a lengthy postposed subject, preceded by a lengthy adverbial phrase, as we can see in Ex. 11, where the relevant part has been italicised:

Ex. 11    Η Ελένη δεν πήγε ποτέ στην Τροία· *μαζί με τον Πάρη έμενε, όλη εκείνη τη φοβερή δεκαετία της ανθρωποσφαγής, ένα είδωλο, ένα φάντασμα της Ελένης που είχαν βάλει στη θέση της πραγματικής οι θεοί.*
i eleni den pige pote stin tria; me ton pari emene oli ekini ti foveri dekaetia tis anthroposfagis ena idolo, ena fantazma tis elenis pu ihan vali sti thesi tis pragmatikis i thei.
(The Helen not went never to-the Troy; together with the Paris was-staying, all that the atrocious decade of-the manslaughter, one

---

[11] The test items also involved some aspect-related issues in the two languages but I will not be discussing them here.
[12] This forms part of a larger study. In this chapter I will be focusing on aspects relevant to my discussion.

104    Chapter Five

image, one ghost of-the Helen that had put in-the place of-the real
the gods)

It was hypothesized that students might be tempted to retain the existing order in their translation, affected, among other things, by the length of the clause-initial phrase as well as of the subject.

The test was replicated with shorter postposed subjects as well as with post-nominal adjectives in poetry and in prose. Items 1 and 2 (see Appendix B) were given to 71 students while item 3 to 73. Overall, it was thought that it would be interesting to see if faithfulness persists well into the more advanced levels of L2 development.[13]

## 4. Results and discussion

Learner outputs for task 1 are grouped by category. I begin by presenting the post-verbal subject category. The orders obtained for post-verbal subject items appear in Table 2 further below. As we can see, there is a substantial amount of fluctuation within each sentence and across sentences (chi-squared, differences in values within items reached significance, with $p<0.001$) but the overall image is one of an impressively robust presence of the faithful post-verbal order in the first column. For a start, this means that learners, quite independently of level, retain the existing order in their translation, even if it is not legitimate, that is, they rank FAITHFULNESS highly, often at the expense of ACCEPTABILITY. It is also clear from these results that learners do not resort to the *there*-dummy subject construction to avoid the empty pre-verbal subject slot. This is, then, perhaps something they need to be shown, as a bridge between the two languages, before they become fully aware of the overwhelming pre-verbal subject occurrence in English. The dummy *there* form would be salutary in the case of *erhete sjopi* (*comes silence*), for instance, which could be rendered as *there comes silence*.

Let us now see if the faithful post-verbal renderings are differentiated across items. If we look at column 1, we can see that verb-subject ranged from 12.2% in item 4a (*vuliazi o kozmos*), where the verb appears sentence-initially and there is no "alibi" for an inversion in English, to an impressive 71% in item 2 (*apo tin pikni filosia ton dentron kseprovale ena parakseno prosopo*), where the prepositional phrase opening and the emergence verb license its presence. The difference may suggest that

---

[13] Students were also asked to comment on the difficulties they had in translating. Interestingly, hardly any student raised the issue of form. Most comments related to lexical problems.

learners are generally aware of contextual restrictions on post-verbal subjects in L2—the second lowest incidence is in 8, where again the verb is sentence-initial.

|         | VS[14]      | SV          | There/*itVS | Other      | Total        |
|---------|-------------|-------------|-------------|------------|--------------|
| Item 2  | 93 (71.0%)  | 30 (22.9%)  | ---         | 8 (6.1%)   | 131 (100%)   |
| Item 3  | 51 (38.9%)  | 72 (55.0%)  | 2 (1.5%)    | 6 (4.6%)   | 131 (100%)   |
| Item 4a | 16 (12.2%)  | 113 (86.3%) | ---         | 2 (1.5%)   | 131 (100%)   |
| Item 4b | 28 (21.4%)  | 96 (73.3%)  | 5 (3.8%)    | 2 (1.5%)   | 131 (100%)   |
| Item 4c | 31 (23.7%)  | 91 (69.5%)  | 4 (3.1%)    | 5 (3.8%)   | 131 (100%)   |
| Item 6a | 34 (26.0%)  | 91 (69.5%)  | 3 (2.3%)    | 3 (2.3%)   | 131 (100%)   |
| Item 6b | 38 (29.0%)  | 89 (67.9%)  | 1 (0.8%)    | 3 (2.3%)   | 131 (100%)   |
| Item 7  | 44 (33.6%)  | 69 (52.7%)  | ---         | 18 (13.7%) | 131 (100%)   |
| Item 8  | 25 (19.1%)  | 100 (76.3%) | ---         | 6 (4.6%)   | 131 (100%)   |
| Item 9  | 58 (44.3%)  | 60 (45.8%)  | 7 (5.3%)    | 6 (4.6%)   | 131 (100%)   |
| Item 10 | 30 (22.9%)  | 73 (55.7%)  | 13 (9.9%)   | 15 (11.5%) | 131 (100%)   |
| Item 11 | 50 (38.2%)  | 67 (51.1%)  | ---         | 14 (10.7%) | 131 (100%)   |
| Item 13 | 49 (37.4%)  | 48 (36.6%)  | 1 (0.8%)    | 8 (6.1%)   | 106 (100%)   |
| Item 14 | 46 (35.1%)  | 37 (28.2%)  | 7 (5.3%)    | 16 (12.2%) | 106 (100%)   |

Table 2. *Translation task 1*: Orders obtained for post-verbal subject items

---

[14] **VS** refers to post-verbal subjects, **SV** to pre-verbal ones, **there/*itVS** to post-verbal subjects with a dummy **it** (ungrammatical) or **there** (grammatical) in pre-verbal position, and **Other** to non-classifiable instances.

On the other hand, even within the plot of legitimate VS items in English, 2 and 9 for instance, the differences are substantial—71% as opposed to 44.3% respectively, which may mean that there is a certain amount of randomness in learner behaviour. Lakshmanan (2006) suggests that the fact that a specific order persists could mean that the constraints leading to the target order are viewed as optional. I would add that the fact that they can vary more or less freely may also be due to the same reason. In any case, it is evident that, as hypothesised, in a non-breach of faithfulness, learners may produce highly marked forms, such as *sinks the world* or *comes silence*.

Let us now go over to CONSISTENCY, the third of my constraints. Crosstabulation revealed that learners were generally consistent in their behaviour with regard to items 4b and 4c, evidently recognizing the consistency of the L1 input (*erhete sjopi* and *irthe i nihta* respectively) as well as with regard to 6a and 6b (*tote genithike i thalasa* and *anadithike i afroditi*). In Optimality-theoretic terms, then, we would mark instances like *From the thick foliage of the trees emerged/appeared a strange face, like a ghost* as optimal, in the sense that they observe both FAITHFULNESS and ACCEPTABILITY, that is they violate the fewest constraints, while the dummy subject sequence *there emerged* [...] or *there appeared* [...] would be marked as the next optimal form in that it is an in-between case as regards FAITHFULNESS, and is also ACCEPTABLE. Erroneous orders like *changed the mood again* would then have to be treated as ranking FAITHFULNESS higher than ACCEPTABILITY while consistent outputs, like *silence comes, night came* would also be optimal in the sense of observing both CONSISTENCY and ACCEPTABILITY. We would thus have a principled way of evaluating outputs and deciding how they can be brought closer to target structures.

If we consider what happens with post-verbal subject orders in the second translation task, where learners are expected to be much more mature linguistically, we will see that FAITHFULNESS is still in a non-negligible number of cases ranked more highly than ACCEPTABILITY. Thus, item (11) in section 3.2 above yielded a relatively high post-verbal percentage (9%), as in Ex. 12a, as well as a surprisingly high percentage (38%) of what resembles a dummy *she*-subject, with the bulk of the subject phrase following Ex. 12b:

Ex. 12a   *With Paris stayed ... an image, a ghost of Helen.*

Ex. 12b   *She lived with Paris ... an image, a ghost of Helen.*

Similarly, in item 1 in Appendix B, 27% of post-verbal subjects were obtained as against 25% for item 2.

Let us now turn to adjectival modification and see how it fared. We had hypothesized that post-nominal adjectives, highly marked in English, might be transferred. Indeed, while pre-nominal adjectives were never moved to post-modifier position, post-nominal adjectives were replicated in the translation. Percentages ranged from 7.6% (10 subjects) for the definite nominal in item 10 to 31.3% (41 subjects) for the lengthier adjectival phrase in 9 (*vrahos psilos ke kataprasinos*), length probably amplifying the predicational properties of the post-modifier. In the advanced group, post-nominal adjectives varied from 6% for *hand whispering* to 17% for *point poisonous*, to an impressive 34% for the lengthier *an evening dim and silent*. So, once again, FAITHFULNESS had not given way to ACCEPTABILITY when required.

Finally, genitive modification generally acted along the lines of FAITHFULNESS along with ACCEPTABILITY, and variation was reduced. The interesting point, however, was in sentence 11, where the two post-nominal genitives were converted into pre-nominals in 30.5% (40 subjects) and 31.3% (41 subjects) of the cases respectively, even though *nature's beauty*, sounds rather more marked than its post-nominal counterpart. On the other hand, the pattern was observed, as was also generally the case with item 7.

All in all, then, FAITHFULNESS is pretty high on the learners' ranking,[15] quite often at the expense of ACCEPTABILITY, while CONSISTENCY is generally observed, though learners' behaviour as a whole is not really consistent.

## 5. The pedagogical imprint: A conclusion

On the basis of the continuum established by observance of the FAITHFULNESS constraint boosted by the literary context of the present study, such data could be the stepping-stone to designing one's teaching so that affinities between the two languages are illustrated, learners are made to notice, and solutions are sought—*there*, as suggested in the previous

---

[15] As a matter of fact, learners' conservatism can be illustrated in a number of ways. According to Calfoglou (1998), the increased use of resumptives, as in *the train that I saw it*, in the relative clause output of (L1) Greek learners of (L2) English suggests resisting changes, resumption being very common in learners' L1. Interestingly, if resumptive relatives are marginally *acceptable* in spoken English (see Biber *et al.* 1999, emphasis added), this means we have a further illustration of the deviance-non-deviance continuum referred to in this chapter.

section, being one such solution. Other structures, such as passives or pseudo-clefts, could also be introduced as legitimate alternatives conforming to the FAITHFULNESS constraint when relevant. A passive or pseudo-cleft rendering of an object-verb-subject sequence in Greek, for example, would approximate FAITHFULNESS more than a mainstream active pre-verbal subject ordering. Constraints could therefore act as a unifying thread for the joint presentation of a number of apparently diverse structures in the target language.

Of course, word order is just one area in which such affinities can be observed. There are several others, such as aspectual differences, which can be treated in similar ways. In a language pair like Greek and English this is a particularly fertile area. Most importantly, however, different pairs of languages may produce very different outputs, with more or less friction, lesser or greater convergence. In the case of post-nominal adjectives in French, for instance, markedness values have to be reset, since adjectives in French typically follow the noun, so in the French-English pair, for example, ACCEPTABILITY would compete with FAITHFULNESS. German word order with its verb-second properties, on the other hand, would compare with Greek in interesting ways. Generally, the varied ranking of constraints such as the ones postulated in this chapter would help establish interesting associations among languages. Moreover, the constraints proposed could be further fine-tuned to serve the particular needs of the specific language pair at issue.

Overall, it appears that the processes learners may engage in when required to translate between languages yield data that shed precious light on the still opaque area of learners' interlanguage. Importantly, literary translation, lending itself to increased form-related experimentation, seems to be a particularly rich source of information. Further research, replicated among a larger and more varied sample of learners in a number of different contexts, might therefore prove particularly enlightening. A cross-sectional implementation might also reveal interesting developmental features of L2 acquisition. Translation may thus be made to step into the foreign language class dynamically both as a research and as a teaching tool, comforting learners by letting them draw on their L1 potential in a number of ways.

## Works cited

Alexiadou, Artemis. 1999. "On the Properties of Some Greek Word Order Patterns". In *Studies in Greek Syntax,* edited by Artemis Alexiadou, Geoffrey Horrocks, and Melita Stavrou, 45–66. Dordrecht: Kluwer.

Alexiadou, Artemis, Liliane Haegeman, and Melita Stavrou. 2007. *Noun Phrase in the Generative Perspective.* Berlin: Mouton de Gruyter.
Archangeli, Diane. 1997. "Optimality Theory: An Introduction to Linguistics in the 1990s". In *Optimality Theory,* edited by Diane Archangeli, and D. Terence Langendoen, 1–32. Oxford, MA: Blackwell.
Biber, Douglas, Stig Johansson, Geoffrey Leech, Susan Conrad, and Edward Finegan. 1999. *Longman Grammar of Spoken and Written English.* Harlow, Essex: Pearson.
Butzkamm, Wolfgang. 2011. "Why Make Them Crawl if They Can Walk? Teaching with Mother Tongue Support." *RELC* 42(3):379–391.
Butzkamm, Wolfgang, and John A. W. Caldwell. 2009. *The Bilingual Reform: A Paradigm Shift in Foreign Language Teaching.* Tübingen: Narr.
Calfoglou, Christine. 2014. "Iconic Motivation in Translation: Where Non-fiction Meets Poetry?" In *Literary translation: Redrawing the Boundaries*, edited by Jean Boase-Beier, Antoinette Fawcett, and Philip Wilson. London: Palgrave Macmillan.
—. 2010a. "An Optimality Approach to the Translation of Poetry". In *Translation: Theory and Practice in Dialogue*, edited by Antoinette Fawcett, Karla L. Guadarrama García, and Rebecca Hyde Parker, 85–106. London: Continuum.
—. 2010b. "Translating History Timelines or 'Negotiating-in-Iconicity'." *Synthèses* 3:75–97.
—. 2004. "The 'Peripheral' Gains Dominance: Verb-Subject Order in Poetry". In *The Periphery Viewing the World*, edited by Christine Dokou, Evi Mitsi, and Bessie Mitsikopoulou, 226–236. Athens: Parousia.
—. 2000. "Translating D. P. Papaditsas and A. Nikolaides: A Linguistic Approach." MA thesis, University of Athens.
—. 1998. "The Acquisition of Major Constituent Order in Restrictive Relative Clauses by Adult Greek Learners of English as a Foreign Language." PhD thesis, University of Athens.
Chen, Rong. 2003. *English Inversion: A Ground-Before-Figure Construction.* Berlin & NY: Mouton de Gruyter.
Cook, Guy. 2010. *Translation in Language Teaching.* Oxford: Oxford University Press.
Cook, Vivian. 2001. "Using the first language in the classroom," *Canadian Modern language Review* 57 (3): 399–423.
Dillon, George. 1980. "Inversions and Deletions in English Poetry." In *Linguistic Perspectives on Literature*, edited by Marvin Ching, Michael Haley, and Roland Lunsford, 213–233. London: Routledge.

Enkvist, Nils Eric. 1981. "Experiential Iconicism in Text Strategy". *Text* 1(1):77–111.
—. 1989. "Connexity, Interpretability, Universes of Discourse, and Text Worlds." In *Possible Worlds in Humanities, Arts and Sciences*, edited by Sture Allen, 162–186. Berlin & NY: Walter de Gruyter.
Fischer, Olga. 2006. "On the Position of Adjectives in Middle English," *English Language and Linguistics* 10(2):253–288.
—. 2001. "The Position of the Adjective in (Old) English from an Iconic Perspective." In *The Motivated Sign. Iconicity in Language and Literature 2*, edited by Max Nänny, and Olga Fischer, 249–276. Amsterdam & Philadelphia: Benjamins.
Haegeman, Liliane, and Jacqueline Guéron. 1999. *English Grammar: A Generative Perspective.* Oxford, MA: Blackwell.
Hassan, Bahaa-eddin A. 2011. *Literary Translation: Aspects of Pragmatic Meaning.* Newcastle upon Tyne: Cambridge Scholars Publishing.
Howatt, Anthony Ph. R., and Henry G. Widdowson. 2004. *A History of English Language Teaching* (2nd Edition). Oxford: Oxford University Press.
Howatt, Anthony Ph. R. 1984. *A History of English Language Teaching.* Oxford: Oxford University Press.
James, Carl. 1998. *Errors in Language Learning and Use: Exploring Error Analysis.* London & NY: Longman.
—. 1980. *Contrastive Analysis.* Harlow: Longman.
Kager, René. 1999. *Optimality Theory.* Cambridge: Cambridge University Press.
Källkvist, Marie. 2008. "L1-L2 Translation vs. No Translation: A Longitudinal Study of Focus-on-Forms within a Meaning-focussed Curriculum." In *The Longitudinal Study of Advanced L2 Capacities*, edited by Lourdes Ortega, and Heidi Byrnes, 182–202. London: Routledge.
—. 2004. "The Effect of Translation Exercises vs. Gap Exercises on the Learning of Difficult L2 Structures: Preliminary results of an empirical study." In *Translation in Undergraduate Degree Programmes*, edited by Kirsten Malmkjær, 173–184. Philadelphia: Benjamins.
Lakshmanan, Usha. 2006. "Child Second Language Acquisition and the Fossilisation Puzzle." In *Studies of Fossilisation in Second Language Acquisition*, edited by ZhaoHong Han, and Terence Odlin, 100–133. Clevedon: Multilingual Matters.
Lascaratou, Chryssoula. 1989. *A Functional Approach to Constituent Order with Particular Reference to Modern Greek. Implications for*

*Language Learning and Language Teaching.* Athens: Parousia Journal Monograph Series, 5.

Laufer, Batia, and Nany Girsai. 2008. "Form-focussed Instruction in Second Language Vocabulary Learning: A Case for Contrastive Analysis and Translation." *Applied Linguistics* 29(4):694–716.

Pesetsky, David. 1997. "Optimality Theory and Syntax: Movement and Pronunciation." In *Optimality Theory*, edited by Diane Archangeli, and D. Terence Langendoen, 134–170. Oxford, MA: Blackwell.

Prado-Alonso, Carlos. 2013. "Verb Phrase Inversion in Fictional and Nonfictional Written English." *English Studies* 94:n.p.

—. 2011. *Full-verb Inversion in Written and Spoken English.* Bern: Peter Lang.

—. 2008. "The Iconic Function of Full Inversion in English." In *Naturalness and Iconicity in Language*, edited by Klaas Willems, and Ludovic De Cuypere, 149–166. Amsterdam & Philadelphia: Benjamins.

Prince, Alan, and Paul Smolensky. 1993. "Optimality Theory: Constraint Interaction in Generative Grammar." RuCCs Technical Report #2, Rutgers University Center for Cognitive Science, Piscataway, N.J.

Prince, Alan, and Paul Smolensky. 2004. *Optimality Theory: Constraint interaction in generative grammar.* Oxford, MA: Blackwell.

Prince, Alan, and Paul Smolensky. 2006. "Optimality: From Neural Networks to Universal Grammar." In *The Harmonic Mind*, edited by Paul Smolensky, and Géraldine Legendre, 123–143. Cambridge, MA: The MIT Press.

Scott, Clive. 2010. "Re-theorizing the Literary in Literary Translation." In *Translation: Theory and Practice in Dialogue*, edited by Antoinette Fawcett, Karla Guadarrama García, and Rebecca Hyde Parker, 109–127. London: Continuum.

Smolensky, Paul, Géraldine Legendre, and Bruce Tesar. 2006. "Optimality Theory: The Structure, Acquisition and Use of Grammar." In *The Harmonic Mind*, edited by Paul Smolensky, and Géraldine Legendre, 453–544. Cambridge, MA: The MIT Press.

Stavrou, Melita. 1996. "Adjectives in Modern Greek: An Instance of Predication, or an Old Issue Revisited." *Journal of Linguistics* 32:79–112.

—. 1999. "The Position and Serialization of APs in the DP: Evidence from Greek". In *Studies in Greek Syntax*, edited by Artemis Alexiadou, Geoffrey Horrocks, and Melita Stavrou, 201–226. Dordrecht: Kluwer.

Tabakowska, Elzbieta. 2003. "Iconicity and Literary Translation". In *From Sign to Signing*, edited by Wolfgang G. Müller, and Olga Fischer, 361–378. Amsterdam & Philadelphia: Benjamins.

Tesar, Bruce, and Paul Smolensky. 2000. *Learnability in Optimality Theory*. Cambridge, MA: MIT Press.

Yau, Jia-ling Charlene. 2011. "Roles of Mental Translation in First and Foreign Language Reading," *International Journal of Bilingualism* 15(4):373–387.

## Appendix A

### Translation Task 1

Please, translate the following:
1. Πάντα ταξίδευα σε χώρες μακρινές με τη φαντασία μου.
   panta taksideva se hores makrines me ti fantasia mu.
   (Always was-travelling-I to countries distant with the imagination my).
2. Από την πυκνή φυλλωσιά των δέντρων ξεπρόβαλε ένα παράξενο πρόσωπο, σα φάντασμα.
   apo tin pikni filosia ton dentron kseprovale ena parakseno prosopo, sa fantazma.
   (From the thick foliage of-the trees emerged one strange face, like ghost).
3. Και ξαφνικά ήρθε η άνοιξη, με κοίμισαν η λάμψη των αστεριών και ένα φως μαγικό, μια γλυκειά ζεστασιά.
   ke ksafnika irthe i aniksi, me kimisan i lampsi ton asterion ke ena fos magiko, mja glikia zestasia.
   (And suddenly came the spring, me lulled the spark of-the stars and one light magical, one sweet warmth).
4. Βουλιάζει ο κόσμος, έρχεται σιωπή, ήρθε η νύχτα, νύχτα σκοτεινή.
   vuliazi o kozmos, erhete sjopi, irthe i nihta, nihta skotini.
   (Is-sinking the world, is-coming silence, came the night, night dark).
5. Η των χρωμάτων ομορφιά πλημμύρισε τα πάντα.
   i ton hromaton omorfia plimirise ta panta.
   (The of-the colours beauty flooded everything).
6. Τότε γεννήθηκε η θάλασσα και αναδύθηκε η Αφροδίτη.
   tote genithike i thalasa ke anadithike i afroditi
   (Then was-born the sea and was-emerged the Aphrodite).
7. Σε δελφινιών ράχες πατώντας, με ποιητών φωνές και στεναγμούς μεγάλωσε ο κόσμος.
   se delfinion rahes patontas, me piiton fones ke stenagmus megalose o kozmos.
   (On dolphins-of backs stepping, with poets-of voices and sighs grew the world).
8. Άλλαξε η διάθεση ξανά κι οι ώμοι σήκωσαν βουνά.
   alakse i diathesi ksana ki i omi sikosan vuna.
   (Changed the mood and the shoulders carried mountains).
9. Πέρα μακριά υψώνεται βράχος ψηλός και καταπράσινος.
   pera makria ipsonete vrahos psilos ke kataprasinos.

# An Optimality Translation Proposal for the Foreign Language Class 113

(Far away is-rising rock tall and all-green).
10. Περπατώ ώρες πολλές και δε φάνηκε ακόμη εκείνο το φως το λαμπερό.
perpato ores poles ke de fanike akomi ekino to fos to lambero.
(Walk-I hours long and not appeared yet that the light the bright).
11. Μπροστά στην ομορφιά της φύσης θολώνει ο νους τ' ανθρώπου.
brosta stin omorfia tis fisis tholoni o nus t'anthropu.
(In front of-the beauty of-the nature dims the mind of-the human being).
12. Και με το φως της μέρας οι σκέψεις επανέρχονται.
Ke me to fos tis meras i skepsis epanerhonte.
(And with the light of-the day the thoughts return).
13. Ψηλά στον ουρανό φάνηκε ένα αστέρι.
psila ston urano fanike ena asteri.
(High in the sky appeared one star).
14. Κανείς τους δεν ταξίδεψε. Με το καράβι ταξίδευε για χρόνια πολλά ένα φάντασμα, δημιούργημα της φαντασίας τους.
kanis tus den taksidepse. Me to karavi taksideve gia hronia pola ena fantazma, dimiurgima tis fantasias tus.
(None of-them didn't travel. With the boat was-travelling for years many one ghost, figment of-the imagination their)

# Appendix B

## Translation task 2

1. Και παντού προβάλλει το σημείο
το ίδιο πάντοτε
στίξη φαρμακερή και αντίστιξη.
ke pantu provali to simio
to idjo pantote
stiksi farmakeri ke antistiksi.
(And everywhere emerges the sign
the same always
point venomous and counterpoint)
2. Στο πρόσωπό σου σέρνεται
χέρι ψιθυριστό.
sto prosopo su sernete
heri psithiristo.
(On-the face your creeps
hand whispering)[16]
3. Ήταν σα να σκοτείνιαζε, κ' έπεφτε σιγαλά το βράδυ—ένα βράδυ θολό και σιωπηλό που ακολουθούσε και σφράγιζε μια μέρα που πέρασε γοργά και ανώφελα κ' έσβηνε τώρα αργά και μελαγχολικά.

---

[16] Both examples are from Aristotelis Nikolaides.

itan sa na skotiniaze, k'epefte sigala to vradi—ena vradi tholo ke sjopilo pu akoluthuse ke sfragize mia mera pu perase gorga ke anofela k'esvine tora arga ke melanholika.

(Was as if was-getting-dark, and was-falling gradually the evening—one evening dim and silent that was-following and was-sealing one day that passed fast and pointlessly and was-fading now slowly and melancholically)[17]

---

[17] From *To fthinoporo* (*Autumn*), by Konstantinos Hatzopoulos.

# CHAPTER SIX

## THE ENGAGING NATURE OF TRANSLATION: A NEXUS ANALYSIS OF STUDENT-TEACHER INTERACTION

## MARIE KÄLLKVIST

### 1. Introduction

This chapter presents the results of action research on classroom student-teacher interaction engendered by a translation task (Swedish (L1) into English (L2)) and a composition task (written directly in English). Data were collected in three English-as-a-foreign-language (EFL) classes within an authentic course at a Swedish university, combining an ethnographic approach with experimental methodology.

The focus is on classroom interaction and translation used as a means for facilitating L2 learning. Engaging in interaction in L2 provides a crucial source of input and is a pre-requisite for learning (Ellis 2008, 205). Interaction and translation tasks have been linked recently as several applied linguists and L2 educators suggest that translation may have particularly good potential to foster interaction in L2 learning contexts (Allford 1999; G. Cook 2007, 2010; Cunico 2004; Danan 2010; Duff 1989; Klapper 2006; Malmkjær 1998, 2004; Schjoldager 2003; Sewell 2004; Witte, Harden and Harden 2009). If interaction is in the L2 and there are high levels of student initiative and engagement (Tudor 2001; van Lier 2008) during task completion, there is thus reason to believe that translation tasks can facilitate learning. However, the publications by applied linguists and educators listed above have not been matched in number by published empirical research on the effect of translation tasks on L2 teaching and learning. Such studies are conspicuously lacking (G. Cook 2010), as is research on advanced-level L2 users who aim for professional-level L2 language proficiency (CEFR level C2) (Ortega and

Byrnes 2008a; though see Leaver and Shekhtman 2002; Ortega and Byrnes 2008b; Shaw and McMillion 2011).

Given the scarcity of research, the project (Källkvist 2008, 2013) within which the present study takes place was designed. Its overall aim is to begin building a theoretically informed empirical basis that can provide guidance as to when and how translation tasks may facilitate L2 learning among advanced-level L2 users who need superior or distinguished levels of L2 proficiency to pursue their career choices.

The study presented in this chapter builds on Källkvist (2013) by examining in greater detail qualitative interaction data on student and teacher agency and by suggesting an explanation that draws on nexus analysis—a discourse analytic approach developed to analyse human social actions such as interactional turns.

## 2. Nexus Analysis

Nexus analysis (Scollon and Scollon 2004, 2007) draws on traditional ethnographic methodology and was developed over several years through research in tertiary educational settings. It is a theory and meta-methodology that uses tools from interactional sociolinguistics, ethnography of communication and critical discourse analysis (cf. Hult 2010). The unit analysed is human social action, taking "the constitution of human social groups and languages as a problem to be examined" (Scollon and Scollon 2007, 608), which makes it a suitable conceptual framework for researching events in L2 classrooms. In addition to different tertiary-level learning contexts, nexus analysis has been used to study language shift and identity in minority language communities (Lane 2009, 2010), the relationships between languages, language users and social contexts in a school bilingual programme (Dressler 2012), linguistic landscape analysis (Hult 2009), educational language policy (Hult 2010) and societal multilingualism (Pietikäinen *et al.* 2011).

The term *nexus* signifies that a social action is seen to take place at an intersection where three main elements are at play: *discourses in place* (i.e. beliefs/ideologies that are circulating through the nexus at the moment of the social action), the social actors' *historical bodies* (life experiences that are relevant to the social action) and the *interaction order* (the social arrangement at the nexus, such as the way interaction is typically conducted in a committee meeting or a classroom). These three elements intersect at the moment of the social action in contexts referred to as *nexus of practice*. In this chapter, the nexus of practice is an EFL classroom setting at a Swedish university, studied in three instantiations called *sites of engagement*: three EFL classrooms at a Swedish university, described in greater detail below.

Nexus analysis identifies three phases in the research process: *engaging the nexus of practice*, which means identifying the social issue and practice to be studied as well as placing the researcher as a participant observer within this practice; *navigating the nexus of practice*, which involves data collection and the subsequent analysis of the data, and *changing the nexus of practice*, which may occur and be observed in longitudinal nexus analyses such as those carried out by Scollon and Scollon (2004), or may transpire through recommendations provided once a nexus analysis has been completed (e.g. Dressler 2012).

## 3. Aims, methodology and participants

### 3.1 Engaging the nexus of practice

The social actions examined in this chapter are student and teacher interactional turns with the aim of tracing, documenting and explaining how student-teacher classroom interaction is initiated and how it unfolds when translation is used compared to a similar task (the composition task) that was targeting the same morphosyntax but which did not involve translation. The focus is on student agency, which was operationalized as student-*initiated* (as opposed to teacher-prompted) turns during teacher-led classroom interaction.

An ethnographic and experimental action approach was made possible at one of Sweden's universities where the syllabi did not require the use of translation to teach or assess English proficiency. Through temporarily joining the teaching staff of this university, I was a participant observer lecturer for a total of 17 weeks teaching the module on English grammar and written English proficiency to three different groups of students in their first semester of English.

### 3.2 Navigating the nexus of practice: participants and data

Apart from the lecturer, the participants were 75 undergraduate students of English, divided into three groups. All three groups were taught by me in order to control for an effect on student-teacher interaction that could be attributable to differences in teaching style. An experimental design was possible for two of the three groups, and these two groups were formed based on matched-pair random assignment (cf. Hatch and Lazaraton 1991) on the basis of the students' English proficiency levels as measured through an in-house multiple-choice placement test. Matched-pair random assignment ensured that both groups included students at different proficiency levels, in this case low, middle and high performers on the departmental placement test.

Each of these two groups was then randomly assigned to one of two different sets of task that would consistently be used as work sheets supporting the grammar content of the course. The tasks were either a) a mixture of tasks, *including* translation, and the group where these tasks were used will henceforth be referred to as the TE group (for: Translation Experimental group), or b) a mixture of tasks, but *excluding* translation, and this group will be labelled NoTE (for: No Translation Experimental group). Students were told to remain in their assigned group throughout the semester.

The third group was an intact group of 25 students who were studying English as part of the teacher-training programme at the same university. This group's schedule could not be coordinated with that of the two experimental groups due to them simultaneously taking an education module and the group was, therefore, kept intact. They were also provided with a mixture of tasks, *including* translation and will be referred to as the TI group (for: Translation Intact group). Each set of tasks targeted the same English morphosyntax, which was also covered by the bilingual grammar book used as set reading.

Students ranged in age from 19 to 37, but few were older than 25. They had all been having classroom exposure to English for 9 or 10 years, and 25 of them (33%) had also spent at least one month in an English-speaking country. They were all starting their first semester of English at university level, at which they have typically reached CEFR level B2 (Granfeldt, Gyllstad and Källkvist 2012). Seventy-one of them (90%) had grown up in Sweden, been exposed to Swedish since birth, and had had all their prior education in Sweden. The remaining four participants (10%) had grown up abroad and had different language backgrounds but they still had a good knowledge of Swedish since completed upper-secondary-level courses in Swedish are required for university entry. Three students were L1 speakers of English: one student in group TE moved to Sweden at the age of 15; two students in group TI moved to Sweden at the age of 27 and 33 respectively. Both of them had completed all their prior education in an English-speaking country. Students' target uses of English were academic writing and research (if they continued in post-graduate education in English) and professional-level proficiency and knowledge of English (if they chose to enter the workforce with an undergraduate degree in English).

Relevant aspects of my historical body include being a Swedish-dominant sequential bilingual in Swedish and English, and having four-year lecturing experience. My experience teaching similar courses at other universities in combination with my beliefs about L2 learning at university level had shaped important priorities that probably impacted on the interaction order of my classes. One was to kindle students' interest in English linguistics in general and English grammar in particular by making the course content suitably challenging and creating a supportive classroom atmosphere in which students would feel comfortable speaking and discussing grammar as well as any other aspect of English usage. Another important aim relates to students' future professional needs: to develop their explicit knowledge of grammar in such a way that they would be able to explain practical English usage to others while feeling confident in doing so.

Data in the form of audio-recordings were collected while I was teaching the course on English grammar and written proficiency. This included a grammar component which contributed 15% of the overall first-semester course and had a written exam at the end. The data reported on in this study come from 3 out of a total of 19 recorded lessons, one for each of the three groups. All recordings were transcribed following an adaptation of Jefferson's transcription notation (cf. Rogers 2004).

Table 1 provides details of the data in terms of the number of students present in each group at the time of data collection and the time spent on whole-class interaction of each task.

| Student group | Number of students present | Translation Time on task (minutes) | Composition Time on task (minutes) |
|---|---|---|---|
| TE (Translation Exp. Group) | 26 | 59 | NA |
| NoTE (No Translation Exp. Group) | 24 | NA | 26 |
| TI (Translation Intact group) | 25 | 34 | NA |

**Table 1. Student group sizes and time-on-task**

This data set allows for an analysis of i) interaction patterns during teacher-led interaction in two different student groups (TE and TI) completing the same translation task, and ii) interaction patterns developed in group NoTE, who did the composition task which targeted the same morphosyntax without requiring students to translate.

## 4. Analysis and results

### 4.1 Discourses in place

Discourses in place are ideologies/beliefs that are circulating through the nexus of practice at the time when the social actions studied are taken. In the three classrooms studied here, the discourses in place emerged partly as a result of topics that are pre-set by the syllabus or other documents and then controlled by the lecturer in class (Scollon and Scollon 2004). Discourse analysis of the syllabus, which prescribes the content and aims of the course as well as the reading list, and the classroom interaction (which is controlled mainly by the lecturer) were therefore carried out in order to identify relevant discourses in place in the three classrooms.

Two general aims were stated in the syllabus: a) students should develop a high level of comprehension and production proficiency in spoken and written English, and b) a good knowledge of English pronunciation, English grammar and variation in present-day English (my translation). Through analysis of the course content and the reading list, the following discourses emerged:
1. There is variation in present-day English,
2. Spoken and written language are equal in status but more practice is needed for writing than speaking,
3. Vocabulary, phraseology, grammar, textual structure and stylistics are the highlighted components of language at the text level,
4. Links to the L1 facilitate the learning of pronunciation, vocabulary and grammar (but not necessarily learning about literature and culture in the English-speaking world).

The discourses in place in the three classes were identified through an analysis of the transcribed audio-recordings of the three lessons, and they emerged as (i) *accuracy*, (ii) *variation*, (iii) *student activity is conducive to learning,* (iv) *explicit information on potential difficulty in the English language is helpful,* (v) *links to the L1 are facilitative*, and (vi) *rules apply more to grammar than to vocabulary.* The discourse *links to the L1* is an inherent aspect of choosing to use translation tasks, but it is traceable also in the classroom where translation was not used as both students and I occasionally drew on L1 resources when discussing grammar as well as lexical aspects of English.

## 4.2 The interaction order

The interaction order in all three classrooms had the characteristics of "a traditional university class" (Scollon and Scollon 2004, 39): a platform event featuring the lecturer, who is in charge of events in the classroom, desks and a whiteboard (Scollon and Scollon 2004). The actual procedures during task completion in the three classes were somewhat different, however.

### 4.2.1 Group TE: the translation task

The translation task consisted of a coherent text containing eight sentences in Swedish to be translated into English, targeting the same morphosyntax as the composition task. The students worked individually, in pairs or in small groups for 22 minutes (which was as long as they needed). I then asked two students to individually write their English translations on the whiteboard, and these translated versions were then the subject of whole-class discussion. Once the two translations of the first sentence had been written on the board, I drew two simple scales on the board relating to two of the discourses in place, namely *accuracy* and *variation* (one scale ranging from incorrect to correct and idiomatic, and the other ranging from formal to informal in style). I then stated that these would be two baselines according to which each translated sentence would initially be discussed, prior to dealing with other potential alternatives to the translated versions that the students may have. Whole-class interaction lasted 59 minutes. This long discussion reflects the intersection between the discourses of *accuracy*, *variability* (which led to numerous student queries) and *student activity is conducive to learning* and aspects of the interaction order: ample time was devoted to the queries.

### 4.2.2 Group TI: the translation task

Students worked on the same translation task, i.e. the eight sentences to be translated into English for 25 minutes; then followed teacher-led, whole-class discussion for 34 minutes. An important difference from group TE was that one student at a time was asked to read his/her translation, which I wrote on the whiteboard and then asked students first to comment on correctness (and idiomaticity and style etc., whenever applicable). Following this, students were encouraged to ask questions or make comments on any aspect of the text on the whiteboard. The two scales (drawn on the whiteboard) relating to *accuracy* and *variation* were referred to in the same manner as in the TE group.

### 4.2.3 Group NoTE: the composition task

As stated above, the composition task targeted the same morphosyntax as the translation task. Five essay topics designed to elicit text of a similar kind to that elicited by the translation task were provided along with a list of sample structures (covered in the previous eight class meetings) and vocabulary (similar to that used in the translation task). Students were divided into five groups and were asked to jointly write a short text on the given topic, using the structures and vocabulary provided. They worked in groups for 11 minutes, then wrote their texts on the whiteboard and discussed them again, often making a few changes before considering them final. This took another 15 minutes. I then initiated the discussion in the same way as with the TI and TE groups when doing translation: "Let's start off by discussing this box here relating to question 4 regarding the state of Sweden's education, and let's first decide: Is everything in this box correct or is there anything that needs to be changed? Feel free to ask any question."

When conducting the discussion, the same scales relating to *accuracy* and *variation* were drawn on the board and referred to. The discussion then moved from text (each about five sentences long) to text similar to how discussions of translations in TE and TI progressed from sentence to sentence.

## 4.3 The three sites of engagement

There are striking similarities in the interaction order and discourses in place in the three classrooms studied. In each, there is text on the whiteboard, and in all three groups students were asked first to comment on accuracy, which emerged as a pervasive discourse in place along with variation. Once everyone agreed on accuracy, students were encouraged to ask questions about or comment on any linguistic feature of the text on the board. Another strongly present discourse in place was my ideology that student activity is conducive to learning, which intersects with the interaction order, yielding interactional turns on my part that show that it was more important that students discuss aspects of any feature of English language use on the whiteboard than to focus solely on the targeted grammar. The results in Källkvist (2013) revealed that gap tasks, which were part of the task sets and used in other lessons with these three groups, were used in order to achieve the desired focus on the targeted grammar.

I used virtually the same phrases in all three groups to encourage and prompt student participation, but there are differences in the frequency of the prompts. During whole-class discussion of the composition task, students were prompted 18 times during the 26-minute discussion (i.e. 0.69 prompts per minute) to ask questions or comment. In the TI group, where whole-class discussion lasted 34 minutes, there were 17 similar prompts, i.e. on average 0.5 prompts per minute, and in the TE group (where there were always two alternative translations on the whiteboard) there were 27 prompts in the 59-minute whole-class discussion, i.e. a mean of 0.46 prompts per minute. Another difference is that the prompts used were followed by longer pauses in the NoTE group. This is a sign of more student questions when translation was used; indeed, students were queuing to raise their questions.

Student-initiated turns are particularly interesting as they provide an indication both of what students were focusing on and how they were approaching the task, e.g. finding out factual information from the teacher or trying to understand grammar and practical English usage in general. Again, analysis revealed that the three classrooms had a great deal in common. Students asked questions to gain factual information when they thought there was an error in the text on the board or when asking about alternative translations. Ex. 1 is from the NoTE group (i.e. the composition task) and Ex. 2 is from the TI group (i.e. the translation task):

Ex. 1   **Student:** *on taxpayers money* should there not be an apostrophe? (NoTE)

Ex. 2   **Student:** could you use the conjunctive (.) *it is important that Sweden educate engineers?* (TI)

The difference between the composition and the translation task groups is not in the existence of this type of student-initiated query on facts, but rather in the frequency with which it occurs; there were considerably more instances in the TE (69) and TI (31) groups than in the NoTE group (8).

There may be several reasons for this difference. When discussing the composition task, there was only one target text at a time in the classroom to be discussed, and this text was on the whiteboard. In the translation groups, there were either two target texts on the board (written by two different students in group TE) or one (in TI, written by the teacher on the basis of what one student said), but, in addition, there were several target texts on students' desks, and it is likely that these target texts were not identical. An interaction order developed where several students in groups TE and TI asked questions regarding the acceptability of alternative translations they had written in their own texts, often starting with "I wrote...", the implicit question being whether this is correct or not. Examples from TE and TI are in (3) and (4):

Ex. 3     **Student:** I wrote *you will hope* (TE)

Ex. 4     **Student:** I wrote *domestic industrial production* (TI)

By this time – this was the ninth meeting in this module – students may have developed historical bodies in this class and become accustomed to asking questions whenever they felt the need to do so.

Another difference inherent in the two types of task is that the translation task requires a correct, idiomatic and stylistically appropriate text that, in addition, is an accurate rendering of the Swedish source text. The phase of comparison between the source and target texts led to additional questions in the TE and TI groups of the kind illustrated by Ex. 5 and 6:

Ex. 5     **Student:** Is *arts subjects* a correct translation of *humaniora* (TI)

Ex. 6     **Student:** *Universiteten och högskolorna* [code-switch meaning *the universities and the university colleges*] (TE)

The turn in (6) is implicitly a question to me to provide translation equivalents of *universiteten och högskolorna* (*the universities and university colleges*). These student turns testify to the fact that there was more work to do for students when translating than when writing the short composition directly in English, leading to more student-initiated questions on aspects where they felt challenged. Ex. 5 and 6 also illustrate the fact that the lexical content of the source text impacted on the number of student questions. *Humaniora* (*arts subjects* or *the humanities*) is a rather specialized, infrequent vocabulary item. The nouns *universiteten* and *högskolorna* encode a distinction between different kinds of higher education institutions in Sweden, also requiring rather specialized knowledge as well as knowledge of English translation equivalents that encode a similar difference.

A further difference with regard to the content of students' questions is that the interaction in the TI and TE groups was richer in turns which contained a true information gap and were followed by a turn-wise discussion extending over several turns. There were 10 such episodes in group TI and 3 in group TE compared to 1 in the NoTE group. These extended-turn episodes seem to appear as a result of an intersection of the discourses in place (*accuracy, variation* and *student activity*), relevant aspects of the historical bodies (students' L1 and my lecturing experience) and the interaction order (ample time left for student participation): analysis revealed that eight out of the ten episodes in the TI group involved the two native-English-speaking students who had moved to Sweden relatively late. They assumed an increasingly active role in the classroom over the period of time the course was running. This was encouraged by me; I had previously taught groups which included one or more native speakers of English, and had experienced the positive effects of engaging them in discussion (see Ex. 7).

Ex. 7   **Anna[1]:** [providing her suggested translation] *We are looking forward to this showing at Swedish universities*
**Lecturer:** That doesn't sound quite idiomatic to me (.) Dennis[2] and Alex what do you think (.) if I may pick your brains on this?
**Dennis:** I wrote *for this to have an effect*
**Lecturer:** Yes
**Alex:** *showing up*
**Lecturer:** *Showing up* yeah
**Alex:** Not *showing*
**Lecturer:** That would be towards unacceptable I think
**Anna:** Why can't you have *showing?*
**Lecturer:** Ehm (.) well (.) when it comes to choice of vocabulary it's harder to give rules (.) ehm (.) that's why we need dictionaries so much (.) ehm (.) dictionaries are very thick books often because they contain so much information (.) *showing* isn't used in that sense (.) *showing* is a very active verb (.) you can show something to somebody (.) *noticed* or *noticeable* is much more passive (.) *märkas* [Swedish for 'being noticed'] you can see the difference between *märka* ['notice'] and *visa* ['show']?
**Anna:** Yah
**Lecturer:** Yah ok (.) so *being noticed* or *being noticeable*

This extract also illustrates Anna's engagement with the task. She remains in the conversation and asks "Why can't you have *showing*", a sign that

---

[1] All names are pseudonyms. Pauses are indicated by (.).
[2] Dennis and and Alex are the pseudonyms for the two L1 speakers of English in group TI.

her involvement goes beyond obtaining just factual information, which in turn suggests that she was engaging in a deep rather than surface approach towards the task (Biggs and Tang 2007).

In Ex. 7, we also see an instance of translanguaging (García 2007, Creese and Blackledge 2010): After hesitating, I code-switched, referring to two Swedish verbs while responding to Anna's question regarding why *showing* does not work well in her translated sentence. It seems as if the use of translation provides incentive to draw on a larger knowledge base than the L2 only, namely the multi-competence (V. Cook 2007) that multilingual people possess. Judging from Anna's reply (her last turn in Ex. 7), she understands the difference between *showing* and *being noticed* after having been presented with the analogy of the two verbs in Swedish, her L1. This suggests an intersection of relevant aspects of Anna's historical body and mine (both of us having native-speaker command of Swedish), the interaction order (ample time devoted to discussion) and a discourse in place (links to the L1 can be facilitative).

Another sign of the potential of translation tasks to engender high engagement levels in students is illustrated by Ex. 8 below. As students have translated the sentence *Vi ser fram emot att detta ska märkas på de svenska universiteten* (*We look forward to this showing up at Swedish universities*), Tomas initiates a discussion with me:

Ex. 8   **Tomas:** Objections your honour (.) the way I read this sentence is that *we are looking forward to the people at the Swedish university will notice this*
**Lecturer:** That's what I mean
**Tomas:** Because I read the Swedish sentence like that the outlet (sic) of courses will be adapted to the new situation
**Lecturer:** Yeah I think you could interpret it in both ways (.) I wrote this again I was a bit (.) well
**Tomas:** It is not the Swedish university that decides what sort of courses they will have
**Lecturer:** No
**Tomas:** The way people at Swedish universities read papers and notice things is rather irrelevant
**Lecturer:** *Being noticed at (.)* I'm not quite sure what you mean now (.) what I meant was or what was meant in the article was that we hear in the news that the Swedish economy is doing well (.) but for me as being employed and as working with students I see no sign of it (.) yet (.) at Swedish universities.

Tomas was otherwise a quiet student who rarely spoke in class, but when his understanding of the sentence in Swedish, his L1, deviated from mine, he did initiate discussion. An observation from my field notes relates to this: on occasions when Swedish-L1 students were discussing meaning and usage relating to Swedish, they would often adopt a more assertive posture, probably as a result of feeling they were experts on their native language. Again, this suggests an intersection between the historical bodies (native command of Swedish) and the interaction order (questions explicitly encouraged).

Let us now (see Ex. 9) consider the one instance in group NoTE, where the composition was used, where a student initiated a question which then led to discussion extending over several turns.

Ex. 9     **Lisa:** [on considering a text on the whiteboard] I don't really get the meaning of the last sentence (.) I don't understand
**Lecturer:** No (.) can we ask the group who wrote it to explain
**Benny:** Högre levnadsstandard ['higher living standards']
**Lecturer:** I think what Lisa is not quite understanding is how it relates to the future (.) is that what you mean
**Lisa:** Yeah
**Lecturer:** That's what I thought as well (.) it is not really talking about the future but we can leave it at that and just discuss it as a piece of language (.) I think now this is correct (.) I can't find anything else (.) Any questions? Things that you would like to improve? (.) I think the definite article could go (.) *differences* is a count noun in the plural (.) it is differences in general so *differences between the classes (.) The structure of Swedish industry would be changed through privatization of public enterprises (.)* I thought that was a very nice vocabulary item
**Jessica:** In the last sentence we were thinking of futurum preteriti ['the future in the past']
**Lecturer:** Yeah (.) futurum preteriti (.) the future in the past
**Jessica:** So that's why we wrote that sentence.

This kind of communication breaks the mechanical Initiation-Response-Feedback (IRF) pattern that is common in classrooms (van Lier 2008; Johnson 1995) and strongly associated with traditional form-focused methodology (Ellis 2003). The episode in Ex. 9 was the only one where there was extended information-gap discussion in group NoTE, where the composition was used. As stated above, there were ten such episodes in group TI and three in group TE.

## 5. Concluding discussion

Using the nexus analysis elements *discourses in place, historical body* and *interaction order* to analyse and propose an explanation of social actions in human social groups, this study has focused on student agency, operationalized as student-initiated turns, in a very common type of communicative event in the traditional L2 classroom, namely teacher-led, whole-class discussion. The analysis suggests that there are two task-inherent factors that impacted on students' readiness to initiate questions relating to two prominent discourses in place, *accuracy* and *variation*: firstly, there is a comparison phase between the source language text and the target language text that is not necessarily present in a composition task, and secondly, there was challenging vocabulary in the translation task, leading to numerous student-initiated questions concerning that.

The interaction patterns in the two groups that did the same translation task displayed both similarities and differences; the discourses in place were identical (*accuracy, variability, student activity is conducive to learning*, and *the use of the L1 can facilitate learning*), but the interaction order was somewhat different in that in group TE two students wrote their versions on the whiteboard whereas in group TI, the lecturer wrote one student version on the whiteboard. The interaction order in group TE (two different student versions on the board) was more time-consuming because the two sentences on the board elicited more student questions than the single sentence in group TI.

The analysis also suggests that relevant aspects of the historical bodies of students influenced agency. In the TI group, two native-English-speaking students, who moved to Sweden relatively late, continually took an active part in lessons, commenting on accuracy, alternative translations and translation equivalence between Swedish and English. They had had all their pre-tertiary education in English and were highly English-dominant sequential bilinguals in English and Swedish. Their native-Swedish-speaking fellow students were the opposite, i.e. highly Swedish-dominant sequential bilinguals. Thus, group TI includes two sub-groups of students with regard to relevant aspects of their historical bodies, one with native-speaker command of English and the other with native-speaker command of Swedish. This suggests an intersection between four discourses in place (*accuracy, variation, student activity is conducive to learning* and *links to the L1 can facilitate learning*), students' historical bodies (i.e. L1 background), my historical body (having previously taught student groups which included native speakers of English) and the interaction order (my decision to allow ample time for student-initiated comments and questions on any aspect of the English language). This was noticeable particularly in some of the students' more assertive behaviour in the classroom and in the quiet student, Tomas, suddenly initiating and maintaining interaction with me when his understanding of the meaning of text in Swedish differed from mine. These findings suggest that having the feeling of being an expert may affect one's agency.

An interesting finding is that the composition task engendered the same type of student-initiated interaction about English language use, but not as frequently despite the fact that the interaction order was highly similar, as were the historical bodies of the students and the lecturer in groups TE and NoTE. Thus, in the case of the composition task used in this study, fewer matters gave rise to student comments and questions than when the translation task was used. When the composition was used, there was only one single text to consider at a time (five in total), and this text did not need to be considered against a source text. When the translation tasks were used, there were potentially as many unique texts as there were students in the classroom.

There is little previous research on the use of translation in L2 interaction studies against which findings in this study can be discussed, but Danan (2010) provides a synthesis of research on L2 learners' language gains through subtitling tasks, which involve a translation phase, and qualitative results from a series of case studies of adult L2 learners of Dari, Farsi and Pashto in the United States. The research on L2 learning through subtitling tasks reviewed by Danan suggests that students benefit from doing translation in terms of "incidental learning, improved listening comprehension, and vocabulary acquisition as well as greater enjoyment and increased motivation" (2010, 444). In her study of students' working on dubbing tasks, in which they were required to translate from L1 into L2 as well as use software to record their translations, Danan reports that the tasks led to "interesting class analysis and discussion" (2010, 448) and engendered high levels of enthusiasm, although no transcripts of the interaction are provided. Nevertheless, her observations accord with the findings presented in this chapter; the classes had consistently high levels of attendance and analysis and discussion were consistent features when translation was used, particularly when the tasks were challenging through the inclusion of either culture-specific or in other ways challenging vocabulary or when they were rich in tokens of the targeted morphosyntax.

A discussion by Sewell (2004) of why translation classes are popular with undergraduate students of French in Britain is also relevant here. In her experience, university students favour translation because it is a closed-ended, predictable activity, which makes students feel comfortable as well as rewarded by completing a concrete product, which in the end can be measured against the source text and a suggested, correct and idiomatic translation, serving as a "visible yardstick" (Sewell 2004, 158). Danan (2010), Sewell (2004) and the data presented in this chapter thus jointly suggest that translation tasks are suitable communicative tasks in university-level foreign/second language education in contexts where knowledge of the L1 is shared. In Danan's study and in the subtitling studies reviewed in her article, translation was used to the specific end of producing subtitling or dubbing in video-clips. The present study has shown that translation tasks can also be used to engender high levels of student engagement in discussions of features of L2 grammar, vocabulary, phraseology and translation equivalence in a context where students typically are at the CEFR B2 level and aim for a career where professional-level knowledge of English is needed.

The data presented in this chapter show that students in the sample were particularly motivated to initiate and engage in communication in the L2 during teacher-led discussion that was based on a translation task. In conjunction with Danan's findings, this suggests that translation may have particular value as an ice-breaking activity in student groups where engendering communication involving many of the students present is a high priority.

As the goal of L2 courses is always mastery of the L2 without necessary mediation through the L1, there comes a point when students become so proficient in the L2 that systematic links to their L1 are no longer needed, and translation then becomes superfluous. Further research in different learning contexts is still needed before we have a refined understanding of when, how and when not to use translation in different contexts to facilitate L2 learning. The results presented in this chapter may have arisen partly due to my historical body and teaching style and to the interaction order typical of classrooms in Swedish higher education. A further restriction is the sole focus on teacher-led interaction. While working on tasks in preparation for whole-class discussion, audio or video-recordings of the interaction taking place between students would have provided interesting further data about student-student interaction during the process of translating. Quantitative and in-depth qualitative studies of student attitudes would also enrich our understanding of when to use translation for the purposes of L2 learning. Building a more firm theoretical and empirical basis enables us to develop teaching practices that are solidly evidence-based.

# Works cited

Allford, Douglas. 1999. "Translation in the Communicative Classroom." In *Teaching Modern Languages at Advanced Level*, edited by Norbert Pachler, 230–250. London: Routledge.

Biggs, John, and Catherin Tang. 2007. *Teaching for Quality Learning at University*. Maidenhead: McGraw Hill.

Cook, Guy. 2007. "A Thing of the Future: Translation in Language Learning." *International Journal of Applied Linguistics* 17:396–401.

—. 2010. *Translation in Language Teaching*. Oxford: Oxford University Press.

Cook, Viviane. 2007. "The Goals of ELT: Reproducing Native-speakers or Promoting Multicompetence among Second Language Users?" In *International Handbook of English Language Teaching*, edited by Jim Cummins, and Chris Davison, 237–248. Norwell: Springer.

Creese, Angela, and Blackledge, Adrian. 2010. "Translanguaging in the Bilingual Classroom: A Pedagogy for Learning and Teaching?" *Modern Language Journal* 94:103–115.

Cunico, Sonia. 2004. "Translation as a Purposeful Activity in the Language Classroom." *Tuttitalia* 29:4–12.

Danan, Martine. 2010. "Dubbing Projects for the Language Learner: A Framework for Integrating Audiovisual Translation into Task-based Instruction." *Computer Assisted Language Learning* 23:441–456.

Dressler, Roswita A. H. 2012. "Simultaneous and Sequential Bilinguals in a German Bilingual Program." PhD diss., University of Calgary.

Duff, Alan. 1989. *Translation*. Oxford: Oxford University Press.

Ellis, Rod. 2003. *Task-based Language Learning and Teaching*. Oxford: Oxford University Press.

—. 2008. *The Study of Second Language Acquisition*. Oxford: Oxford University Press.

García, Ofelia. 2007. "Foreword." In *Disinventing and Reconstituting Languages*, edited by Sinfree Makoni, and Alastair Pennycook, xi–xv. Clevedon: Multilingual Matters.

Granfeldt, Jonas, Henrik Gyllstad, and Marie Källkvist. 2012. "Linguistic Correlates to Communicative Proficiency Levels of the CEFR: The Case of Syntactic Complexity in L2 English and L3 French." Paper presented at ASLA-symposiet, Linneaus & Linköping Universities, May 1–12.

Hatch, Evelyn, and Anne Lazaraton. 1991. *The Research Manual: Design and Statistics for Applied Linguistics*. New York: Newbury House.

Hult, Francis M. 2009. "Language Ecology and Linguistic Landscape Analysis." In *Linguistic Landscape: Expanding the Scenery*, edited by Elana Shohamy, and Durk Gorter, 88–104. London: Routledge.
—. 2010. "Analysis of Language Policy Discourses across the Scales of Space and Time." *International Journal of the Sociology of Language* 202:7–24.
Johnson, Karen E. 1995. *Understanding Communication in Second Language Classrooms*. Cambridge: Cambridge University Press.
Källkvist, Marie. 2008. "L1-L2 Translation vs. No Translation: A Longitudinal Study of Focus-on-Forms within a Meaning-focussed Curriculum." In *The Longitudinal Study of Advanced L2 Capacities*, edited by Lourdes Ortega, and Heidi Byrnes, 182–202. London: Routledge.
—. 2013. "Languaging in Translation Tasks Used in a University Setting: Particular Potential for Student Agency." *The Modern Language Journal* 97:217–238.
Klapper, John 2006. *Understanding and Developing Good Practice Teaching Languages in Higher Education*. London: CILT.
Lane, Pia. 2009. "Identities in Action: A Nexus Analysis of Identity Construction and Language Shift." *Visual Communication* 8:450–468.
—. 2010. "'We Did What We Thought Was Best for our Children: A Nexus Analysis of Language Shift in a Kven Community." *International Journal of the Sociology of Language* 202:63–78.
Leaver, Betty Lou, and Boris Shekhtman, eds. 2002. *Developing Professional-level Language Proficiency*. Cambridge: Cambridge University Press.
Malmkjær, Kirsten. 1998. "Introduction: Translation and Language Teaching." In *Translation and Language Teaching: Language Teaching and Translation*, edited by Kirsten Malmkjær, 1–11. Manchester: St. Jerome.
Malmkjær, Kirsten, ed. 2004. *Translation in Undergraduate Degree Programmes*. Amsterdam: John Benjamins.
Ortega, Lourdes, and Heidi Byrnes. 2008a. "The Longitudinal Study of Advanced L2 Capacities: An Introduction." In *The Longitudinal Study of Advanced L2 Capacities*, edited by Lourdes Ortega, and Heidi Byrnes, 3–20. New York: Routledge.
Ortega, Lourdes, and Heidi Byrnes, eds. 2008b. *The Longitudinal Study of Advanced L2 Capacities*. New York: Routledge.
Pietikäinen, Sari, Pia Lane, Hanni Salo, and Sirkka Laihiala-Kankainen. 2011. "Frozen Actions in the Arctic Linguistic Landscape: A Nexus

Analysis of Language Processes in Visual Space." *International Journal of Multilingualism* 8:1–22.

Rogers, Rebecca. 2004. "A Critical Discourse Analysis of Literature Identities across Contexts: Alignment and Conflict." In *An Introduction to Critical Discourse Analysis in Education*, edited by Rebecca Rogers, 51–78. Mahwah, NJ: Lawrence Erlbaum.

Schjoldager, Anne. 2003. "Translation for Language Purposes: Preliminary Results of an Experimental Study of Translation and Picture Verbalization." *Hermes* 30:199–213.

Scollon, Ron, and Suzie Wong Scollon. 2004. *Nexus Analysis: Discourse and the Emerging Internet*. New York: Routledge.

Scollon, Ron, and Suzie Wong Scollon. 2007. "Nexus Analysis: Refocusing Ethnography on Action." *Journal of Sociolinguistics* 11:608–625.

Sewell, Penelope. 2004. "Students Buzz around the Translation Class like Bees Round the Honey Pot—Why?" In *Translation in Undergraduate Degree Programmes*, edited by Kirsten Malmkjær, 151–162. Philadelphia: Benjamins.

Shaw, Philip, and Alan McMillion. 2011. "Components of Success in Academic Reading Tasks for Swedish Students." *Iberica* 22:141–162.

Tudor, Ian. 2001. *The Dynamics of the Language Classroom*. Cambridge: Cambridge University Press.

van Lier, Leo. 2008. "Agency in the Classroom." In *Sociocultural Theory and the Teaching of Second Languages*, edited by James P. Lantolf, and Matthew E. Poehner, 163–186. London: Equinox.

Witte, Arnd, Theo Harden, and Alessandra Ramos de Oliveira Harden. 2009. "Introduction." In *Translation in Second Language Learning and Teaching*, edited by Arnd Witte, Theo Harden, and Alessandra Ramos de Oliveira Harden, 1–12. Oxford: Peter Lang.

# CHAPTER SEVEN

# RESURRECTING TRANSLATION IN SLT: A FOCUS ON YOUNG LEARNERS

# SILVA BRATOŽ AND ALENKA KOCBEK

## 1. Introduction

Several authors (Cook 2010; Witte, Harden and Harden 2009; Widdowson 2003; Malmkjær 1998) have recently pointed out that translation has been unjustly neglected in second language teaching (SLT) for too long. The use of translation for SLT purposes has been negatively affected by its association to the Grammar-Translation Method, which was characterised by its primary focus on formal accuracy in writing, an extremely restricted view of translation equivalence, and a complete disregard of language use in communication. However, it is safe to say that today there is a wide, if not total, consensus among linguists on the ineffectiveness and unsuitability of the original method for SLT purposes, including those overtly advocating the use of translation in foreign language teaching (cf. Cook 2010; Widdowson 2003; Malmkjær 1998). In addition, rather than being viewed as a viable alternative to the current SL teaching methods and practices, the Grammar-Translation Method is mainly discussed from a historical perspective and examined within a broader framework of the social and educational change of the time in which it was developed and used (Howatt and Widdowson 2004).

On the other hand, translation is still largely seen as posing a threat to the effectiveness of task-based and communicative approaches. In such sensitive climate, we believe it might be beneficial to lay out what we are not advocating, and thus avoid potential misapprehensions. First of all, we are not arguing in favour of reintroducing the 19th century concept of grammar-translation as a SLT method. This paper proposes to view translation not as a comprehensive teaching method but as a pedagogic tool or strategy aimed at increasing the effectiveness of other successful

SLT approaches, as well as an indispensable component of cross-cultural communicative competence. Secondly, we are not advocating a more prominent or widespread use of the mother tongue in SLT settings, such as for example in classroom interaction or explaining grammar. Contrary to this, we see clear benefits in maximizing the amount of second language exposure, and recognize, for example, the intrinsic potential offered by classroom communication for enhancing second language acquisition (Žefran and Bratož 2012).

The paper proposes drawing on an interdisciplinary framework by combining two theoretical perspectives which shed light on the various dimensions of using translation for SLT purposes, i.e. the translation and cognitive perspective. The former brings to the fore recent findings from translation studies, while the latter looks at the key concepts in the area of cognitive linguistics and the ways in which they can be applied to second language learning and teaching. A case will be argued in favour of re-examining translation as a teaching tool at the earliest levels of foreign language learning, i.e. with young learners, with a view to encouraging learner autonomy and raising learners' awareness of the cross-cultural and linguistic differences between the first and second language. Examples, in which the first language is Slovene (L1) and the second English (L2), will be given, and several aspects of language, which can be dealt with through translation and contrastive activities in early-level foreign language instruction, will be examined.

## 2. Translation theory and practice

Since the downfall of the grammar translation method, we have seen a burgeoning development in translation theory and practice. Among the approaches which are in line with the scope of this research we would like to highlight the functionalist perspective with the Skopos theory (Reiss and Vermeer 1984), according to which translation can take a number of forms and pursue different strategies depending on its purpose, and will thus be essential to enable effective cross-cultural communication. Furthermore, we suggest applying the concept of "cultureme"[1], as elaborated by Kocbek (2012) following Oksaar (1988), and use it as a tool for enhancing cross-cultural communicative competences. Another related theory which endorses the use of translation in SLT is "the theory of memes" where translation is seen as the only possible vehicle for

---

[1] The concept was later adopted in a slightly modified form by the functionalist approaches to translation (Vermeer 1983, 8; Nord 1997, 34).

transferring culturally-bound concepts, ideas, cultural practices (i.e. "memes") across cultural and linguistic boundaries (Chesterman 1997).

In its initial stages translation studies were mostly concerned with the concept of equivalence, i.e. finding target language means which enable the transferring of the source text (or any other relevant language segment) into the target language, corresponding to an understanding of translation which can be embraced by learners at all levels. Although different scholars have essentially viewed equivalence in the light of a binary opposition between two contrasting types, e.g. formal vs. dynamic (Nida 1964), semantic vs. communicative (Newmark 1981), overt vs. covert (House 1981), documentary vs. instrumental (Nord 1991), while others introduced alternative concepts which were still centred on a more or less pronounced degree of "sameness", it was the functionalist approach that decidedly shifted the focus from equivalence to the purpose of translation (i.e. the "skopos"). From the functionalist perspective "skopos" is seen as the factor defining the translation strategy to be applied and the type of translation to be produced, as well as justifying a wide range of different renderings of the source text. A further important concept advocated by the functionalist approach is that of the cultural embeddedness of language, according to which a message can be fully understood only if embedded in the context of the culture underlying it. The idea of the fundamental interrelatedness of language and culture was also at the core of the so-called "cultural turn" in translation science, a stance advocated by Bassnett and Lefevere (1990) and best rendered by the following metaphor:

> No language can exist unless it is steeped in the context of culture; and no culture can exist which does not have at its center, the structure of natural language. Language, then, is the heart within the body of culture, and it is the interaction between the two that results in the continuation of life-energy. In the same way that the surgeon, operating on the heart, cannot neglect the body that surrounds it, so the translator treats the text in isolation from the culture at his peril.[2]

In order to be able to effectively translate from one language into another, the cultures underlying the source and the target languages thus need to be taken into account. Moreover, to fully grasp the interrelatedness of language and culture, communicative situations need to be viewed in the light of the "cultureme theory", where "culturemes" are defined as patterns of communicative behaviour, i.e. as a socio-cultural category,

---

[2] Bassnett 1991, 14.

which is realised through realisational and regulatory "behaviouremes". "Realisational behaviouremes" refer to verbal (choice of linguistic means), paraverbal (pitch, tone, prosody) and non-verbal (e.g. gestures, body language) aspects of a communicative act, while "regulatory" ones involve extra-linguistic factors, such as time, space, status, social order, culturally-specific norms and conventions, etc. (Oksaar 1988, 26–27).

We believe that when applied in SLT settings, the functionalist approach would enable learners to understand that a text or a message in L1 can be transferred into L2 in different ways depending on the communicative purpose. In order to communicate effectively, the speaker does not only need to choose the most adequate verbal elements in L2, but also take into account the behaviouremes forming a particular cultureme in the target culture. For instance, in teaching L2 greeting customs, the learners' attention is drawn to the linguistic means available in L2, taking into account parts of the day and the hierarchical differences between the communicating parties as regards their age, status, gender, etc. (e.g. polite forms of address by using special verb forms or titles). In addition, the conventional gestures or body movements accompanying the act of greeting (shaking hands or bowing one's head), the habitual voice pitch, intonation, as well as other paraverbal and nonverbal behaviouremes will be made prominent. At the linguistic level, learners will be able to grasp that even when the communicative purpose is maintained (i.e. when there is function constancy between utterances in L1 and L2), the linguistic means of expression may not be equivalent. For example, when rendering the greeting formula "good afternoon" in Slovenian, an alternative solution will have to be adopted, as the Slovenian language does not have a special formula referring to afternoon, and most probably the more general greeting *dober dan* (*good day*) will be used or *dober večer* (*good evening*) in the late afternoon hours. While young learners obviously do not need to be acquainted with the theoretical concept of culturemes, they can develop the ability to map and bridge differences between them by being made aware of the multifaceted nature of communication.

When teaching a second language by consistently linking it to its underlying culture, teachers might have to deal with culturally specific ideas, conventions, concepts and cultural practices (such as festivities, traditional folk and fairy tale characters or culinary traditions), which have no corresponding counterpart in the learners' culture and can be seen as memes. Within one culture, memes can be transmitted through imitation and language, while their transmission across cultural and linguistic boundaries only occurs through translation. Thus, translation serves as "a survival machine for memes" (Chesterman 1997, 7) and the very need for translation proves the existence of a cultural boundary. Translation will therefore be indispensable for effectively presenting prototypical features of the L2 culture to its learners. Moreover, translation as advocated by the theory of memes can actually provide an effective tool for highlighting the intercultural dimensions of SLT and expanding the learners' cultural horizon.

## 3. Cognitive linguistics and SLT

Relying heavily on the interrelatedness of language and culture, and the prototypical character of memes, the memetic approach to translation can be related to several findings in the area of cognitive linguistics. One of the main assumptions underlying the cognitive linguistics investigations is that languages are embedded in cultural contexts, which implies that there are clear benefits in dealing with the cross-linguistic differences between L1 and L2 in an explicit way. Several scholars have recently discussed different ways in which the key claims from the cognitive linguistics framework can be effectively applied to the area of second language acquisition and pedagogy (Littlemore 2009; Achard and Niemeier 2004; Boers 2000; Bratož 2011). Among the fundamental principles developed by the cognitive linguistics movement the ones particularly relevant for the area of second language teaching are the concept of categorisation, the scope of metaphor and metonymy, and the principle of encyclopaedic knowledge.

### 3.1 Categories across languages and cultures

There are differences in the way people structure their experiences through language, in other words, different languages construe a variety of phenomena in different ways. One of the areas in which languages differ on the conceptual level is the way phenomena are divided up into categories. Lakoff (1987) argues that linguistic (and conceptual) categories show "prototype effects", which means that some members of the category are more prototypical than others. Categories may overlap and boundaries between them are more often than not "fuzzy". In addition, they are culture specific, for example, the category "sports" will have a different radial structure in different languages and cultures: while football may be at the very centre of the category for both Slovene and British people, skiing and rugby will hardly share the same place in the two cultures.

Taken as an overriding principle, categorization accounts for the common difficulties in trying to provide one-to-one correspondences between two languages. A case in point is the category *professor* (Slo. *profesor*) which is usually considered a prototypical *university teacher* in English, but has a much wider semantic span in Slovene where it is also used for primary and secondary school teachers and is often synonymous with *teacher*. When, in the light of the Skopos theory, the category of primary or secondary school teacher is rendered in Slovenian with *profesor*, the communicative purpose realized may either be maintained (function constancy with differing linguistic means) or it may be widened by including the culturally conditioned and implied meaning of showing respect and/or acknowledging the status of the person addressed in this way (the hierarchical position of *profesor* is higher than that of *učitelj*). Littlemore (2009, 28–29) points out that languages also vary according to the number of categories into which a particular phenomenon can break up. For example, in English we have *woods* and *forests* whereby the former are supposed to be slightly smaller than the latter, while in Slovene this distinction is not represented in language by two separate categories and would have to be expressed with adjectives *small* and *large* (*manjši gozd, velik gozd*). This has clear implications for second language learning, especially in the area of vocabulary development.

## 3.2 The scope of metaphor and metonymy

According to the cognitive view of metaphor developed by Lakoff and Johnson (1980) and elaborated by many other scholars, metaphors do not function merely at the linguistic level but also on the conceptual, physical, and socio-cultural level, which means they are likely to be subject to variation across languages. This has significant ramifications for SLT especially since learners might not be aware of the differences in which metaphors are processed and applied in the two languages respectively. Let us take as an example the metaphor in which body parts are commonly conceptualised as parts of objects, producing linguistic metaphors such as *the leg of a table* or *the head of a nail*, which exist both in Slovene and English. Based on the analogy suggested by the conceptual metaphor, a Slovene learner of English might conclude that it would apply also to other examples, such as *the hand of a clock*, which, however, is not directly translatable into Slovene in which the rotating pointers on a clock are not called *hands* but *forefingers*. The strategies used by language learners for processing and using L2 metaphors often differ from those used by native speakers. For example, learners might not recognize some common L2 metaphors as everyday and conventional, and treat them as highly novel and creative. On this account, Littlemore (2009, 94) stresses that even advanced learners tend to avoid using metaphorical senses of words and prefer to use more literal expressions.

Metonymy is, like metaphor, also regarded as a fundamental component of human cognition, a cognitive-linguistic mechanism which allows us to take one aspect of a thing or an event and use it to stand for the whole thing or event. Unlike metaphor which makes use of similarity and substitution, metonymy draws on relations of contiguity. Littlemore (ibid., 117) argues that some uses of metonymy may be problematic for language learners, especially when they rely heavily on cultural scripts and require the activation of large chunks of cultural knowledge. A case in point is the use of the word *tea* as in the question *Have you had your tea yet?* which in English metonymically refers to the custom (i.e. meme) of taking a light meal in the afternoon or early evening which may or may not include the drinking of tea[3]. And if tea is included, the prototypical kind is traditionally the earl gray. In contrast, the Slovene practice of *piti čaj* (*to drink tea*) evokes an entirely different cultural scenario in which *drinking tea* does not involve meals but refers to events such as warming up on a cold winter day or recovering from illness, with fruit or herbal varieties at the heart of the category, preferably with a spoonful of honey.

The above examples suggest that there may be strong arguments for including the development of metaphoric and metonymic competence in SLT, and that there are clear benefits in systematically focusing on L2 metaphors and metonymies from the perspective of memes and in an explicit fashion.

### 3.3 Encyclopaedic knowledge

The claim that knowledge is encyclopaedic in nature contrasts with the so called dictionary view by arguing that lexical concepts are not neat catalogues of disparate meanings of words but rather serve as "points of access to vast repositories of knowledge relating to a particular concept or conceptual domain" (Evans, Bergen and Zinken 2007, 8). From an SLT perspective, this means that acquiring L2 vocabulary knowledge involves learning integrated networks based on word associations rather than lists of unrelated words, bearing in mind that

> [...] L2 learners will already have built up a complex network of encyclopaedic knowledge, which is reflected in their L1 mental lexicon; when they learn a second language, they do not need to build up their

---

[3] The different customs related to having tea vary according to the part of the country or social class.

encyclopaedic knowledge from scratch. What they are more likely to try and do, at least in the early stages of L2 acquisition, is to map their L2 mental lexicon onto the existing structure, thus creating links that resemble those used in their L1.[4]

However, this mental process can have a two-pronged effect; on the one hand, by building on their well-established L1 networks, learners can efficiently create links in the L2 lexicon and thus augment L2 acquisition; on the other, this may lead to negative transfer, especially in areas which are subject to variation across languages and cultures. This suggests that there are strong arguments for explicitly focusing on both similarities and differences between L1 and L2 in SLT.

Another important aspect of encyclopaedic knowledge is that it always depends on the context in which it is activated. According to the model of frame semantics developed by Fillmore (1982), a lexical item activates a frame of semantic knowledge, i.e. a coherent conceptual structure of concepts which are related in such a way that without knowledge of all of them, we do not have complete knowledge of any one. One of the examples he gives is the word *weekend* which only makes sense in the context of the seven-day cycle in the calendar, devised by our civilization as a system of organizing time. It represents a social category which works because it is divided up into two complementary parts, one of which is the work-free part stretching over two days. Indeed, if the work-free part took only one day, we wouldn't need to have a special word for it; the name of that day would be enough. In addition, Fillmore (ibid., 191) points out that many concepts can only be grasped against the social and cultural background in which they occur, such as the concept "vegetarian", which only makes sense considering the frame of a culture in which eating meat is also common practice.

Littlemore (2009, 76–79) suggests that valuable insights can be gained by employing frame theory findings in SLT, especially when trying to account for the different ways the connotations of a word are structured and the points where the frames vary in the two languages. This is more likely to happen with words which have memetic connotations, such as for example the lexical item *chrysanthemum* which in some European countries (including Slovenia) evokes strong associations of funerals, lamentation and death, but is regarded as positive and cheerful in other countries, such as the United Kingdom. Time and again, these points suggest that there are clear benefits in dealing with differences explicitly.

---

[4] Littlemore 2009, 73.

## 4. Translation as a communicative competence

The prevalent teaching methods of the last decades have overtly rejected the use of L1 in second language instruction, advocating a "the less L1, the better" attitude and thus promoting a doctrine of monolingualism. This stance is clearly reflected in the communicative approach and its application in the form of communicative language teaching (CLT), one of the, if not the most, prominent methodology in SLT in the last forty years. Born out of the inefficiencies and shortcomings of the Grammar Translation and the Audio-Lingual methods but also the structural and behaviourist approaches and methods of the time, it changed the focus from the teaching of the foreign language as a system to teaching the language as communication (Howatt and Widdowson 2004). According to the fundamental principles of CLT, a language is best learnt by being used to communicate. Learners can achieve communicative competences in ESL settings by engaging in meaningful communication, using authentic materials which reflect real life situations (or culturemes). Based on these postulates, communicative SLT is geared towards setting the conditions which enable learners to comprehend, negotiate and express meaning in order to attain a communicative goal (or "skopos") by using a variety of linguistic and/or non-linguistc means which, despite pursuing the same communicative purpose, may differ considerably in different cultural settings. Several of the claims advanced by CLT have been examined critically. Bax (2003), for instance, argues that CLT has promoted a methodology-driven approach which was supposed to work in different contexts worldwide, completely ignoring any local varieties and contexts in which teaching takes place. He goes on to suggest that the area of SLT has been informed and pervaded by a "CLT attitude" according to which there is only one right and proper way of learning a foreign language. It is easy to see how the use of L1 and translation of any kind would interfere with the "CLT attitude".

Aside from the perspective assumed by the "CLT attitude", it is by no means clear why translation could not be seen as a legitimate means of achieving the communicative goals implied by the communicative approach or why translation would be at odds with the communicative principles in the first place. An important pedagogical argument in favour of using translation in SLT is that translation skills are connected with language competence in the sense that they aid L2 acquisition. For example, Vermes points out that

> [...] translation is not only structure manipulation; it is primarily a form of communication. And as such, it necessarily involves interaction and

cooperation between people, which makes it a potentially very useful device in foreign language teaching.[5]

However, there is another argument for including translation in foreign language classes which does not explicitly refer to the acquisition of L2 skills but is related to translation itself as a useful and necessary communicative competence. In other words, a competence which would not only enable learners to use the foreign language efficiently but also, as Cook (2010, 100) suggests, empower learners "to move back and forth between L1 and L2". This point raises some fundamental questions about the actual communicative needs of an L2 learner.

The model of communicative competence set out in the Common European Framework of Languages (CEFR) defines "communicative language competences" as those which "empower a person to act using specifically linguistic means" (Council of Europe 2001, 9). It is broken down into separate components (i.e. linguistic, sociolinguistic and pragmatic competences, which largely correspond to the various dimensions or behaviouremes of communicative acts viewed as culturemes), each of which encompasses particular knowledge, skills and know-how. It is stressed that the linguistic competences, made up of lexical, phonological, syntactical knowledge and skills and other dimensions of language as system, do not only refer to the range and quality of knowledge but also to the ways the knowledge is organised, stored and accessed (for example, by activation or recall), which may vary from individual to individual and may depend on a variety of factors, such as his or her knowledge of other languages or a person's cultural background. Sociolinguistic competences are concerned with sociocultural conditions of language use which are susceptible to social conventions, including, for example, rules of politeness, norms governing relations between generations, sexes, classes and social groups, and other social codes. It is here that the communicative language competences come closer to cross-cultural differences, as they are expressed through language, which may require, as suggested by the Skopos theory, using non-equivalent linguistic means of expression in order to achieve the intended communicative purpose. Pragmatic competences are concerned with a variety of interactional exchanges and require learners to demonstrate discourse competence (being able to arrange sentences in sequence in order to produce coherent stretches of language), functional competence (i.e. the use of spoken discourse and written texts in communication for particular functional purposes), and

---

[5] Vermes 2010, 91.

design competence (i.e. knowledge of the design conventions in a community).

In addition to these, CEFR introduces another dimension which sheds fresh light on the importance of translation in SLT, namely the development of "plurilingual competence", i.e. the capacity of a person to communicate using his or her complete linguistic repertoire, including their mother tongue. The reasoning behind this new perspective is that when acquiring a second language, learners do not turn off their own mother tongue and the associated culture. By acquiring a new language, learners do not develop a completely new way of communicating and acting, incongruous with the ones already acquired. Quite the contrary,

> [...] the linguistic and cultural competences in respect of each language are modified by knowledge of the other and contribute to intercultural awareness, skills and know-how [...][6]

enabling learners to "mediate, through interpretation and translation, between speakers of the two languages concerned who cannot communicate directly" (ibid.). In this vein, we may conclude that rather than seeing translation as conflicting with the fundamental principles of the communicative approach, its application in foreign language teaching can be perceived as an integral part of the communicative perspective, enhancing rather than hindering the attainment of communicative competence.

A major objection levelled against the use of translation in SLT is that it is unnatural and that it produces interference (Malmkjær 1998). One of the most prominent assumptions advanced by teaching methods such as CLT, the direct method and others is that language teaching should be informed by language which is "real", "authentic" and "natural". Today, this is clearly reflected in the wealth of EFL course books which claim almost without exception that they are based on real-life and authentic language sources and genuine uses of language. This can be clearly seen in comments advertising EFL course books, such as "it brings real life into the classroom" (*English Unlimited Elementary Coursebook*) or "real-world speaking skills" (*New Headway Elementary*). However, it is not always clear what is meant by "authentic" or "real-life". Taylor (1994) argues convincingly that the concept of authenticity is ambiguous since it is not clear whether what is meant is authenticity of "language", authenticity of "task", or authenticity of "situation". In addition, what is real and authentic for a native speaker of English may be (and often is)

---

[6] Council of Europe 2001, 43.

unreal and inauthentic for a L2 learner. In fact any kind of communicative activity in the foreign language classroom which is not carried out in their mother tongue is by definition a simulation for the language learners. And conversely, the only real and authentic situation for them would be one in which they would use their mother tongue to discuss the foreign language. In this context, Cook (2010, 32) argues convincingly that "authenticity is less a quality of the language itself than of the communication which makes use of it".

## 5. Young learners, young translators

Discussions about using translation in SLT tend to avoid the level of young learners and there are some obvious reasons for this. First of all, it is easy to see how translation might be seen as too complex a process for children to comprehend and make use of. Translation activities usually involve a certain amount of metatalk, i.e. talking about language and communication, which young children have not grasped or acquired yet. Six-year old children still struggle with basic language concepts like *word* or *sentence*, so how can we expect them to understand the highly complex cognitive process of translating? When trying to understand a second language, children will transfer the language strategies used for L1 acquisition to make sense of L2 sentences (Cameron 2001, 14–15). However, the transfer of strategies from L1 to L2 may not always be effective and may lead to negative transfer, which can be dealt with explicitly through translation activities. Nevertheless, for children (like any other language learners) who have already acquired a certain level of L1, it is natural to try and relate to what they already know when struggling with L2; we could say that translation comes to them naturally.

An eloquent example of how children spontaneously engage in the translation activity is the phenomenon of language brokering. Namely, with the intensification of the migration flows L2 speakers more and more often assume the roles of "natural translators" (Nord 1997, 16) as they volunteer to act as translators and/or interpreters in situations when professional translation or interpreting is not available or when they intervene upon request of family members or members of the same cultural community who feel more at ease when translation/interpreting is provided by someone they know rather than by professionals. This phenomenon has been acknowledged by several studies which clearly indicate that children and adolescents from immigrant families, who tend to become proficient in L2 more rapidly than their parents, increasingly take on the role of language and culture mediators.[7] This has important ramifications for language teaching policies which should support and integrate these developments rather than simply ignore them (cf. Belpoliti and Plascencia-Vela, this volume).

The second reason for questioning the use of translation with young learners is that it is so easy to avoid using translation. Compared to teaching teenagers and adults, SL teachers of young learners have the benefit of working with uninhibited, spontaneous, extremely receptive beings who do not mind singing at the top of their voices or imitating monkeys. This makes it easier for teachers to capitalise on maximising L2 exposure. However, this does not necessarily go against using translating activities in class. Cameron (2001, 212) suggests that children take pleasure in making comparisons between different languages, looking for words that are similar or different, for example. In addition, the very fact that they are unrestrained in their spontaneity allows them to be open and frank about what they learn, which can be effectively used in making the most of the discussions about differences between the languages and cultures involved. In this context, we will discuss three aspects in which translation can fruitfully be used with young learners. These aspects are related to three major SLT objectives, i.e. raising cross-cultural awareness, raising cross-linguistic awareness and expanding vocabulary, while at the same time paving the path for a profounder understanding and more conscious use of translation at a later stage.

## 5.1 Activities aimed at raising cross-cultural awareness

As we have seen above, communicative language competences incorporate also cross-cultural differences as they are expressed through language. By developing sociolinguistic competence and thus taking into account the regulatory behaviouremes of L2 culturemes, learners acquire the use of language which is reflected in social conventions, such as rules of politeness and other accepted norms. The use of translation activities lends itself easily to developing the awareness of the numerous differences in L1 and L2 sociolinguistic practices. An eloquent example which can be dealt with explicitly through translation is the T-V distinction for varying the levels of politeness in Slovene, where the 2nd person singular form is used for informal address and the 2nd person plural form for formal

---

[7] The reference here is to papers presented at the 1st International Conference of Non-Professional Interpreting and Translation which took place from 17 to 19 May 2012 in Forlì, Italy.

address. So, for example, in Slovene, the question *How are you?* can be rendered in two different ways depending on the addressee (informal *Kako si?* and formal *Kako ste?*), which also accounts for the uneasiness the learners sometimes feel using the politeness-neutral form in English after they have learnt in Slovene that teachers are to be addressed formally.

However, aside from raising learners' awareness of the culturally-determined speech practices and norms, the SL classroom offers innumerable opportunities for focusing on cross-cultural differences between the two or more cultures in question. Here are some of the topics which can be examined in class through meme-oriented translation activities: culture-specific festivals and celebrations (e.g. looking for translation equivalents related to the sociolinguistic practices of celebrating Mother's Day in the USA or Women's Day in Slovenia), mythological and legendary figures (e.g. discussing the translation of the Slovene expression *Dedek mraz*[8] and other related social and linguistic routines), literary characters, e.g. when translating names from or into L2, such as the name of the main character in the Slovene story *Muca copatarica*, (*The Slipper Cat*), recipes and other culinary practices (e.g. translating measuring units, special ingredients, etc.) and others. What is more, these activities can be used as a springboard for more comprehensive discussions of specific cultural practices, such as the tradition of celebrating Mother's Day in the USA or the role of the *Slipper Cat* and the all-pervasive practice of *wearing slippers* in the Slovene culture.

## 5.2 Bridging activities

We refer to translation activities aimed at overcoming the barriers of linguistic differences between L1 and L2 as "bridging" activities with translation playing a primarily facilitative role of helping learners to bridge the gaps between the two languages identified as differences in various cultureme aspects. This is especially worth considering in cases of negative transfer which can occur at different levels of language. At the level of phonology (i.e. paraverbal behaviouremes), for example, the learners may not be able to distinguish between the long and short vowels in English and therefore not recognise the difference between *feel* and *fill*, for instance. At the syntactic level, they may transfer the L1 word order, as for example in the sentence *Today is nice weather* which reflects a typical

---

[8] *Dedek mraz* is usually translated into English either with the Russion expression *Ded Moroz* or the English translation *Father Frost*, although *dedek* is actually *grandfather*, so *Grandfather Frost* would be a closer equivalent.

Slovene structure. At the lexical level (i.e. verbal behaviouremes), negative transfer may occur in false cognates, for example the Slovene word *biskvit* (*pastry*) and the English *biscuit*, the Slovene *tabla* (*blackboard*) and *table*), or collocations such as *sladka voda* (*sweet water*) for *fresh water* (when referring to rivers) and idiomatic expressions (e.g. the Slovene idiom *vleči za nos* is literally translated as *pull one's nose* rather than *pull one's leg*). At the pragmatic level, transfer is likely to occur in the use of language for particular functional purposes, complying with the relevant regulatory behaviouremes, such as when the Slovene interactional pattern *hvala-prosim* is literally rendered in English with *thank you-please* rather than *thank you-you're welcome* or when *dober tek* (*good appetite*) is used to start off a meal according to the established social convention in Slovenia.

Benson (2002) argues that teachers can raise consciousness of the differences between L1 and L2 by focusing on particular points in an explicit way and eliciting awareness and suggests that translation can be used either with sentences illustrating particular points and predicting transfer errors or with whole texts containing potential transfer errors. In addition, translation activities can be either form-focused or more communicative in nature. A good example of a communicative translation activity would be asking learners to look at the different functions in which the response *you're welcome* is used in English, and translate it into Slovene accordingly (i.e. in accordance with the given skopos). This may involve learners to contemplate and discuss language in active ways as eloquently illustrated by Cook (2010, 142–143) with the example of the Italian word *prego* whose possible translations into English triggered several enthusiastic discussions among English learners of Italian. Indeed, Cook (ibid., 142) suggests that the actual process of talking about language may "feed directly into improved language use". We would like to argue that all these examples can be used in various types of translation activities also with young learners; they are either common, everyday functions usually dealt with in beginners' classes (e.g. thanking) or relevant for young learners because they are related to their other subjects (e.g. they learn about water sources) or relate to classroom equipment and realia (e.g. whiteboard).

## 5.3 Expanding vocabulary

Translation has traditionally been used for introducing and developing vocabulary, especially with young learners and students at the beginner's level. While providing or eliciting the translation of vocabulary for learners may not always be the best teaching strategy, it is still the fastest and most efficient way of explaining the meaning of L2 words and expressions. However, this is only true in cases when there are clear one-to-one correspondences (semantic equivalence) between words in L1 and L2. Course books and other teaching materials aimed at young and very young learners are based on teaching sets of vocabulary which lend themselves easily to translation and categorisation, with lexical areas such as animals, colours, family members, body parts, etc. This overt focus on the lexical level has some clear practical advantages; learners are presented with clear-cut categories and one-to-one correspondences. However, as we have argued above, real-life categories are often fuzzy and translation highly dependent on context or purpose. But are young learners not too young to be able to grasp the fuzziness of language?

We would like to argue that translation can be used as a strategy for developing vocabulary and at the same time raising awareness of the differences between L1 and L2 even with young learners. Once they have mastered the basic categories, young learners may gradually be introduced to the differences between L1 and L2, and several possible translation equivalents, as well as to the multifaceted character of communication seen as a sequence of culturemes. For example, once they have learnt about the parts of the body, they may be asked to compare their conventionalised metaphoric uses in the two languages looking for similarities and differences: English and Slovene both refer to *the legs of the table* or the *head of the nail* but they differ in referring to the pointers on the clock. Another example is the idiom *the eye of a needle*, the Slovene equivalent being *the ear of a needle (šivankino uho)*. Drawing on the conceptual metaphor BODY PARTS ARE OBJECTS, this activity capitalises on both the similarities and differences between L1 and L2 and can be extended to include other lexical items always bearing in mind the learners' level. Metaphors are thus seen as a rich source and useful tool for learning new vocabulary. In addition, Boers (2000) argues convincingly that language learners can benefit from an enhanced metaphorical awareness also in terms of greater vocabulary retention. The reasoning behind this claim is, first, that the learning of new vocabulary through image processing paves an extra way for later recall; second, that the cognitive effort employed to identify the relevant source domain enhances memory storage; and third, that conceptual metaphors function as structured frameworks which help organizing the vocabulary to be learnt.

## 6. Conclusion

We have attempted to argue that valuable insights into the relevance of translation in foreign language instruction can be gained by drawing on findings in cognitive linguistics and recent trends in translation studies. Attempting to narrow the gap between theory and practice, the chapter presents some of the ways in which translation can be sensibly used for different SLT purposes.

If we understand communicative competence as laid out by CEFR, then there is little doubt that translation and contrastive analysis are not just an alternative but an indispensable tool for developing communicative competence, in which meanings are negotiated not just within one language but also across languages and cultures. Translation is increasingly coming to be seen as a natural and necessary competence in its own right or, to borrow McConnell-Duff's (1989, 6) words, "translation happens everywhere, all the time, so why not in the classroom?". In this respect, a case has been argued in favour of introducing translation as a viable pedagogic tool at the earliest levels of SL instruction.

In conclusion, while we are well aware that more research is necessary to fully explore the potential of translation in SLT, we cannot but agree that the Cinderella of language teaching has to be granted the position it justly deserves in the palace of accepted language teaching practices from which it has been unjustly banished for too long.

## Works cited

Achard, Michel, and Suzanne Niemeier, eds. 2004. *Cognitive Linguistics, Second Language Acquisition, and Foreign Language Teaching*. Berlin: Mouton de Gruyter.
Bassnett, Susan. 1991. *Translation Studies: Revised Edition*. London & New York: Routledge.
Bassnett, Susan, and André Lefevere, eds. 1990. *Translation, History and Culture*. London & New York: Pinter.
Bax, Steven. 2003. "The End of CLT: A Context Approach to Language Teaching." *ELT Journal* 57(3):278–287.
Belpoliti, Flavia, and Amira Plascencia-Vela. 2013. "Translation Techniques in the Spanish for Heritage Learner's Classroom: Promoting Lexical Development." In *Translation in Language Teaching and Assessment*, edited by Dina Tsagari, and Georgios Floros, this volume. Newcastle upon Tyne: Cambridge Scholars Publishing.

Benson, Cathy. 2002. "Transfer/Cross-linguistic Influence." *ELT Journal* 56(1):68–70.
Boers, Frank. 2000. "Metaphor Awareness and Vocabulary Retention." *Applied Linguistics* 21(4):553–571.
Bratož, Silva. 2011. "Metaphors as Tools for Facilitating Learning and Comprehension." In *La investigación y la enseñanza aplicadas a las lenguas de especialidad y a la tecnologia,* edited by María L. Carrió, Josefa Contreras, Françoise Olmo, Hanna Skorczynska, Inmaculada Tamarit, and Debra Westall, 445–452. València: Unversitat Politècnica de València.
Cameron, Lynne. 2001. *Teaching Languages to Young Learners.* Cambridge: Cambridge University Press.
Chesterman, Andrew. 1997. *Memes of Translation.* Amsterdam & Philadelphia: Benjamins.
Council of Europe. 2001. *Common European Framework of Reference for Languages: Learning, Teaching, Assessment.* Strasbourg: Council of Europe Publishing. Accessed November 22, 2012. http://www.coe.int/t/dg4/Linguistic/Source/Framework_EN.pdf
Cook, Guy. 2010. *Translation in Language Teaching.* Oxford: Oxford University Press.
Evans, Vyvyan, Benjamin Bergen, and Joerg Zinken. 2007. *The Cognitive Linguistics Reader.* London: Equinox.
Fillmore, Charles. 1982. "Frame Semantics". In *Linguistics in the Morning Calm,* edited by the Linguistic Society of Korea, 111–137. Seoul: Hanshin Publishing.
House, Juliane. 1981. *A Model for Translation Quality Assessment.* Tübingen: Narr.
Howatt, Anthony P. R., and Henry G. Widdowson. 2004. *A History of English Language Teaching.* Oxford: Oxford University Press.
Kocbek, Alenka. 2012. "Memes and Culturemes as Tools in Translating Contracts". In *Translation Studies: Old and New Types of Translation in Theory and Practice,* edited by Lew. N. Zybatow, and Alena Petrova, 79–85. Frankfurt am Main: Peter Lang.
Lakoff, George. 1987. *Women, Fire, and Dangerous Things: What Categories Reveal about the Mind.* Chicago: University of Chicago.
Lakoff, George, and Mark Johnson. 1980. *Metaphors We Live By.* Chicago: University of Chicago Press.
Littlemore, Jeannette. 2009. *Applying Cognitive Linguistics to Second Language Learning and Teaching.* Basingstoke: Palgrave Macmillan.
McConnell-Duff, Alan. 1989. *Translation.* Oxford: Oxford University Press.

Malmkjær, Kirsten, ed. 1998. *Translation and Language Teaching: Language Teaching and Translation*. Manchester: St. Jerome.
Nida, Eugene A. 1964. *Toward a Science of Translating*. Leiden: Brill.
Newmark, Peter. 1981. *Approaches to Translation*. Oxford: Pergamon Press.
Nord, Christiane. 1991. *Text Analysis in Translation*. Amsterdam & Atlanta: Rodopi.
—. 1997. *Translating as a Purposeful Activity: Functionalist Approaches Explained*. Manchester: St. Jerome.
Oksaar, Els. 1988. *Kulturemtheorie: Ein Beitrag zur Sprachverwendungsforschung*. Hamburg: Joachim Jungius Gesellschaft der Wissenschaften.
Reiß, Katharina, and Hans J. Vermeer. 1984. *Grundlegung einer allgemeinen Translationstheorie*. Tübingen: Niemeyer.
Taylor, David. 1994. "Inauthentic Authenticity or Authentic Inauthenticity?" *TESL-EJ* 1(2):1–12.
Vermeer, Hans J. 1983. "Translation Theory and Linguistics." In *Näkökohtia käänämisen tutkimuksesta*, edited by Pauli Roinila, Ritva Orfanos, and Sonja Tirkkonen-Condit, 1–10. Joensuu: University of Joensuu.
Vermes, Albert. 2010. "Translation in Foreign Language Teaching: A Brief Overview of Pros and Cons." *Eger Journal of English Studies* X:83–93.
Widdowson, Henry G. 2003. *Defining Issues in English Language Teaching*. Oxford: Oxford University Press.
Witte, Arnd, Theo Harden, and Alessandra R. Harden, eds. 2009. *Translation in Second Language Learning and Teaching*. Bern: Peter Lang.
Žefran, Mojca, and Silva Bratož. 2012. "Redefining the Role of Classroom Discourse in Early Foreign Language Instruction." In *Nastava i učenje: ciljevi, standardi, ishodi*, edited by Snežana Marinković, 679–690. Užice: Učiteljski fakultet.

# CHAPTER EIGHT

## FROM *INTERCULTURAL SPEAKER* TO *INTERCULTURAL WRITER*: TOWARDS A NEW UNDERSTANDING OF TRANSLATION IN FOREIGN LANGUAGE TEACHING

### RAPHAËLLE BEECROFT

### 1. Introduction

Using German Translation Studies research as well as the status quo in Foreign Language Teaching (both in research and practice) in Germany as a situational framework, this chapter will set out to explore the differences in understanding the process of translation between these two contexts. I will then make a call for a shift in the perception of translation in Foreign Language Teaching towards one more in harmony with that of Translation Studies, namely of translation as a functional, communicative and inter- and transcultural process. In so doing, I aim to highlight the didactic potential of this understanding for the secondary English L2 classroom.

Section 2 will provide an overview of selected translation theories which reject the understanding of translation as an *equivalent* interlingual code transfer. In section 3, I will reconstruct how these translation theories have led to calls for a *communicative turn* in translator education. To do so, I will focus on the initiatives taken in this direction by various scholars at the Faculty of Translation Studies, Linguistics and Cultural Studies at the University of Mainz (Germany), one of the country's leading centres in the field. Section 4 will focus on communicative language teaching and intercultural communicative competence (ICC) as the main pillars of contemporary foreign language teaching (FLT). I will also highlight developments in the didactics of foreign language cultural studies towards a more discourse-oriented, affective form of teaching and learning. At the same time, however, I will demonstrate that in German foreign language theory and practice the understanding of the translation process is at odds with the didactic developments mentioned above. It seems that they only focus on the structural linguistic benefits of written translation as an interlingual code transfer for language learners.

The aforementioned elements will form the basis for my main argument in section 5. In this section, I will propose that, parallel to the calls made by translation scholars for a more communicative approach to translation didactics, a more communicative approach to and grasping of the translation process in FLT could be very productive. This can be in the context of considering FLT as a hybrid space for discourse and action. I will argue that the inclusion of the translation process in the EFL classroom can create these hybrid spaces. The didactic potential of such spaces can then be channelled through complex translational tasks, thus promoting the development of ICC in learners. The final part of the chapter (section 6) will give an example of one such complex translational task whose methodology is based on that used in translation didactics. The task was developed as part of a seminar on translation in the EFL classroom delivered by the author at Karlsruhe University of Education, Germany, in 2011. In the outlook (section 7), I will make suggestions for further interdisciplinary cooperation between Translation Studies and Foreign Language Teaching.

## 2. Translation theories

The emergence of Translation Studies as a discipline engendered a reflection by scholars on the facets of the process of translation and of the translated text itself. This reflection signified a shift away from what Dizdar (2006, 15) calls the "narrow" understanding of translation based on the assumption that signifiers from different languages (all corresponding to one and the same signified) are interchangeable. This understanding is, according to Dizdar (ibid.), often used to demonstrate that translation is impossible, not desirable, and/or an assimilation tactic which denies difference and destroys concepts of otherness. Such an understanding creates boundaries for the act of translation and the translated text. It is often described in the form of a vessel/transportation metaphor: two riverbanks and a freight vessel with its contents. The vessel and its contents must arrive at the opposite riverbank in exactly the same state as when they left (cf. Dizdar 2008, 54–55). The role of the translator in this metaphor is that of the freight carrier (Arrojo 1997, 25–26), whose only duty is to see to that the freight arrives intact at its destination (cf. Dizdar

2006, 271). Dizdar (ibid., 15) calls for a deconstruction of both this understanding and its accompanying metaphor as well as of scholarly texts on translation. His aim is to engender a continuous reflection process in Translation Studies, and transform the position of the discipline both in society and scholarly debate.

Several strands of Translation Studies challenge this narrow understanding of translation (without deconstructing it). One of these is Vermeer's *Skopos Theory* (1978, 1986, 1992, 1996) which can be said to have formed the basis for a paradigm shift in Translation Studies through its function-oriented approach (Dizdar 1999, 104). This approach positioned the goal (Skopos) of the translation at the forefront of the translation process and assigned the responsibility of reaching this goal to the translator. This is opposed to the translator being solely a freight carrier, and to the "freight" having to remain identical from one riverbank to another. In Vermeer's theory, Skopos can be seen as twofold: As the goal of the translator when translating, and as the goal of the text which reaches the target culture. It is, accordingly, the responsibility of the translator to know what is required in the target culture, and what the intention of the source text was. It is also the translator's responsibility to have the ability to reconcile these two in order to enable intercultural communication. This entails the ability to make decisions and remain flexible with regard to these decisions. The theory highlights the historical, cultural and situational contexts of the translator as important factors in the translation process. It also requires critical awareness on the part of the translator of factors which influence the translation process (ibid.). Vermeer's theory thus emphasised the role of the translator and the importance of the situational and cultural contexts a) from which the source text stems, b) within which the translator translates, and c) for which the translation is destined. This resulted in a shift in the understanding of translation towards a functional, action-oriented and communicative perspective, where translation was considered a "particular type of interaction and, as part of this, communication" (Vermeer 1992, 43, my translation). In this perspective, the reason for the existence of translation is intercultural communication (cf. Dizdar 1999, 105).

The above perspective also paved the way for approaches in Translation Studies which highlighted and discussed the relevance of culture in the translation process, addressing, in particular, the role of the translator as an expert in and between cultures (cf. Witte 2000, 24). Witte emphasises that although comparing putative cultures is often seen as an intrinsic part of the translation process, the designation of what stands as a "culture-specific" item can only stem from the translator's own socio-cultural background. Thus, the item can only stand for a particular construct in a particular context and not as synecdoche for a whole culture. Witte further warns that these "culture-specific" items can only emerge through a comparison and do not stand alone. Witte refers to an awareness of this, and the responsibility on the part of the translator, which engenders as "translatorial cultural competence" (ibid., 75, my translation). She furthermore emphasises the need for translator education to distance itself both from the view that "a culture" can be taught as such and from relating putative "static" facts about a culture (cf. ibid., 83, 102) as a way of "teaching" it.

The focus on culture in Translation Studies paved the way to a broader *cultural turn* (Bachmann-Medick 2004, 449) which aimed to analyse the variety of socio-cultural contexts present in the world and their relationship to one another. This both engendered new categories in translation, such as cultural transfer, otherness, cultural differences and power relations (cf. ibid.), and enabled a rapprochement of translation with (postcolonial) cultural studies in a way that Dizdar (see above) had called for. Here, too, the emphasis is on the hybridity and internal dynamics of cultures. Cultures in themselves can be seen as translation processes as opposed to static, homogenous identities which can be represented in a synechdochical manner through writing. The spaces of overlap which occur through this hybridity of culture(s) and identity/ies are called *third spaces* by Bhabha (1994, 53). They inspire creativity and productivity (cf. Bachmann-Medick 2004, 456) similar to the freedom and creativity Vermeer assigns to the translator, knowing that "a text will not 'be' the same to everyone forever" (Vermeer 1996, my translation). Bachmann-Medick (2004, 455) makes a plea for highlighting these cultural *third spaces* from a translation perspective in order to make them a breeding ground for discourse. Cook also highlights the relevance of these spaces for translators:

> [W]ith increased mobility and international communication, the process of contact between communities and languages becomes for many people as important as their separate static identities. The translator should no longer inhabit an unacknowledged no-man's land between 'source language' and 'target language'. The spaces in between are becoming bigger than those on either side of them.[1]

---

[1] Cook 2010, 79.

## 3. Translation didactics

Both the understanding of translation as a functional process of inter- and transcultural communication as well as the highlighted position and responsibility of the translator made it necessary to re-think an important issue. This issue involves the ways in which translation theory and practice, and the linguistic competence required for such practice, were being taught at university (tertiary) level, where Translation Studies was most visibly emerging as a discipline.

In the late 1990s Dizdar called for a change in translation didactics. He argued that if the understanding of the teaching matter had changed, then the teaching methods should be adjusted accordingly. She based her argument on the claim that essentialist and knowledge-transfer oriented teaching methods dominated the field of translation didactics—just as an essentialist understanding of translation as one-to-one transfer of meaning from one language into another, and of theory as a way of "transferring truth", pervaded translation studies (cf. Dizdar 1998, 254). Arguing along the same lines, Kiraly claimed that, similar to the situation in translation didactics, the methods used to teach translation were characterised by "an objectivist belief in the transferable nature of knowledge" (2000, 165). He remarked that

> the still pervasive pedagogical view of translation as an interlingual transcoding process [has] perpetuated the stranglehold of transmissionist teaching approaches in translator education.[2]

Underlining the parallel use of the vessel metaphor both in translation theory and didactics, Kiraly refers to "[s]tudents […] being treated like empty vessels that need to be filled with knowledge" (ibid., 185). As an alternative to the above, he calls for "teaching methods and approaches that are geared toward the development of authentic communicative competence", thus mirroring the "contemporary consensus view from the scholarship in translation studies that professional translation is an act of communication" (ibid., 182). The methods and approaches he proposes are of a social-constructivist ilk, emphasising, under the communicative paradigm, the holistic, somatic, emotional and personal nature of language learning. They also promote ways of fostering group learning processes to which each individual can contribute in a way that corresponds to their learning style. These methods and approaches include authentic group

---

[2] Kiraly 2000, 181.

translation projects, in which each student chooses a particular role/task to take on, as well as reflection exercises, such as Think-Aloud-Protocols.

Still with regard to translation practice, Bahadır (2007) echoes this call when describing her understanding of teaching language and culture as focusing not only on the fostering of cognitive abilities, but also on emotional and personal dimensions, which should be given greater priority (cf. ibid., 254). As an interpreter, interpreting scholar and interpreting trainer, Bahadır applies such principles to her own teaching. They include dynamic theatre methods (improvisational theatre, forum theatre) to channel the holistic, spontaneous and ephemeral character of interpreting (ibid., 249).

Teaching translation came on the scene also as part of the general adaptation process which was required in Germany as a result of the introduction of Bachelor and Master's degree programmes. The area most affected by this adaptation is the acquisition of language competence. Students now have to be at level B1 (Common European Framework of Reference) in their first and second languages to embark on translation studies (cf. Hassel 2009, 179). Before that, it was expected of students to acquire their linguistic competence parallel to their translation studies. In order to be able to meet these new demands, it was necessary to devise new ways of teaching language competence. This presented the opportunity to re-structure teaching methods and contents to match the tenets of communicative language teaching, and become functionally oriented towards acquiring language competence from a translator's perspective. This would mean that the main teaching focus would be the various linguistic skills needed to engage in the act of translation. This would do away with the "compartmentalization of knowledge" (Kiraly 2000, 181) identified in language teaching within Translation Studies. Hassel (2009) developed a typology of exercises geared to this. She defines *translation-oriented foreign language teaching*, as

> [...] a form of Foreign Language Teaching which is communicative, learner-focused and action-oriented as well as being directly related to translation processes in that it trains the competences required by translators.[3]

The typology consists of six different competences, which are thought to cover the linguistic skills required of translators, including what Hassel terms "culture-related understanding" (ibid., 188, my translation). This means raising awareness of the fact that every utterance is linked to its

---

[3] Ibid., 187, my translation.

speaker's culture (ibid., 189; see also Nord 1999). Hassel suggests the use of models employed in "pure" translator training, such as scenes-and-frames semantics, to promote this understanding in language learners.

The new understanding of translation as a communicative and functional process across cultures, triggered a rethinking of teaching methods and contents to become more communicative, holistic, and (functionally) oriented towards translator training. This in turn spawned the use of methods which had not been exploited in translator training before. These include authentic translation project group work, Think-Aloud-Protocols, theatre methods and scenes-and-frames-semantics.

## 4. Communicative language teaching, intercultural communicative competence and translation

The calls for more communicative teaching methods in translation didactics can be seen as part of general developments in foreign language teaching in Germany over the last forty years towards *communicative language teaching*. This has culminated in ICC being deemed the overriding principle in foreign language teaching at both secondary and tertiary education levels (cf. Müller-Hartmann and Schocker-von Ditfurth 2004, 18). ICC is codified in the guidelines of the federal state curricula for modern foreign languages (MFL) (e.g. those of Baden-Württemberg). The guidelines stipulate that ICC entails openness, empathy, respect and tolerance to (culturally) diverging ways of life. ICC also entails the ability to take on different perspectives and reflect upon how one's own socio-cultural context influences the constitution of one's own identity and personality. Furthermore, the guidelines recommend that the contents of the MFL syllabus should be re-structured so that learners are able to observe, analyse and compare socio-cultural contexts beyond reproducing facts about the target culture. (Ministerium für Kultus, Jugend und Sport Baden-Württemberg 2010, 84)

In formulating their aims regarding ICC, the guidelines draw heavily on Byram's homonymous concept. He proposes that students should be fostered into becoming "intercultural speakers" (Byram 1997, 31). Their ability to be interculturally and communicatively competent is expressed in their various "savoirs" (ibid., 34) on different affective and cognitive-linguistic levels. These savoirs allow them to successfully engage in situations of intercultural interaction, fostering awareness and the potential for reflection. Distancing himself from the concept of the native speaker, and dismissing the ideal of "native speaker linguistic competence" as "imprecise" (ibid., 32), Byram summarises his model as follows:

It is this function of establishing relationships, managing dysfunctions and mediating which distinguishes an 'intercultural speaker', and makes them different from a native speaker.[4]

While ICC remains the overriding principle in foreign language teaching in Germany, the idea of interculturality itself has become a subject of discussion, in particular in the field of postcolonial cultural studies in foreign language teaching didactics (cf. Freitag, Stroh and von Reinersdorff 2008, 4–5). For some scholars in this field, interculturality is taken to imply the existence of static cultures with definite borders and inviting essentialist and dichotomous comparisons. However, proponents of intercultural foreign language teaching in Germany (cf., for example, Bredella and Christ 2007) argue that the notion of interculturality implies the moment of crossing borders as well as the process of mutual understanding that occurs on that moment. This requires a reassessment of original positions, thereby making the categories of *own* and *other* dynamic and relational, rather than static and essentialist (cf. Freitag, Stroh and von Reinersdorff 2008, 5). Furthermore, cultures are seen as "historically grown, discursively constructed, culturally heterogeneous and politically contested entities" (Delanoy 2006, 241). Accordingly, the aim of intercultural foreign language teaching should be "transcultural awareness" (Freitag, Stroh and von Reinersdorff 2008, 5) of the different perspectives and voices within one putative culture. Scholars in the field (cf., for example, Bredella 2001, Nünning 2001) call for didactic tasks which focus on differentiating, navigating and coordinating between perspectives. Hallet (2002, 34ff) calls for the classroom to be considered as a hybrid space for discourse and action. In this classroom, opportunities for negotiating meaning between various text-based, individual and cultural points of view should be provided. Thus, learners are in a position to recognise, relate and develop cultural expressions of meaning (cf. ibid., 34).

However, written translation as a functional, inter- and transcultural process of communication, does not yet seem to have found its place within the didactic context of Germany. A cursory look at relevant grammar school (*Gymnasium*) textbooks reveals that ten years ago translation was considered a skill to be trained through the translation of texts and grammatical structures. But this perspective no longer features in the current edition (cf. Derkow Disselbeck *et al.* 1999a, 1999b; Abbey *et al.* 2008, 2009). Nonetheless, calls for translation to be given more attention in foreign language teaching in Germany have been made recently. The understanding of translation promoted by such calls is "as a

---

[4] Bayram 1997, 38.

much more complex phenomenon at the basis of human communication" (Taviano 2010, 129). Furthermore, a non-representative study carried out by Gnutzmann and Bohnensteffen (2012) at German grammar schools revealed that both teacher and student informants had a positive attitude to translation. Nevertheless, what translation is understood to entail still seems to differ greatly from that discussed within Translation Studies.

In their article, Gnutzmann and Bohnensteffen use grammar and translation as a collocating pair, pointing to the historical methodological connection of the two terms. They define translation as "the meaning transfer of written or spoken texts from one language to another" (ibid., 52), and identify three areas where translation can be said to take place in the classroom: grammatical structures, texts, and classroom discourse (cf. ibid., 49). The focus thereby seems to be very much on the cognitive-linguistic dimension of the translation process. In particular, they see the benefits of translation in that it a) expands learners' knowledge of language, b) tests reading comprehension, and c) contributes to the improvement of L1 competence (cf. ibid., 52–55). The authors also deploy categories rejected by translation scholars, such as "the phenomenon of untranslatability as in the case of proverbs, metaphors or idioms" (ibid.). The use of these categories again points to an understanding of translation as interlingual transfer and not as a functional, inter- and transcultural communicative process. Further on in their paper, the authors consider grammar and translation not "able to develop learners' communicative competence" (ibid., 58).

Interestingly, the process of mediation has begun to feature prominently in curriculum guidelines and textbooks (cf. Abbey *et al.* 2008, 2009, 2011; Derkow Disselbeck *et al.* 2012) across all school types in Germany as "the fifth communicative skill alongside listening-comprehension, speaking, reading and writing" (Gnutzmann and Bohnensteffen 2012, 52). The process of mediation is used

> [...] in plurilingual settings when two people do not share a common language and need a third person who has access to both languages and thus can act as a mediator to ensure understanding between the other two.[5]

Perhaps because of its oral, obviously communicative nature, mediation is considered as furthering ICC and as having transformed the understanding of the translation process:

---

[5] Ibid.

[T]ranslation is no longer viewed as the mere transference of linguistic structures from one language to the other, but has rather taken on a functional-communicative meaning exemplified by the concept of mediation.[6]

Taking into consideration the informant responses to the survey on mentioned above, this can really be said to apply only for mediation itself and not for its written counterpart. In Translation Studies however, this understanding encompasses both kinds of translation. At the same time, Gnutzmann and Bohnensteffen call for "the development of interlingual exercises that fill the gap between exclusively monolingual exercises and traditional translation exercises" due to "the increase in intercultural communication situations" (ibid., 53). Although the focus here is still on "interlingual" exercises, the distancing of the authors from "traditional" translation exercises could signify a call for written translation tasks which foster ICC.

## 5. Complex translational tasks as a means of fostering intercultural communicative competence

After discussing the role of translation and the understanding of cultural studies within foreign language teaching, I propose to re-introduce written translation into the secondary English language classroom. I follow the translation scholars' perspective on translation as a functional, communicative, inter- and transcultural process. Echoing Dizdar's statement that teaching methods should match teaching matter, I would suggest that translation can be used as a means of promoting ICC in learners. Translation is seen here as a process of intercultural communication in itself in the form of a complex task (Ellis 2003). The translation process as a functional type of communication, according to Translation Studies, requires (intercultural) communicative competence. I would argue, therefore, that a didactic design of translation may be used to foster ICC in learners.

The *third spaces* which emerge through the process of translation can contribute to the embodiment of the foreign language classroom as a hybrid space for discourse and action. The potential of these spaces for learning and experiences is channelled in a productive manner. Furthermore, the translation process requires skills not only at the linguistic level (cf. Gnutzmann and Bohnensteffen 2012), but also at the

---

[6] Ibid., 58.

affective level, which is of equal importance. An example of the latter is the "translatorial cultural competence" described further above (Witte 2000).[7] I propose to channel the potential of these third spaces through complex translational tasks in the secondary foreign language classroom. The methodology for these tasks should match the communicative aspect of the translation process with a communicative teaching methodology.

Whilst the goal of these complex translational tasks reflects the aims of FLT and ICC as a whole, it seems that they can also contribute to the learners' development into *intercultural writers*. This is a combination of Byram's *intercultural speaker* and Witte's[8] notion of the translator as an *expert* in and between cultures. In this way, learners can act as *cultural agents* with tasks designed according to task-based language learning (with a pre-task and a post-task) (cf. Ellis 2003, 351). This structure promotes phases of awareness raising and reflection, helping learners negotiate meaning between various text-based, individual and cultural points of view. Thus, learners are in a position to recognise, relate and develop cultural expressions of meaning. Furthermore, the learners' role as translators who have to make explicit choices whilst carrying out the tasks should help them realise that putative culture-specific phenomena only occur through the act of comparison. Therefore, these phenomena are neither absolute nor representative, thus contributing to one of the goals of ICC to raise awareness of the fictitiousness of essentialist concepts of culture and identity.

## 6. An example of a complex translational task based on the scenes-and-frames model

This section will present a practical example of how the didactic potential of the spaces emerging during the translation process can be harnessed in the form of a complex translational task. This task is based on the *scenes-and-frames* model, a method used in translation didactics. It aims to develop the skills necessary for the students to become intercultural writers in the terms set out by Byram and Witte: awareness of the hybridity and dynamicity of cultural expressions of meaning, as well as flexibility and the ability to critically reflect on their own actions as

---

[7] I consider these skills to be similar to the "savoirs" proposed by Byram (1997) in his model of ICC to create an "intercultural speaker".
[8] The notion of the *intercultural writer* as a follow-on term from the *intercultural speaker* was also the topic of a one-day event hosted by the International Association for Languages and Intercultural Communication (IALIC) in 2009.

translators. The following example, together with further tasks such as Think-Aloud-Protocols and group translation processes, were devised and used in 2011 as part of a seminar on *translation as an (inter)cultural and communicative process in the foreign language classroom* at Karlsruhe University of Education. Their overall aim was to raise trainee teachers' awareness of this issue. The first part of the section will focus on the scenes-and-frames model itself, so as to explain its applicability to the task, which will then be outlined in the second part of the section.

Fillmore's (1977) concept of *scenes* and *frames* was applied to the translation process by Vannerem and Snell-Hornby (1986) and further modified by Vermeer and Witte (1990) as a theoretical and methodological possibility of describing (inter)cultural communication processes. The model postulates that communication partners have a "scene" in their heads of what they want to say before they actually express it. In expressing this "scene", either verbally, para- or non-verbally, they create a "frame" which the other communication partner receives and, again, creates a "scene" in his/her head based on the way he/she has received his/her partner's "frame" (cf. Witte 2000, 110). For translation purposes, the realisation that the scenes in the communication partners' heads as well as the frames through which they are expressed are context- and situation-specific, is highly relevant. The reason is that, due to this specificity, no partner involved in the communication process can have the same "scene" in his/her head (cf. ibid., 111). Translators and, I would add, intercultural writers should possess the skills which will enable them to make decisions on what the "source" and "target" scenes could look like and how to construct the "frame" in which the "target" scene should be depicted (cf. ibid., 114).

Witte claims that the scenes-and-frames model should be used in translation didactics in order to raise awareness of the translator's decisions and actions during the translation process. This model also raises awareness of potential essentialist notions and value judgements which could influence the translation process. Moreover, Witte adds that the model can help translators identify gaps in their declarative knowledge regarding both linguistic and sociocultural aspects (cf. ibid.). Hassel (2009, 190) also identifies the potential of the scenes-and-frames model with regard to vocabulary learning through the use of mind-maps. The mind-maps could include L1 and L2 words which can then be compared and discussed, leading to the realisation that social experiences, habits and value-judgements are contained in the connections and associations that are made between words.

The scenes-and-frames model could, in my opinion, be incorporated into a 45-minute lesson (the usual length of a language lesson in German schools) and worked into a *task-cycle*: A 15-minute-awareness raising pre-task could be designed as follows:
- In small groups (e.g. 4 pupils), the learners write down what they associate with [*school in Germany*] (the learners' *scenes*), in German (the learners' *frames*) (List 1).
- The learners then attempt to translate these words into English *frames* (List 2). They should find that some words will be "easy" to translate, whilst others may not.
- As a next step, the learners based on their own knowledge (their *scenes*) make a list of words which they associate with [*school in the United Kingdom*], for example, in English (the learners' L2 *frames*) (List 3).
- The three lists are then compared with one another and the reasons why the interlingual "equivalent" translation of some words did not work are discussed.
- The learners then discuss whether the words they found difficult to translate could be replaced by words from List 3. Thus, they channel the *spaces* occurring during the translation process. In this way, awareness is raised of the dependence of *scenes* and *frames* on contextual-cultural perceptions and of the importance of not accepting these as static facts, but rather as phenomena occurring through the translation process.

The next, longer part of the lesson could consist of a textual translation. Learners are given the opportunity to coordinate between perspectives, and recognise, relate and develop cultural expressions of meaning, as a way of raising transcultural awareness and fostering ICC. The text in question could be taken from a British teenage magazine, if learners are teenagers. This text-type, which is written with the direct aim of appealing to its readership, is advantageous in that teenage magazines can also be found in Germany, having a similar structure and subject matter. One category which can be found in both German and British teenage magazines is a column in which readers write about embarrassing situations they have found themselves in. In Germany's *Bravo* magazine the column is called *Voll daneben*! (*So wrong!*, my translation) and in British *Mizz* it is called *Cringe!*. The stories focus on the teenagers' worlds, mostly featuring love and school affairs as causes for embarrassment. In *Mizz*, the stories are rated according to the level of embarrassment triggered by the event. The learners, again in small groups, could be asked to translate one of these British stories (averaging around 50 words) into German. One could choose a story with features which might be unknown to learners in Germany. Below are two examples of such stories taken from *Mizz* (No. 604, July 10$^{th}$-23$^{rd}$ 2008):

> Ex. 1    *Calm down dear!*
> It was our end-of-term assembly at school and people were getting prizes for attendance and working extra-hard in lessons. When the teacher called out my name, I instantly leapt out of my seat and hurried to the front to eagerly accept my prize. As I did, one of the teachers told me I'd be given it later on. I had to shuffle back to my seat in front of the entire school! Hope it's forgotten by next term...
>
> Ex. 2    *Call me stupid*
> When my little brother pestered me to take him to the park this afternoon, I was more than happy to, as I knew my crush would be playing football on the pitch there. When we arrived, he noticed me right away but I wanted to play it cool and pretended to be talking on my phone. Then, to my horror, my phone actually rang. I looked like I was crazy and he and his gang had a good laugh at me!

The above examples demonstrate aspects of a teenager's life which learners may be able to relate to, but which they may also experience as "foreign" or not quite fitting into their everyday "scenes". A first step in the group translation process would be to discuss the scenes which occur in learners' heads when reading these texts (the frames) and to identify terms which perhaps do not even trigger any kind of scene to the learners. A second step would be to discuss in a group what kind of scene would be appropriate for a German teenage magazine such as *Bravo*. A third step would be to formulate the frame, i.e. the text in German, which should trigger the intended scene for the *Bravo* readership. As in all translation processes, the learners should have parallel texts at their disposal, both English and German, in order to inform themselves of possible frames, so as to formulate their respective scenes. In this way, the learners do not merely transfer linguistic codes from one language to another, but they also reflect upon the different interpretation possibilities of a text. Moreover, they make informed decisions on how to formulate a translation based on their reflection. For more advanced classes, it may be possible to repeat the process from German into English, requiring perhaps more informed reflection and decision-making on the part of the learners.

   The third part of the lesson, the *post-task*, could be used for a reflection of the whole class on the experiences triggered by the translation process.

This would enable a double outcome: on the one hand the translated text, and, on the other, increased learner inter- and transcultural awareness.

## 7. Outlook

The renewed interest in oral and written translation processes in the German FLT context makes a dialogue between Translation Studies and FLT more than necessary. Teaching practitioners and scholars need to be aware of the theoretical framework of both oral and written translation processes as well as of the skills these require. Also, translation scholars should be informed of and reflect upon the implications of the wider contexts in which translation is taught and carried out.

Bearing the above in mind, this chapter was intended as a contribution to the discourse on *reinstating translation in the foreign language classroom*, provided that translation is understood as a functional, communicative, inter- and transcultural process. New task-oriented language learning formats need to be developed to assist learners in becoming intercultural speakers, or writers in reflecting upon and making informed decisions on intercultural actions on their part to ensure successful, open and tolerant communication processes. The example of a complex translational task, as outlined above, is just one of the many possibilities to channel the didactic potential of the spaces created by the translation process in the classroom. It would be desirable to carry out further interdisciplinary research in the fields of Translation Studies and Foreign Language Teaching both at undergraduate and graduate level, as well as during in-service teacher training. In this way, both disciplines could come together through collaborative undergraduate seminars or teacher workshops. In such a framework, each discipline could contribute its expertise towards designing further translational tasks for everyday classroom use and preparation for oral exams. This would ensure that the outcome of the designed tasks would be firmly anchored in translation theory and foreign language didactics, which should, in turn, promote ICC in learners as the goal of both disciplines.

# Works cited

Abbey, Susan, David Christie, Barbara Derkow Disselbeck, Laurence Harger, and Allen J. Woppert. 2009. *English G21*, Vol. A4, edited by Hellmut Schwarz. Berlin: Cornelsen.
Abbey, Susan, Barbara Derkow Disselbeck, Laurence Harger, and Allen J. Woppert. 2008. *English G21*, Vol. A3, edited by Hellmut Schwarz. Berlin: Cornelsen.
Abbey, Susan, Barbara Derkow Disselbeck, Allen J. Woppert, and Laurence Harger. 2011. *English G21*, Vol. D2, edited by Hellmut Schwarz. Berlin: Cornelsen.
Arrojo, Rosemary. 1997. "Pierre Menard und eine neue Definition des 'Originals'." Translated by Johanna Klemm. In *Übersetzungswissenschaft in Brasilien. Beiträge zum Status von "Original" und Übersetzung*, edited by Michaela Wolf, 25–33. Tübingen: Stauffenburg.
Bachmann-Medick, Doris. 2004. "Übersetzung als Medium interkultureller Kommunikation und Auseinandersetzung." In *Handbuch der Kulturwissenschaften*, Vol. 2, edited by Friedrich Jaeger and Jürgen Straub, 449–465. Stuttgart & Weimar: Metzler.
Bahadır, Şebnem. 2007. *Verknüpfungen und Verschiebungen, Dolmetscherin, Dolmetschforscherin, Dolmetschausbilderin*. Berlin: Frank & Timme.
Bhabha, Homi. 1994. *The Location of Culture*. London & New York: Routledge.
Bredella, Lothar, and Herbert Christ, eds. 2007. *Fremdverstehen und interkulturelle Kompetenz*. Tübingen: Narr.
Bredella, Lothar. 2001. "Zur Dialektik von Eigenem und Fremdem beim interkulturellen Verstehen." *Der Fremdsprachliche Unterricht Englisch* 53:10–14.
Byram, Michael. 1997. *Teaching and Assessing Intercultural Communicative Competence*. Clevedon: Multilingual Matters.
Cook, Guy. 2010. *Translation in Language Teaching*. Oxford: Oxford University Press.
Delanoy, Werner. 2006. "Transculturality and (Inter-)Cultural Learning in the EFL-Classroom." In *Cultural Studies in the EFL Classroom*, edited by Werner Delanoy, and Laurenz Volkmann, 233–248. Heidelberg: Winter.
Derkow Disselbeck, Barbara, Laurence Harger, Allen J. Woppert, and David W. Bygott. 1999a. *English G 2000*. Ed. A, Vol. 3, edited by Hellmut Schwarz. Berlin: Cornelsen.

Derkow Disselbeck, Barbara, Laurence Harger, Michael Macfarlane, and Allen J. Woppert. 1999b. *English G 2000*. Ed. A, Vol. 4. Edited by Hellmut Schwarz. Berlin: Cornelsen.
Derkow Disselbeck, Barbara, Allen J. Woppert, Susan Abbey, Laurence Harger, and Claire Lamsdale. 2012. *English G21*. Vol. B5, edited by Hellmut Schwarz, and Wolfgang Biederstadt. Berlin: Cornelsen.
Dizdar, Dilek. 1998. "Wer hat den Überblick? – Überlegungen zum Unterrichtsfach Translationstheorie." In *TEXTconTEXT 12, 3+4*, 251–261. Heidelberg: TEXTconTEXT.
—. 1999. "Skopostheorie." In *Handbuch Translation*, edited by Mary Snell-Hornby, Hans G. Hönig, Paul Kußmaul, and Peter A. Schmitt, 104–107. Tübingen: Stauffenburg.
—. 2006. *Translation. Um- und Irrwege*. Berlin: Frank & Timme.
—. 2008. "Translation zwischen den Disziplinen." *Natur und Geist, Forschungsmagazin der Johannes Gutenberg-Universität* 24(2):54–57.
Ellis, Rod. 2003. *Task-based Language Learning and Teaching*. Oxford: Oxford University Press.
Fillmore, Charles J. 1977. "Scenes-and-frames-semantics." In *Linguistic Structure Processing*, edited by Antonio Zampolli, 55–81. Amsterdam: North Holland.
Freitag, Britta, Silke Stroh, and Uta von Reinersdorff. 2008. "Szenische Interpretationsverfahren. Cultural Identities on the Move." *Der fremdsprachliche Unterricht Englisch* 42:2–5.
Gnutzmann, Claus, and Markus Bohnensteffen. 2012. "Grammar and Translation—A Comeback?" *Anglistik International Journal of English Studies* 23(1):49–60.
Hallet, Wolfgang. 2002. *Fremdsprachenunterricht als Spiel der Texte und Kulturen. Intertextualität als Paradigma einer kulturwissenschaftlichen Didaktik*. Trier: Wissenschaftlicher Verlag.
Hassel, Ursula. 2009. "Fremdsprachenlernen, Übersetzen und Dolmetschen: Das Konzept einer translationsorientierten Fremdsprachendidaktik." In *Wie kann man vom 'Deutschen' leben? Zur Praxisrelevanz der interkulturellen Germanistik*, edited by Ernest W. B. Hess-Lüttich, Peter Colliander, and Ewald Reuter, 179–202. Frankfurt am Main: Peter Lang.
Kiraly, Don. 2000. *A Social Constructivist Approach to Translator Education, Empowerment from Theory to Practice*. Manchester & Northhampton, MA: St Jerome.
Ministerium für Kultus, Jugend und Sport Baden-Württemberg. (2010). *Bildungsplan 2010 Werkrealschule*. Available online at

http://www.bildung-staerkt-menschen.de/service/downloads/ Bildungsplaene/wrs2010/BP_WRS.pdf (08.12.2012).

Müller-Hartmann, Andreas, and Marita Schocker-von Ditfurth. 2004. *Introduction to TEFL*. Stuttgart: Klett.

Nord, Christiane. 1999. "Fertigkeit Übersetzen." Studienbrief des Goethe-Instituts. Pre-release version. Munich.

Nünning, Ansgar. 2001. "Fremdverstehen durch Literatur." *Der Fremdsprachliche Unterricht*, Special Issue 53.

Taviano, Stefania. 2010. "English as an International Language and the Pedagogy of Translation." In *EIL, ELF, Global English: Teaching and Learning Issues*, edited by Cesare Gagliardi, and Alan Maley, 127–140. Bern: Peter Lang.

Vannerem, Mia, and Mary Snell-Hornby. 1986. "Die Szene hinter dem Text, 'scenes and frames semantics' in der Übersetzung." In *Übersetzungswissenschaft – eine Neuorientierung. Zur Integrierung von Theorie und Praxis*, edited by Mary Snell-Hornby, 184–205. Tübingen: Francke.

Vermeer, Hans J., and Heidrun Witte. 1990. *Mögen Sie Zistrosen? Scenes & frames & channels im translatorischen Handeln*. Heidelberg: Julius Groos.

Vermeer, Hans J. 1978. "Ein Rahmen für eine allgemeine Translationstheorie." *Lebende Sprachen* 3:99–102.

—. 1986. *A Skopos Theory of Translation (Some Arguments for and against)*. Heidelberg: TEXTconTEXT.

—. 1992. *Skopos und Translationsauftrag – Aufsätze*. Frankfurt am Main: Verlag für Interkulturelle Kommunikation.

—. 1996. *Die Welt, in der wir übersetzen. Drei translatologische Überlegungen zu Realität, Vergleich und Prozess*. Heidelberg: TEXTconTEXT.

Witte, Heidrun. 2000. *Die Kulturkompetenz des Translators, Begriffliche Grundlegung und Didaktisierung*. Tübingen: Stauffenburg.

# CHAPTER NINE

## THE DIDACTIC USE OF TRANSLATION IN FOREIGN LANGUAGE TEACHING: A PRACTICAL EXAMPLE

## ANNA KOKKINIDOU AND KYRIAKI SPANOU

### 1. Introduction

A very important function of translation lies in the fact that it contributes to the achievement of a high level of proficiency in a foreign language, as well as to foreign language learning in general. Diachronically speaking, translation has been a primary means of exercising foreign language skills. Since the very invention of the written word, translators have been building bridges among nations, races, languages, cultures and periods of time (cf. Delisle and Woodsworth 1995, 13), while the art of translation has been synonymous with attainment of L2 proficiency. Additionally, translation lies upon something more than the transfer of the text from L1 to L2 as it is realizable because of the deep-seated universals, genetic, historical and social components "from which all grammars derive" (Steiner 1975, 77). Thus, translation is a means of paramount importance especially when working on these common elements, and transcending the exterior disparities of two languages (cf. Steiner 1975, 77).

Especially literary translation has had a long tradition as a means of teaching a foreign language and constitutes the oldest teaching method. It is particularly loved for its contribution to the enrichment of the target language (cf. Richards and Rodgers 2001, 4–7), being at the same time the breeding ground for the "free" or "unfaithful" translation. Generally speaking, translation has given rise to a significant number of heated debates within the framework of second language teaching/learning. More specifically, translation was the dominant practice in the field of foreign language teaching up to the 1950s (see Larsen-Freeman 1986 for a list of the most common techniques in the Grammar-Translation Method), and it has been revisited lately as it still constitutes a privileged method of evaluating second language proficiency (cf. Cook 2001).

Even today, this well-known method, whose role and value in the modern teaching world has been repeatedly questioned by experts and teachers, still applies in learning dead languages.[1] Within the framework of this method, students are often required to practice in the foreign language through direct translation (from source to target language) or through reverse translation (from target to source language). The texts used in this type of translation are, mostly, literary.

Linguistically speaking, literary translation drills and activities can be considered to be a means of contrastive analysis (CA) of two languages when discussing the differences and similarities as well as the language transfer process between the Source Text (ST) and the Target Text (TT). In a more comprehensive manner, this sort of analysis may be seen on the level of the respective pair of languages as enabling the researcher to draw comparative conclusions on the structure of the languages involved, especially in the case of literary translation. The relationship between translation and CA is bidirectional (Baker 1998, 49) as translation of specific texts may provide data for CA while the latter may offer explanations for the translation process. Hence, translation can work as a methodological tool that emphasizes the importance of language universals and facilitates the instruction of common and differentiated structures and, thus, foreign language acquisition.

The present chapter examines the paramount importance of the role of translation in foreign language learning and teaching through a brief discussion of the implementation of translation in a foreign language classroom and the presentation of the results of a small-scale study involving foreign language teachers.

## 2. On the application of translation in foreign language teaching

Historically speaking, translation has not only served as a means of L2 learning but also contributed to the development of national language as well. A fine example of this is Woolfell (ca. 311–383 AD), who invented the gothic alphabet in order to translate the Holy Bible and Christianize the

---

[1] Note that the Grammar-Translation Method was developed for the study of "dead" languages, namely, ancient Greek and Latin (Kellerman 1984).

Goths. The Woolfell Bible constitutes the oldest "monument" of the German language and an exquisite example of the power of translation. Additionally, the practice of translating STs into the second language (L2) was for centuries a traditional medium of instruction for second/foreign languages. It was so widespread that it has been applied even by contemporary researchers and teachers (cf. Duff 1989). In fact, in some cases, teachers of the "traditional school" supported this method against more communicative approaches. In the field of teaching methodology, it was established as the "Grammar-Translation Method", but it is also called the "Prussian method" or "Cicero's method". In the past, this method, now considered to be a kind of conservative, traditional and "sterile" tool, was characterized by the following (Richards and Rodgers 2001, 3–4):

1. The objective of learning foreign languages was to learn the language in order to study its literature or in order to capitalize on the mental discipline and intellectual development arising from the study of foreign languages.
2. Reading and writing were the focus of the process, while little or no importance was given to speaking and listening.
3. Vocabulary was learnt through the translation of the texts used, and words were taught through bilingual lists by studying the dictionary and memorizing.
4. The sentence was the basic unit in teaching and language practice. Most of the course was devoted to translating sentences to and from the target language.
5. Emphasis was placed on the correctness of the translated texts. Students were expected to perform outstandingly in translation due to the high priority attributed to the meticulous correctness criteria.
6. Grammar was taught deductively, i.e. through the presentation and study of grammatical rules that students practice through translation exercises.
7. The language of instruction was the mother tongue of the learner. It was used to explain the new material and to facilitate the comparison between the mother tongue and the foreign language.

Therefore, literary translation was not only a mere means of learning a foreign language, but also the ultimate goal as the foreign language itself was considered to be the means for the study of literature, since

> [...] the goal of language learning is to learn the language in order to study its literature or in order to benefit from the mental discipline and intellectual development that arise from the study of foreign languages.[2]

---

[2] Richards and Rodgers 2001, 3.

Traditionally then, translation and inverse translation have been the most conventional exercises of language practice in the pedagogical profession (Baker 1998, 65). As far as the SL is concerned, this process works outwards, whereas, when it comes to the TL it is inward. According to Ladmiral (1994), L1 to L2 translation is a more efficient practice than the L2 to L1 inverse translation ("theme") given individual variability in linguistic competence.

## 3. Revisiting translation in foreign language teaching

With the prevalence of communicative language teaching and the emphasis placed on the cultivation of the communication capacity, this method was "eliminated" on the grounds of being non-communicative. Quite simply, its use and its conservative implementation, in conjunction with its high level of difficulty, had historically made it the "fear and trembling" of learners (Nord 2005, 155–156). For example, recent handbooks on methodology will not dedicate more than three pages to the presentation/discussion of the Grammar-Translation Method. On the contrary, translation scholars tend to refer more to foreign language learning in the context of the translational act (ibid., 160–161).

Furthermore, translation is often used uncritically as an easy solution and practice by teachers who do not have any translation knowledge. It is common practice in the foreign language classroom to ask learners to translate something from and into their own language, something which is also the case in foreign literature studies, where students are asked to translate demanding literary texts. At the same time, professional translators who are experts in their subject fields often lack the necessary linguistic background in order to view the process taking into consideration the fruitful feedback offered by the field of linguistics.

Translation as a tool in the language classroom is by no means an "easy task" as, according to Newmark, it tends to take students to "ten different directions" (Newmark 1988, 4–5). Therefore, if we do not want to fall into the trap of the "Grammar-Translation method", which obliges language students to achieve unachievable equivalences, we should construct a clear theoretical framework, informed by the current teaching methodology and its principles before using translation in the classroom (cf. Stibbard 1998, 72).

However, since translation, in both its theory and teaching, is a discipline that falls, among others, into applied linguistics and thus constitutes suitable material for language teaching laboratories (cf. Kentrotis 2000, 298), it can be claimed that there is a basis of kinship or relevance between the theoretical and practical developments in the teaching of second/foreign language and the teaching or studying of translation.

Having taken all the above into account, we have constructed a model of translation that will potentially help towards an effective analysis of textual factors and their restoration in the target language, and targets both translation trainees and language teachers who want to integrate translation into their teaching practice. The model is based on the text linguistics approach of Hatim and Mason (1997) and Mona Baker's (1992) systemic approach regarding the way in which utterances are used in communicative situations. Briefly, of great value is the use of translation exercises for practice in textual analysis, as it seems that students find it very interesting to pinpoint the identity of a text by answering the questions: *What kind of text? By whom? To whom? Why? When? For what purpose?* This kind of textual analysis, before we even get to the textual factors and discuss how they can be restored in the target language, is of great interest. Indicatively, the following table demonstrates the main text-linguistic processes to be considered in order to evaluate translation in the context of foreign language learning (see Kokkinidou 2003, adapted from Hatim and Mason 1997, Tatilon 1986; Batsalia and Sella-Mazi 1994).

| ST-processing skills | Transfer skills | TT-processing skills |
|---|---|---|
| Recognition of **intertextuality** | Negotiation strategy through adaptation: | Restoration of **intertextuality** |
| Locating **situationality** | **Efficiency Adequacy Relevance** | Restoration of **situationality** |
| Understanding of **intentionality** | According to the target-audience | Creation of **intentionality** |
| Texture and textual structure | | Understanding of **intentionality** |
| Estimation of informativity (static/dynamic text) within the context of appreciating the impact on the SL target audience | Within the view to attain a rhetorical objective | Organization of textual texture and structure within the context of appreciating the impact on the TL target audience |

**Table 1. Text-linguistic processes to evaluate translation in language learning**

More specifically, the aforementioned table could be useful to the foreign language teacher when evaluating language skills, and especially the transfer skills involved and activated when translating. In general, the text-linguistic approach to both translation and language learning offers a privileged field of shared practices and values which may be of use to both disciplines. The tasks related to translation are determined by text types, by what we know about first and second language learning processes and translation learning processes (Wilss 1996, 206). The common grounds underlying these fields are of a great significance to language and translation teachers alike.

## 4. The didactic use of translation exercises: An example

In this section we present and discuss an example of a translation exercise. The aim was to examine the didactic use of a translation exercise by the target audience, which consisted of the participants in the long distance training program *Routes to Teaching Modern Greek Language* (http://elearning.greek-language.gr), organized and implemented by the Centre for the Greek Language. The specific program addresses an audience of mostly non-native speakers of Greek, who are involved in teaching Greek as a second/foreign language. In this context, a didactic proposal for the use of translation as a tool was discussed through the following steps:
   a. A suitably processed source text in English (or in another native language) was provided.
   b. Trainees were asked to suggest how they could use it in a classroom of Greek as a foreign/second language (e.g. based on linguistic phenomena or as a mediation exercise).
   c. Suggestions from trainees were gathered.
   d. A basic model for translating texts in the classroom was proposed.
Before proceeding to the discussion of our example, a more detailed look at the target audience that we addressed the translation exercise to is in order.

The target audience consisted of twenty teachers of Greek as a second/foreign language in foreign countries who, at the time, participated in an e-learning program. The majority did not have an academic degree in a field relevant to teaching and were, therefore, in need of some type of training in the field. The aim of the program is to teach them the relevant foreign language teaching methodology and to reinforce their Greek language level, which is expected to be C2+ (advanced C2, according to the reference levels set by CEFR). The particularity of the target audience lies in the fact that all teachers reside and work in a wide variety of countries world-wide outside Greece. In fact, their residence abroad, i.e. outside Greece, constitutes a prerequisite for their participation in the program. The program does not include a translation module; however, translation techniques are used to a certain extent in the module that is to do with the fundamentals of second language teaching/methodology.

The purpose of our study was to investigate the beliefs of the participants of the program regarding the potential use of translation in teaching practice. We used two different exercises of translation, which we sent to the participants electronically and we asked them to comment on their potential value in an FL classroom through sets of questions. Our goal was to draw some useful and practical conclusions regarding the introduction and the reinforcement of the use of translation as a teaching tool in foreign language teaching through a more communicative perspective. As the exercises were in English and Greek, we only targeted those participants in the program whose mother tongue was English. Below are the two exercises we used for data elicitation.

Exercise 1: Differentiated rendering of English phrases/words into Greek

*Each of the following paragraphs contains the same phrase, which is rendered differently in Greek. Suggest a Greek version that fits each of these phrases.*

Phrase: *Then there were different terms.*

A. And, then, there were different terms. None of this "three-term-with-a-long-summer-break" business. No, we had four terms and a much shorter holiday period. A much better system altogether, especially judging from the level of students we have now.
B. When Gary and Jane had their first child they agreed that Garry would take a year off to be with the child and work on his novel. But he soon realized that he had no time to get it on to paper. So, then, there were different terms. Gary stayed at home in the morning and Jane took over at three o' clock.

Exercise 2: "False friends"

*Consider the following two texts. The text in the first column is in English and the text in the second one is its translation into Greek. The translation, however, contains some mistakes that mainly come from a misunderstanding of certain words because of their similarity to Greek. Pinpoint the mistakes that have been made and render them correctly in the target language.*

| Source language | Target language |
| --- | --- |
| This would be his last afternoon in the gymnasium. He had spent the whole morning looking into his thesaurus and he wanted some time off. His psychic had warned him: "Don't leave home on Thursday! Your life may be in grave danger!" but he didn't believe in anything apocalyptic anymore. He wanted to become more pragmatic! Enough with the zodiac signs and the astrological maps. But he should have been skeptic. When he lay there in agony, without anyone sympathetic, a pathetic dying man, he remembered his psychic's prediction. The autopsy would reveal the truth … much later, though. | Αυτό θα ήταν το τελευταίο του απόγευμα στο γυμνάσιο. Είχε περάσει όλη τη μέρα εξετάζοντας τον θησαυρό του και ήθελε να ξεδώσει λίγο. Ο ψυχικός του τον είχε προειδοποιήσει: «Μην αφήσεις το σπίτι σου την Πέμπτη! Η ζωή σου θα κινδυνέψει σοβαρά!», αλλά δεν πίστευε πια στην αποκάλυψη. Ήθελε να είναι πιο πραγματικός! Είχε μπουχτίσει με τα ζώδια και τους αστρολογικούς χάρτες. Αλλά έπρεπε να είναι πιο σκεπτικός. Όταν έμεινε έτσι εκεί, μέσα στην αγωνία, χωρίς κανένα συμπαθητικό άνθρωπο, ένας παθητικός άντρας που πέθαινε, θυμήθηκε την πρόβλεψη του ψυχικού του. Η αυτοψία θα αποκάλυπτε την αλήθεια … πολύ αργότερα, όμως. |

The exercises used concern their bilingual competence, but also touch upon their intercultural awareness. The first exercise concerns the elaboration of vocabulary skills. Translation is extremely useful when it comes to retrieving words from our mental lexicon, while the phantom of lexical equivalence or "finding the right words" haunts even experienced translators. Furthermore, recent studies demonstrate that

> […] it may be the case that lexical items from all the languages we may know are potentially interconnected, and that we only manage to find a particular word in one language by suppressing unwanted words for that particular item in other languages familiar to us.[3]

The second exercise proposed pertains to the widely known "false friends" (*faux amis*) and has been designed in such a way as to demonstrate common misconceptions referring to the specific pair of languages. The proposed exercise (see above) includes words or

---

[3] Anderman and Rogers 1996, 7.

expressions which have the same form in two or more languages but convey different meanings (Baker 1992, 25). The false friends chosen in our case are easily spotted and the purpose of the specific exercise is to dissolve common misreading of the words involved. The objective involved in both exercises is to enrich foreign language learning at higher levels of attainment with an interesting translation activity, while closely examining the contextual meaning of words that may get "lost in translation". The examples proposed are as follows:

> *Please respond briefly to the following questions:*
> a) Could you use these translation exercises in the context of a classroom where you teach Greek as a foreign/second language? If so, how?
> b) If you used these exercises, which item/items of the language (grammatical, morphosyntactic, lexical, semantic, stylistic ) would you be able to examine?
> c) How could you use these exercises in a communicative way?
> d) Can you suggest other exercises linked to translation? Please specify.
> e) Identify any other concerns you may have in connection to such activities.

Before moving on to a brief examination of what the respondents told us, we would like to clarify the following. The translation exercises mentioned above have many similarities with language exercises that students come across in a language course at the C2 level. Naturally, the communicative teaching method "forbids" the use and intervention of the mother tongue in learning the foreign language, as the student is introduced to the use of the foreign language from the A1 level. Here, however, the students are not just Greek language students but prospective language teachers themselves, and our goal was to familiarize them with alternative uses of translation. In fact, some of them may work as translators, too, making it easier for them to integrate translation into their classroom. Additionally, it is to be noted that we have not been guiding the responses of the interviewees as the objective has been to be offered an objective insight into the use of translation in the foreign language classroom.

# 5. Results

In this section we examine briefly the responses collected from the trainees who participated in this small-scale study. First, we present each question and then the proposals/responses of trainees along with any other issues that arose. It is to be noted that the answers stated for the purposes of this chapter are an indicative reference to the feedback we received, as the full responses were of a considerable length. Methodologically, each question is followed by the respective answers presented in an "unbiased" manner.

Question 1: *Could you use these translation exercises in the context of a classroom where you teach Greek as a foreign/second language? If so, how?*

Answers:
The trainees would use the specific exercises
- with very advanced students,
- for the purpose of fostering intercultural awareness,
- based on the insofar (unconscious and conscious, formal and informal) experience in translation as a learning process,
- based on very specific teaching objectives,
- in order to understand the underlying structures of the language,
- for vocabulary teaching as they believe that the translation of false friends and polysemic words constitutes a very good vocabulary exercise,
- in a form that would promote "language practice" (e.g. multiple choice exercises or true/false exercises),
- mainly for semantic and pragmatic analysis, but also for grammar/syntax analysis.

Question 2: *If you used these exercises, which item/items of the language (grammatical, morphosyntactic, lexical, semantic, stylistic) would you be able to examine?*

Answers:
- Trainees emphasize that all parts are more or less tested through such an activity.
- They mostly opt for higher levels i.e. pragmatic, semantic and stylistic.
- Others stress the importance of these exercises on the lexical/semantic level, on which the "unilingual" debate cannot directly help in understanding polysemy.
- The exercises have been considered as an effective way to highlight the role of the translator at all levels.
- In general, translation is considered to be a tool of analysis at all levels.

Question 3: *How could you use these exercises in a communicative way?*

Answers:
- Such exercises can be used as they are communicative by nature, and, contrary to popular belief, do not "slow down" learning.

- Trainees stress the fact that older people who learn foreign languages translate (consciously or subconsciously) from their mother tongue into the foreign language. Translation constitutes one of the strategies of their learning process and is included in Communicative Language Teaching.
- They can be used by experienced language students, who will have the opportunity to handle the writing style of certain authors.
- Through the conversion of exercises into communicative ones beyond the "contextualization" with multiple choice options or keywords that will help the interpretation and translation of the sentence.
- In group work, giving the source text to groups and discussing the various translations.
- The teacher can use the translation to facilitate learning, but also to highlight similarities and differences between the two languages. Differences at all levels of linguistic analysis. In this way, translation is or becomes communicative and distances itself from what was once the teaching of foreign languages.

Question 4: *Can you suggest other exercises of this type that are related to translation? Please, specify.*

Answers:
- Exercises with proverbs
  Through proverbs, we understand and approach each other's culture more effectively, we find the common elements in expression and thinking, and we learn vocabulary and understand its use (daily, folk, even scholarly words or phrases). We also learn some of the many common proverbs, translated exactly word for word, because there is almost an exact match. There is a degree of differentiation in linguistic difficulty with expressions and proverbs which present similarities on a lower language level but then differentiate.
- Literary translation, specific extracts (e.g. an English poem into Greek or a Greek poem into English).
- Translation of song lyrics with gaps to be filled.
- Editing and translation of "emergency" texts that are directly related to the interests and activities of students or which the students themselves bring to class, e.g. newspaper articles or magazines, various documents/certificates, the Greek menu on their computer, but also any text that presents difficulties for them and they would like to translate.
- Involvement of students in translation activities in groups and discussion of the different versions.
- Teaching the proper use of bilingual dictionaries.
- Translation for reading comprehension, for purely linguistic practice and textual analysis.

- Translation exercises for words that have the same meaning in Greek, but also for words that have been altered and now mean something different in our language.
- Focus on the "cultural load" of words, translation exercises of culturally characterized of designated units.

Question 5: *Identify any other concerns you may have in connection to such activities.*

Answers:
- Especially for the second type of exercise, if the language has not been mastered at a high level, it is likely to confuse the meanings of words since these meanings are similar.
- "Decriminalisation" of the process: In an effort not to lose grades and to avoid having the teacher think that they have an inadequate knowledge of the language, students do not let their imagination free to "travel" through the words and their meanings (this leads to a poor, sterile translation and a dubious "contact" with both languages). It should be emphasized that the goal is not to achieve the unachievable equivalence.
- There is a wrong impression that the use of the mother tongue intervenes in the main process of learning and delays it due to the translation process.
- A trainee characteristically stated that: "It's time to acquit translation of whatever negative has been attributed to it".

In processing the results, it needs to be noted that effort was made to group together the answers which were similar to one another (i.e. into a general statement).

# 6. Findings

As can be seen from the responses of participants reported in the previous section, they believe that translation can fit comfortably into the language learning process and that, due to its multidimensional nature it can be used in many different contexts. The responses also showed that translation in the form of properly designed exercises/activities can contribute positively to the teaching of foreign languages as an additional language tool.

The responses of trainees indicate that translation could be exonerated from its guilty past as a tedious and laborious chore of compiling bilingual lists and performing "unrelated" translation exercises severed from the context of class and language. The specific issue is more than crucial:

translation should not be presented as an activity which is detached and alienated from common teaching practice. In fact, translation is considered to be a very powerful tool in communicative language teaching. Tatilon (cf. 1986, 153–154) puts it very well when saying that translation is a very useful and practical exercise at all stages of (foreign) language learning, since it serves not only as an illustrative tool for mediation and linguistic interference but also as a monitoring and evaluation tool with regard to both linguistic and cultural knowledge. Hence, translation proves to be a meaningful activity in many cases, but it still depends on how the teacher implements it in the class.

It has already been stated that translation may constitute the "fifth skill" in language learning (Brownlees and Denton 1987), while a large number of researchers and teachers support its use in an imaginative and communicative way within the language lesson. In the same way, it is very important to see translation as an important tool for developing and fostering communication skills, which, as we know, has two dimensions: linguistic and extralinguistic. This means that we are not just interested in the "proper" use of a language form, i.e. the acquisition of the language system, but on its successful application in order to achieve communication, which, in this case refers to communicating in a foreign language through the transfer process and adjustment from the mother tongue. Here, the mother tongue does not function as an obstacle but as an opportunity for an objectively useful and practical activity. Therefore, we are interested in the choice of the correct language form for the specific case.

The sample of answers by practicing and trainee foreign language teachers is indeed limited. However, the discussion triggered by the questions posed and the responses elicited from the proposed exercises have offered useful feedback as regards the use of translation in the very context of the program presented in our study. It is of paramount importance to treat translation as a meaningful task in the foreign language classroom, a task that complies with the notion of

> [...] a structural language learning endeavor which has a particular objective, appropriate content, a specific working procedure and a range of outcomes for those who undertake the task.[4]

According to many translation scholars and following the replies of the interviewees, one of the most important issues for the foreign language teacher, one that may undermine the introduction of a translation task into the classroom, pertains to the goal of the translation exercises. Therefore,

---

[4] Breen 1987, 23.

goal-related translation is increasingly important when discussing the latter as a means of learning a second/foreign language since the "concept of goal is central to the translation teaching methodology" (Wills 1996, 208), while it is essential to design and organize the accommodation of the translation exercises in an appropriate context.

In this light, the choice to include translation exercises into the foreign language learning classroom should not be made arbitrarily and without the appropriate design of the process. In order to do more good than harm, classroom practice should be a welcoming environment for translation exercises and this will only be achieved if teachers realize the significance of translation as an act in the learning context. The problems that come to the fore when discussing the implementation of translation into the foreign language classroom mainly concern the lack of interrelation between translation theory and practice, on the one hand, and foreign language theory and practice, on the other, as the teacher may affront translation as a detached activity. Thus, sound classroom "work plans" are needed, which could gradually integrate translation exercises, from the simple type to the more elaborated one, for instance, from activities concerning lexical meaning to elaborated texts that need specific decision-making and complex semantic analysis. In the context of this discussion, it is noted that the aim of the exercises is by no means to achieve the maximum equivalent but textual analysis, the parallel practice in the known language skills, the interaction among students, and the feedback from teachers. Above all, the aim is to lead the foreign language teacher to serious consideration of the value of translation in his/her classroom. Therefore, teachers should reflect on what is schematically represented in the following table, where attempt has been made to schematically represent the fundamental parameters to be considered.

Finally, it is worth noting that trainees were deliberately given two somewhat "rigid" language exercises. This was done in order to see the communicative dimension that trainees would give, which actually happened while their feedback was very significant for our reflection. It is evident that a more organized approach is necessary in order to implement translation exercises in the foreign language classroom. The exercises given for the purposes of this brief analysis are of a more conventional type given that there has been no previous analysis of the teachers' familiarization with translation.

| Before the translation exercise | During the translation exercise | After the translation exercise |
|---|---|---|
| • the skills they want to develop<br>• the textual factors that they want to emphasize (e.g. intertextuality, coherence, etc.)<br>• the language level they want to emphasize on in connection to various factors (e.g. cohesion and morphosyntax, cohesiveness and semantics/stylistics)<br>• the way in which the exercise will practically enhance the communication skills of participants (exercises can be related to issues of daily life)<br>• clear definition of the target audience | • focus not on correctness but on communicative skills<br>• students should work in groups in order to communicate their choices,<br>• the use of bilingual dictionaries should be encouraged, when appropriate<br>• exercises should meet the teaching objectives and translation should not be a detached activity<br>• discussion of options should take place in the target language,<br>• possibility to alternate skills (e.g. source text in written form, oral presentation of target text) | • evaluation of the process and suggestions for further uses of translation<br>• comparative analysis of the translation versions based not on "best performance" but on the communicative effectiveness and capacity for judgment,<br>• discussion or recording of intercultural conclusions deriving from the process,<br>• assessment of level of communication achievement of the message of the source text in the target text |

**Table 2. Parameters to consider during the translation process**

Overall, the whole effort concentrated in the reception of the teachers' immediate response and reaction to such a proposal. The aforementioned term "unbiased" refers to the open-ended and unguided reception of the teachers' feedback. The primary pre-hermeneutical query concerned the need to decipher the target group's willingness and availability to (re)consider the value of translation in foreign language learning.

## 7. Conclusion

The debate on the communicative aspect and use of translation itself as a tool in order to develop a high degree of linguistic culture and intercultural competence has long been a concern for translation scholars, translators and foreign language teachers. Besides, translation as an inherently complex and multidimensional process, is offered "for all purposes" and it is evident that it can be used in a language classroom, especially within the multitranslating and multitranslated pan-European context. Literary translation may hold a privileged position, especially at higher levels of language proficiency, as it gives a sense of creative freedom to the advanced students of the language. Our goal is to introduce translation with a fresh look into the language classroom. To be able to use it as an effective, direct, and timely communication tool constitutes our high goal for a high art.

Finally, this brief discussion among teachers echoed a most apparent fact: when asked to consider translation exercises, the foreign language teacher replies positively as the answers received have strongly demonstrated. The "problem" refers to the fact that translation does not come to the (foreign) language teacher's mind that often, while the translation teacher takes for granted mastery of the involved languages and does not waste time for such "superfluous" activities. The challenge to be considered here is to awaken involved teachers to an obviousness that tends to be neglected (or taken for granted): translation equally constitutes a window offering an exquisite view on a foreign language and culture. This window should be kept open.

## Works cited

Anderman, Gunilla M., and Margaret A. Rogers, eds. 1996. *Words, Words, Words. The Translator and the Language Learner.* Avon, England: Multilingual Matters.
Batsalia, Freideriki, and Eleni Sella-Mazi. 1994. *Glosslogiki Prosengisi sti Theoria kai ti Didaktiki tis Metafrasis [A Linguistic Approach to the Theory and Teaching of Translation]*, Corfu: Ionian University.
Baker, Mona. 1992. *In Other Words. A Coursebook on Translation.*
London & New York: Routledge.
Baker, Mona, ed. 1998. *Routledge Encyclopedia of Translation Studies.*
London: Routledge.

Breen, Michael, P. 1987. "Learners' Contribution to Task Design." In *Language Learning Tasks*, edited by Christopher N. Candlin, and Dermot F. Murphy, 23–46. Englewood Cliffs, NJ: Prentice Hall.
Brownlees, Nicholas, and John Denton. 1987. *Translation Revisited, Ritorno alla traduzione.* Florence: Cremonese.
Delisle, Jean, and Judith Woodsworth, eds. 1995. *Translators through History*. Amsterdam & Philadelphia: Benjamins.
Duff, Alan. 1989. *Translation*. Oxford: Oxford University Press.
Cook, Vivian J. 2001. "Using the First Language in the Classroom." Canadian *Modern Language Review* 57(3):184–206.
Hatim, Basil, and Ian Mason. 1997. *The Translator as Communicator.* London & New York: Routledge.
Kellerman, Eric. 1984. "The Empirical Evidence for the Influence of the L1 in Interlanguage," In *Interlanguage*, edited by Alan Davies, Clive Criper and Anthony P. R. Howatt, 98–122. Edinburgh: Edinburgh University Press.
Kentrotis, Georgios. 2000. *Theoria kai Praxi tis Metaphrasis [The Theory and Practice of Translation]*. Athens: Diavlos.
Kokkinidou, Anna. 2003. "Keimenoglossologiki Prosengisi sti Didaktiki tis Metafrasis" [A Text-linguistic Approach to the Didactics of Translation]. In *Translating in the 21$^{st}$ Century: Trends and Prospects*, 699–706. Thessaloniki: Faculty of Arts.
Ladmiral, Jean-René. 1994. *Traduire: Théorèmes de la traduction*. Paris: Gallimard.
Larsen-Freeman, Diane. 1986. *Techniques and Principles in Language Teaching*. Oxford: Oxford University Press.
Newmark, Peter. 1988. *A Textbook of Translation*. New York: Prentice Hall.
Nord, Christiane. 2005. *Text Analysis in Translation: Theory, Methodology, and Didactic Application of a Model for Translation-oriented Text Analysis*. Amsterdam: Rodopi.
Richards, Jack C., and Theodore S. Rodgers. 2001. *Approaches and Methods in Language Teaching.* Cambridge: Cambridge University Press.
Steiner, George. 1975. *After Babel*. London: Oxford University Press.
Stibbard, Richard. 1998. "The Principled Use of Translation in Foreign Language Teaching." In *Translation and Language Teaching: Language Teaching and Translation*, edited by Kirsten Malmkjaer, 69–76. Manchester: St. Jerome.
Tatilon, Claude. 1986. *Traduire. Pour une pédagogie de la traduction*. Toronto: G.R.E.F.

Wilss, Wolfram. 1996. *Knowledge and Skills in Translator Behavior*. Amsterdam & Philadelphia: Benjamins.

# PART II

# TRANSLATION AND LANGUAGE ASSESSMENT

# CHAPTER TEN

# TEST ADAPTATION AND TRANSLATION: THE LANGUAGE DIMENSION

# SAMIRA ELATIA

## 1. Introduction

Test Adaptation and Translation (TAT) has forged its place as a distinct measurement discipline partly due to the substantial increase and use of TAT in assessment processes around the world. Tests are often used outside their original geographical locations and in different languages. For educational purposes, the increase is quite remarkable. For instance, the Programme for International Student Assessment (PISA) was administered in 65 nations and territories[1] in 2009. Also, in 2011, the International Mathematics and Sciences Study (TIMSS) was administered in 64 countries and translated into more than 30 languages. With respect to the diploma exams of the International Baccalaureate Organization, Spanish, French and English have always been the three official languages since the establishment of the IBO in the 1960s. Therefore, all development takes place in English and is then translated into the other two languages. Multinational companies, such as IBM and Microsoft, have developed many assessment tools for credentials in various countries where they hold offices. Thus, their tests are translated and adapted to the respective local languages. The trend is not about to change, and, for Hambleton,

> […] more test adaptations can be expected in the future as (a) international exchanges of tests become more common (b) more exams are used to provide international credentials, and (c) interest in cross-cultural research grows.[2]

---

[1] 45 countries participated a decade ago.
[2] Hambleton 2005, 3.

Although translation has become more prevalent in the test development process over the last thirty years or so, it is by no means new to testing. In the late 19th century and early 20th century, psychologists Alfred Binet and Theodore Simon developed in French what is considered the first objective standardized intelligence test. Lewis Terman, a psychologist at Stanford University, "adapted" the test of Binet and Simon to the American context, creating the Stanford-Binet test.[3] Though we cannot speak of a proper TAT process at the time, TAT now provides a research platform for dealing with and working in the translation of tests into new languages and within new contexts.

Within a TAT process, translation becomes part of the adaptation process. Usually, a test is initially developed, administered and analyzed in a given language.[4] The final product is then adapted and translated to another language or languages. Such a practice raises new issues in the measurement field especially regarding fairness. Using a test outside its linguistic and cultural context is a delicate matter. Researchers (Hambleton 1994; van de Vijver and Hambleton 1996) argue that when a test is adapted and/or translated, the construct that it was set initially to measure changes. Stansfield (2003) warns of such use without proposing re-analyses of the test scores. He further claims that in the process of translation and adaptation of a test, the test itself is not necessarily the same as its original version: it changes, and various stakeholders—from test users and test developers to test administrators—need to be aware of this change. In this regard, Gudmundsson adamantly adds that

> [a] translated version of a test cannot be assumed to have the same psychometric qualities as a standardized version in the primary language. The psychometric qualities of a translated test can only be established by empirical and logical evidence. This entails that interpretive material for a standardised test in a primary language—from mere statistics to complex validity assumptions—do not automatically apply to the translated version of the test.[5]

Standard 13.4 of the *Standards of Educational and Psychological Testing* targets the translation of tests because of its importance and the sensitive nature of the process. On this issue, it states:

---

[3] For further information on this test, the following works are recommended: Fancher 1985; Kamin 1995; McGuire 1995; Siegler 1992.

[4] Ironically, for academic or other credential purposes, assessment tools are typically developed first in English and then adapted and/or translated to other languages. Rare are the instances of the other way around.

[5] Gudmundsson 2009, 30.

When a test is translated from one language or dialect to another, its reliability and validity for the uses intended in the linguistic groups to be tested should be established.[6]

Furthermore, two more standards are set in order to ensure that proper testing development is carried out in ways that ensure the validity, reliability and fairness of the assessment instrument, whenever there is a change in the language of the instrument:

> *Standard 6.2.* When a test user makes a substantial change in test format, mode of administration, instructions, **language**, or content, the user should revalidate the use of the test for the change conditions or have a rationale supporting the claim that additional validation is not necessary or possible.

> *Standard 13.6.* When it is intended that the two versions of dual-language tests be comparable, evidence of test comparability should be reported.[7]

It is clear with Standard 13.4 mainly, and with Standards 6.2 and 13.6 secondarily, that the whole process of recalibrating test results must be redone when a test is translated. Moreover, documentation of the whole translation process must be kept meticulously in order to establish validation arguments.

However, whereas the standards warn about an issue and aim to raise awareness of practice, they do not address practical issues of translation, nor do they mention the role that language, with all its nuances, plays in the validity and fairness of an assessment translation. Consequently, several questions arise for practitioners: What translation techniques should be used? How can we adapt a test to a new context while keeping the construct the same? And most importantly, what role does the *language* variable play in this process, regardless of the purpose of the test?

This chapter aims to highlight the intricate relationship between language, language assessment and TAT. Such a relationship is due to the highly sensitive process of TAT, its implication for the validity and reliability of the assessment instrument, and the nuclear role that language and linguistic and cultural variations within a language play in a TAT process. These factors would impact the validity and fairness of the assessment instrument. Hence, in this chapter, first, the TAT process in test development is defined. Focus in this section is on presenting an overview of techniques used in this process: translation and interpretation

---

[6] AERA, APA and NCME 1989.
[7] AERA, APA and NCME 1989, my emphasis.

techniques, cultural sensitivity reviews, etc. Afterward, a review of current literature on TAT is presented, with a focus on the issues that researchers are currently addressing. In the third and major section of the chapter, a discussion of the language dimension in the TAT process is developed: language is a major factor in this process with several issues at stake. The chapter concludes by highlighting the interface between language assessment and TAT. It also highlights the danger emanating from not addressing the different language facets in any test development process relying on test adaptation and translation.

## 2. Understanding TAT

TAT is the process of creating various language versions of the same test or battery of tests. Technically speaking, in TAT, a test is developed in a primary language and serves a specific context; then it is translated to a target language or languages, and adapted to target contexts. Test adaptation and translation are often known as the procedures being used for creating language versions of a test. Hambleton *et al*. (2005) described a TAT concept which involves two steps: a) *test translation*, and b) *test adaptation*. Test translation involves the translation of test items from the primary language to the target language or languages. Test adaptation, in comparison, takes into consideration the cultural and social factors that may affect the results of a test when used in different contexts. Hambleton *et al*. (2005) consider test translation as part of the test adaptation process, whereas before, it was mostly translation without taking any other factors into consideration. With the advent of TAT as a measurement field, researchers began to pay more attention to the adaptation process in order to ensure that the language versions fit culturally into the target language group.

An example of a test that has been translated and adapted into different languages is the SF-36, an instrument used to measure generic health status. SF-36 has been widely researched and translated and adapted into different languages, such as French (Leplège *et al*. 1998), Danish (Bjorner *et al*. 1998). There are also two Chinese versions (Li *et al*. 2003), and a Japanese version (Fukuhara *et al*. 1998). Forward and backward [8] translations were commonly used in the translation process for these versions, and the content of the items was adjusted to fit the target culture as well. For instance, in the Chinese version, activities such as mopping the floor and practicing Tai Chi were used instead of bowling and playing

---

[8] Also referred to in the literature as *front* and *back translation*.

golf in the American version of the test (Li *et al.* 2003). Hence, a proper TAT process goes beyond the translation alone; TAT aims to adapt the items in a test a) linguistically, b) culturally, and c) educationally to their new setting. However, each of the three parts (linguistic, cultural and educational background) presents many challenges because each part is intricately connected to the other parts. From a linguistic perspective, there are many aspects to consider, and each is complex in its own right: syntax, word choice, register, pragmatics, for instance. Educational systems change from one place to another: models, approaches to teaching, the cognitive domains targeted, types of measurement tools, etc. Such diversity makes it hard to assume a standard system that applies everywhere. For instance, a North-American multiple-choice items model of assessment would fit within a context where students are accustomed to constructing their responses, instead of choosing one. As a new field, TAT attempts to address these issues in assessment, and primarily attempts to stay away from literal translation alone.

## 2.1 TAT guidelines

In 2000, the *International Test Commission* published its 22 guidelines for TAT, emphasizing the fact that

> [...] adaptation needs to consider the whole cultural context within which a test is to be used. Indeed, the adaptation guidelines apply wherever tests are moved from one cultural setting to another.[9]

Several professional associations and academic societies[10] contributed to the development of these guidelines. Even though these are *guidelines* (not standards), the ITC strongly recommends using them. They henceforth became a *frame-of-reference*, as Hambleton and de Jong (2003) put it. These guidelines are used by practitioners around the world to build judgmental and empirical arguments to validate an assessment instrument that relies on the TAT process for its development.

---

[9] International Test Commission 2010.
[10] These include: *European Association of Psychological Assessment*, *European Test Publishers Group*, *International Association for Cross-Cultural Psychology*, *International Association of Applied Psychology*, *International Association for the Evaluation of Educational Achievement*, *International Language Testing Association*, and *International Union of Psychological Science* (International Test Commission 2010).

Hambleton (2005) defines two contexts for the use of the ITC guidelines: (1) the translation/adaptation of existing tests and instruments, and (2) the development of new tests and instruments for local and international use. For this last point, the multilingual and multicultural nature of the world mandates the use of various linguistic versions of a test. In Canada, for instance, all assessment instruments are developed in both French and English. In most cases, English is the primary language of test development and French is the target one for the TAT process.

The ITC guidelines for TAT (see Appendix) are straightforward and are adaptable to various testing situations. They are organized into four categories: *Context, Test Development and Adaptation, Administration,* and *Documentation/Score Interpretation.* The ITC guidelines are not relevant only when constructing assessment tools to be used elsewhere in various languages. They also provide a point of reference for research on the context of a test, where test equivalence is of crucial importance (Hambleton 1994, 2005; Hambleton and Patsula 1999; van de Vijver and Hambleton 1996). For Gudmundsson,

> the guidelines focus on various conditions that must be met to increase the likelihood of test equivalence, which would justify comparisons between different countries or cultures.[11]

Overall, the guidelines provide a great help to various stakeholders to understand TAT and its workings. However, they are prescriptive in nature. As Solano-Flores *et al.* (2009, 79) state, ICT guidelines "may not be sufficient to ensure high-quality test translation because they are prescriptive documents, not analytical tools". Consequently, "they are limited in their ability to guide the reasoning used by test translators or test translation reviewers". Moreover, the use of the ICT guidelines remains linked to the discretion of the test user; in other words, their use is not reinforced. Nonetheless, the ICT guidelines have played a seminal role in the research and development of assessment instruments, as well as in establishing a threshold for quality assurance. Lonner stated that

> [a]lthough hundreds of tests and assessment procedures work reasonably well in the Western world, it must be proven and not assumed that they will work equally well in cultures where they were not developed.[12]

---

[11] Gudmundsson 2009, 10.
[12] Lonner 1990, 56.

Test Adaptation and Translation: The Language Dimension 199

The TAT guidelines, along with the standards mentioned above, narrow down what would constitute "proof" that a test would be used justly in another language within a different regional geographical context.

## 2.2 TAT methods: Fairness and bias

At the heart of any TAT is translation. There are two popular and well-established methods used for test translation: (a) forward translation and backward translation (as mentioned earlier), and (b) two independent translations of the same assessment tool or instrument with a comparison study of the two versions carried by a third party. In Hambleton *et al.* (2005), several variations of both methods/techniques are showcased and empirically analyzed. The former approach has been extensively applied in cross-cultural comparative studies. The latter has been applied in large-scale international comparative studies on students' achievement.

However, the translation itself, no matter how it is conducted, is problematic, since it is a) subjective to the person(s) who undertake(s) the translation, and b) unnatural, in the sense that it is not a natural *language* process. Translation activities in test development should never be undertaken lightly. Gudmundsson suggested the following eight steps when translating and adapting a test outside its country of origin:

> (1) selecting an instrument for translation and adaptation, (2) selecting qualified translators, (3) selecting qualified experts in the subject matter of the instrument, (4) selecting the method of translation, (5) applying a proper method of adaptation, (6) applying proper methods for investigating bias in the translated and adapted instrument, (7) applying proper procedures in piloting items, administration instructions and scoring rules, and (8) performing appropriate validity studies.[13]

Brislin (1986) suggested that when a test is intended for translation later, several criteria with regard to language mechanics, such as length and structure of sentences, should be specified during test and item construction in the original version. Geisinger (1994) discussed the general procedures of test translation and adaptation into different languages to ensure test contents and validity would remain the same. Five steps were suggested for researchers to follow when adapting a test: (1) translate and adapt the measure; (2) review the translated or adapted version of the instrument; (3) adapt the draft instrument on the basis of the comments; (4) pilot test the instrument; and (5) field test the instrument. It was also

---

[13] Gudmundsson 2009, 31.

noted that the documentation of research procedures should be provided in detail, so that other researchers can perform evaluations as well.[14]

Differential Item Functioning (DIF) analyses are often used as part of the test adaptation and translation process to determine if two versions of a test are comparable to each other. DIF comes into play when the matters of fairness and bias are being evaluated on a test. DIF applies both substantive and statistical analyses in order to produce optimal results (cf. Gierl 2005). Substantive analysis involves the use of expert judges to evaluate potentially problematic items. Statistical analysis uses statistical procedures to determine the level of DIF. When an item is classified as DIF, it indicates that, even after the test-takers' ability levels are being controlled, the probability for one group to answer an item correctly is different from that for another group (Gierl and Khaliq 2001; Shepard *et al.* 1981). DIF analysis allows for a comparison between the focal and the reference group. The focal group is the group that is thought to be the minority, and the reference group would be the majority group. DIF exists as a result of an item measuring an unwanted secondary dimension, in addition to its intended primary dimension. There are different types of DIF: *uniform DIF* occurs when one group consistently obtains a higher score than the other group at all ability levels, causing the item characteristics curve (ICC) for both groups to parallel to each other; in *nonuniform/crossing DIF*, the probability for the two groups to answer an item correctly is not the same at all ability levels, meaning that the ICC for both groups will not be parallel to each other (Ferne and Rupp 2007).

DIF is widely used to ensure equivalence of translated test versions. Petersen *et al.* (2003) tested the parallelism among the nine translations of the *European Organization for Research and Treatment of Cancer Quality of Life Group* (EORTC QLQ-C30). They have found that seven out of the nine language versions had indications of DIF, and it has been concluded that the DIF was due to translational problems. Another example of using DIF to detect translational difference was that by Gierl and Khaliq with the English and French versions of the Grade 3 and 6 Mathematics and Social Studies Achievement Test items. In this study, four sources of DIF were identified using substantive analyses:

(a) Source 1: omissions or additions that affect meaning, (b) Source 2: differences in the words, expressions, or sentence structure of items that are *inherent* to the language and/or culture, (c) Source 3: differences in the

---

[14] Although this last point seems repetitive, since it is a standard in test development, Geisinger stresses the fact that details should be provided in order to allow for replication but also for language equivalence.

words, expressions, or sentence structure of items that are *not inherent* to the language and/or culture, and (d) Source 4: differences in item format.[15]

Items were then classified by experts into these sources and later *confirmed* by using statistical analyses. In an earlier similar study of blind item review of 60 items including expert analyses from Hebrew-to-Russian translators, Allalouf *et al.* (1999) identified four probable causes of what they labeled "translation" DIF. These causes relate to cultural relevance, changes in the difficulty of words or sentences, changes in the format of the items and test, or changes in the content of the items/test. Auchter and Stansfield (1997a, 1997b) pointed out a few issues to be considered before creating tests for students of different native languages. These issues include the following: (1) the cost of test translation and adaptation, (2) the number of students that may benefit from the process, and (3) the language attitudes and politics of the State. They also highlighted the importance that should be given to the processes of translation and adaptation, which, as they emphasized, must be thoroughly documented.

## 3. Language and TAT

Within a TAT framework, language is central because most tests are developed first in one language, the dominant language, and then they are translated and/or adapted to other languages. Many advocates ask for simultaneous adaptations of tests (Tanzer 2005) where various versions of an assessment instrument are developed simultaneously. ElAtia (2010, 2012) argues that the sociolinguistic complexities inherent to any language would render the TAT process difficult (if not impossible). Language is a sensitive part of TAT. The language dimension becomes more complex since there is an assumption that the final result of a TAT process in two or more languages yields the same constructs, regardless of the language(s) to which the test has been translated or adapted. Van Haaften and van de Vijver (1996) warn about such an assumption due to social and cultural differences, while Davidson strongly argues against the use of a single language model:

> [L]anguage learning theorists have insisted that language is componentially complex. We know the thing we are measuring is supposed to be complicated (theory tells us this), but again and again, we keep finding out that it is not - it is unidimensional.[16]

---

[15] Gierl and Khaliq 2001, 173.
[16] Davidson 1994, 379.

Even when a test has been translated and adapted into another language, it does not mean the two languages versions are necessarily equivalent to each other. Stansfield (2003) strongly argues that a test in its newly adapted and translated version may very well be a different test from the original version. He addressed the issue that a content-specific test may end up not measuring the construct it was set to measure. Instead, such a test would unintentionally focus on measuring the language competency of the examinees. According to Budgell *et al.* (1995), tests may not be equivalent due to the meaning of items that may change during the translation process, and/or the differing importance that items may carry when used from one cultural context to another.

The issue of equivalence among the original and the translated versions of a test has been a central issue in many research projects. Besides front and back translation, several approaches that address test equivalence rely on reviewing the translation by experts, identifying potential problematic items, and re-testing these items by administering them to a sample group of examinees (e.g. Gierl *et al.* 1999; Muñiz *et al.* 2001). For Solano-Flores *et al.* (2009), the "inaccurate translation" of a single term may affect the differential functioning of an item across languages (see also Allalouf *et al.* 1999; Ercikan 2002; Ercikan *et al.* (2004); Gierl and Khaliq 2001). Unfortunately, from a logistical perspective, cost plays a big role in this process, and, due to financial restrictions (see Allalouf 2003), these approaches are unlikely to become a part of standard test translation practices in the near future. As a consequence, translation teams will have to continue depending considerably on cost-effective judgmental review procedures.

An important factor with regard to language in the TAT process is the variations within the same language—for instance, not all "Englishes" are equal and neither are all "Frenches" or "Spanishes". Regarding the English language, when exams are developed in a mainstream unilingual model, they "set forth linguistic norms that do not necessarily represent the rich body of English varieties spoken in contact situations all over the world" (Davidson 2006, 709). Davidson's comment does not apply to English alone. Diverse variation may exist in every language, as in Arabic, for example, which is spoken differently across countries and minority/closed settings within the same country or region. Therefore, it is problematic to assume that one variety of Arabic would be spoken and understood by all Arab-speaking communities around the world. Such variation may help explain the differences in performance among examinees, and is an important factor that needs to be taken seriously in the TAT process.

The diversity of linguistic varieties produces group differences in test performance (cf. ElAtia 2012), as testing becomes more *glocal*. Glocal means that a locally developed test is translated and adapted to be used globally, while it will be administered in local communities. TAT needs to be handled and studied meticulously, given the sensitive linguistic context. Considerations for the variations among any linguistic minority groups need to be laid down for test developers, so that the TAT process is a valid one and does not discriminate against any linguistic minority group. When we work with the assumption that one specific model of a given language is the standard, we are led to what Davidson (2006) refers to as an *interlanguage*. Thus, we discard any richness that the other varieties and dialects of the same language may have. Previous research regarding sociolinguistic bias found that such a phenomenon would occur among examinees of the same language. For example, the French version of the SF-36 was divided into the Canadian French and the French spoken in France, due to linguistic difference (cf. Leplège *et al.* 1998). Wolfram (1983, 26) claimed that when an English test is being used in another population, its variations of structure in the dialects become important: "A linguistically appropriate or 'correct' form may differ from community to community depending on the particular dialect norm." Using a "standard" form of American English could pose a problem for those who speak varieties of such "standard" English, due to cultural and dialectal differences (cf., again, Wolfram 1983).

Special care needs to be given to the methods and procedures used to generate valid test score inferences across different linguistic or cultural groups (Harkness 1998; Hambleton and Kanjee 1995). The nature of a given language, its status in society, and the connotation given to its use all add to the complexity of the TAT task. The situation is further complicated when, within the same multilingual society, as is the case in Canada, a test is developed in a dominant language with the assumption that this is an *interlanguage* throughout Canada. Then, the test is adapted or translated into the language of a minority group where this language tends to be pidginized (cf. Romaine 1994), thus presenting a different variation of the language. The very fact that the languages concerned have a different status within the same society may pose a threat to the validity and fairness of the exam (cf. McNamara and Roever 2007).

Such diversity may produce group differences in test performance not only across regions, but also within the same region (cf. ElAtia 2012). Speakers of different varieties of a language may not be able to communicate effectively because of language differences (Wolfram 2008). Studies in the field of language testing have shown that language variation among test takers produces group differences in test outcomes, and may be the cause of erroneous evaluation of the examinees' language competence (see Davidson 2006; Brown 2004; Davis and Johnsrude 2003; Lowenberg 2000). Sociolinguistic factors become more prevalent, and hence lead to differences in the test performance.

Khan (2006), when examining the IELTS speaking test in Bangladesh, found that it is very difficult to adapt a test into different contexts. In particular, she found that the examinees had difficulty with certain items and tasks. These difficulties include vocabulary and topics that are unfamiliar to the examinees. Such sociolinguistic bias would thus affect the examinees' performance. Moreover, sociolinguistic bias in a test may cause long-term problems. For example, Malgady *et al.* (1987) found that linguistic and cultural bias in mental health assessments was possibly causing a result of a higher rate of mental health "issues" in the Hispanic-American population. Elosua and López-Jaúregui (2007) identified four sources of bias in testing: cultural relevance, translation problems, morphosyntactic differences, and semantic differences. It is common for a translated/adapted test to be different, as different languages often have different ways of expression. Culture also plays an important role for such differences in terms of test content. For example, when translating the SF-36 from English into Japanese, Fukuhara *et al.* (1998) found that there are words and phrases that were irrelevant or nonexistent in Japanese. English phrases such as *nervous/happy person* are considered unnatural by the Japanese. Another example is that instead of using the phrase *the past four weeks*, a time-length indicator commonly used in North American English, it is more appropriate to use *one month* in Japanese (Fukuhara *et al.* 1998). The translation of tests should take such culturally-bound words and phrases into serious consideration.

## 4. An eclectic model for TAT

When used outside their initial context, many tests undergo a literal translation that does not take linguistic difference and cultural context into consideration; hence, they lack *adaptation*. Merenda (2005) warns about this practice. He further highlights that tests would undergo literal translation without any re-standardization of scores, and hence ignore Standards 13.4 (see above). He adds that a lack of re-standardization of scores will have serious consequences on test validity. Van Widenfelt *et al.* (2005) raised the issue that forward and backward translation is insufficient to create a good translation of tests. This is primarily due to a lack of content knowledge and awareness of different cultures. Discussing the translation of the GED test from English into Spanish, Aucher and Stansfield stated that

> [t]ranslation must be expressed in a natural language, or in language that is as natural as the language used in the English original. If it is too literal it will read like a translation as opposed to authentic document in the target language.[17]

Similarly, back-translations have been criticized in the literature. Hambleton (1993) pointed out that when translators are aware that their translation is to be back-translated, they tend to use wording in the translation that is easier to back-translate. Van de Vijver and Leung (1997) endorse this criticism, and add that back-translations emphasize correct grammar and syntax, rather than context, meaning and understanding of a text. Furthermore, Geisinger (1994) argues that adaptation is extensively missing when people back-translate. Even though there has been some research on translation in adapted tests, Gudmundsson (2009) urges that more empirical research should be conducted on the merits and flaws of various translation techniques, as well as on the methods and context where they could best be applied.

An ideal translation within the TAT process would therefore involve a) mastering the languages of translation, b) in-depth knowledge of both the source and target cultures, c) being an expert in the subject matter to be assessed, and d) knowledge of measurement fields (see Fig.1 further below). This proposition is an ideal one, as Stansfield (2003) also highlighted. However, it is a costly one, and thus it may not be feasible in most testing situations. Mastering the language into which a test will be translated, the cultural environment where the test will be administered, and the subject matter and content of the test, is essential for a fair and valid, translated and adapted test. Also, having knowledge of measurement is equally important. However, it is difficult to find specialists who can cope with all the above. Therefore, in most cases, the most appropriate approach would be to have teams working on such processes, as Aucher and Stansfield (1997) have recommended in various panels.

Finally, and even when translation and adaptation are tackled by teams of specialists, the language dimension still represents a major challenge. Language and its socio-linguistic variations add to the complexity of the TAT process. Everyone involved in the development of assessment instruments must be aware of the diversity of each language and the socio-cultural political aspect of testing. Unfortunately, that is not the case in

---

[17] Aucher and Stansfield 1997, 6.

everyday practice. Assessment specialists have not sufficiently focused on the linguistic diversity within a language. We should take a break and consider anew the multidisciplinarity of TAT, which goes beyond translation and measurement as constitutive fields. TAT also includes language acquisition, sociolinguistics, and language testing. The general trend is to adapt and translate a test into the dominant variety of each language and to ignore that there is a bias arising when other varieties are not considered. Thus, examinees ultimately suffer discrimination which is not based on their abilities or skills, but rather on speaking a language variety different from that of the test.

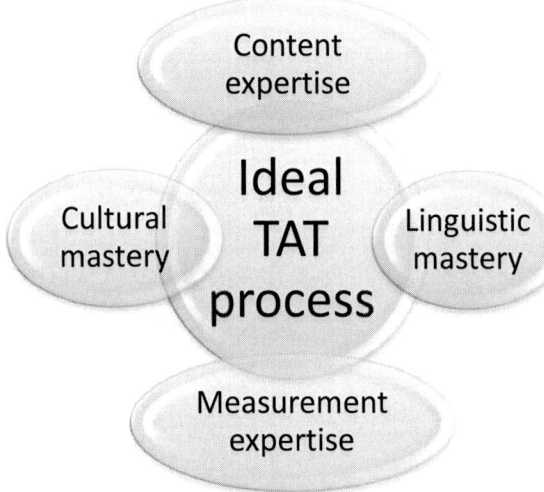

Fig.1. Breakdown of elements necessary for an ideal TAT process

## Works cited

Allalouf, Avi, Ronald Hambleton, and Stephen Sireci. 1999. "Identifying the Causes of Translation DIF on Verbal Items." *Journal of Educational Measurement* 36:185–198.

Allalouf, Avi. 2003. "Revising Translated Differential Item Functioning Items as a Tool for Improving Cross-Lingual Assessment," *Applied Measurement in Education* 19(1):55–73.

American Educational Research Association (AERA), American Psychological Association (APA), and National Council on Measurement in Education (NCME). 1989. *Standards for Educational and Psychological Testing.* Washington, DC: American Psychological Association.

Auchter, Joan, and Charles Stansfield. 1997a. *Linking Tests across Languages: Focus on the Translation and Adaptation Process.* Report to the National Council on Measurement. Washington, DC: National Council on Measurement.

Auchter, Joan, and Charles Stansfield. 1997b. *Developing Parallel Tests across Languages: Focus on the Translation and Adaptation Process.* Report to the National Council on Measurement. Washington, DC: National Council on Measurement.

Bjorner, Jakob, Svend Kreiner, John Ware, Morgens Damsgaard, and Per Bech. 1998. "Differential Item Functioning in the Danish Translation of the SF-36." *Journal of Clinical Epidemiology* 51(11):1189–1202.

Brown, Annie. 2004. *Interviewer Variation in Oral Proficiency Interviews.* PhD diss., University of Melbourne.

Brislin, Richard. 1986. "The Wording and Translation of Research Instruments." In *Field Methods in Cross-Cultural Research*, edited by Walter Lonner and John Berry, 137–164. Newbury Park, CA: Sage.

Budgell, Glen, Numbury Raju, and Douglas Quartetti. 1995. "Analysis of Differential Item Functioning in Translated Assessment Instruments." *Applied Psychological Measurement* 19:309–321.

Davidson, Frederick. 2006. "World Englishes and Test Construction." In *The Handbook of World Englishes*, edited by Braj Kachru, Yamuna Kachru, and Cecil Nelson, 709–717. Malden, MA: Blackwell.

—. 1994. "The Interlanguage Metaphor and Language Assessment." *World Englishes* 13(3):377–386.

Davis, Matthew, and Ingrid Johnsrude. 2003. "Hierarchical Processing in Spoken Language Comprehension." *The Journal of Neuroscience* 23(8):3423–3431.

ElAtia, Samira. 2012. "Evaluating the Effect of Socio-Linguistic Factors on Adapted and/or Translated Educational Achievement Bilingual Tests." Paper presented at the *National Council on Measurement in Education*, Vancouver.

—. 2010. "Sociolinguistic Bias in Educational Measurement in the Two Official Languages." Paper presented at the *Canadian Association of Language Assessment*, Montreal.

Elosua, Paula, and Alicia Lopez-Jauregui. 2007. "Potential Sources of Differential Item Functioning in the Adaptation of Tests." *International Journal of Testing* 7(1):39–52.

Ercikan, Kadriye. 2002. "Disentangling Sources of Differential Item Functioning in Multi-language Assessments." *International Journal of Testing* 2:199–215.

Ercikan, Kadriye, Mark Gierl, Tanya McCreith, Gautam Puhan, and Kim Koh. 2004. "Comparability of Bilingual Versions of Assessments: Sources of Incomparability of English and French Versions of Canada's National Achievement Tests." *Applied Measurement in Education* 17:301–321.

Fancher, Raymond. 1985. *The Intelligence Men: Makers of the IQ Controversy.* New York: W. W. Norton & Company.

Ferne, Tracy, and André Rupp. 2007. "A Synthesis of 15 Years of Research on DIF in Language Testing: Methodological Advances, Challenges, and Recommendations." *Language Assessment Quarterly* 4(2):113–148.

Fukuhara, Shunichi, Seiji Bito, Joseph Green, Amy Hsiao, and Kiyoshi Kurokawa. 1998. "Translation, Adaptation, and Validation of the SF-36 Health Survey for Use in Japan." *Journal of Clinical Epidemiology* 51(11):1037–1044.

Geisinger, Kurt. 1994. "Cross-cultural Normative Assessment: Translation and Adaptation. Issues Influencing the Normative Interpretation of Assessment Instruments." *Psychological Assessment* 6:304–312.

Gierl, Mark. 2005. "Using a Dimensionality-based DIF Analysis Paradigm to Identify and Interpret Constructs that Elicit Group Differences." *Educational Measurement: Issues and Practice* 24:3–14.

Gierl, Mark, and Shameem Khaliq. 2001. "Identifying Sources of Differential Item and Bundle Functioning on Translated Achievement Tests." *Journal of Educational Measurement* 38:164–187.

Gierl, Mark, Todd Rogers, and Don Klinger. 1999. "Using Statistical and Judgmental Reviews to Identify and Interpret Translation Differential Item Functioning," *The Alberta Journal of Educational Research* 45(4):353–376.

Gudmundsson, Einer. 2009. "Guidelines for Translating and Adapting Psychological Instruments." *Nordic Psychology* 61(2):29–45.

Hambleton, Ronald. 2005. "Issues, Designs, and Technical Guidelines for Adapting Tests into Multiple Languages and Cultures." In *Adapting Educational and Psychological Tests for Cross-Cultural Assessment*, edited by Ronald Hambleton, Peter Merenda, and Charles Spielberger, 3–38. Mahwah, NJ: Lawrence Erlbaum Associates.

—. 1994. "Guidelines for Adapting Educational and Psychological Tests: A Progress Report." *European Journal of Psychological Assessment* 10:229–244.

—. 1993. "Translating Achievement Tests for Use in Cross-National Studies." *European Journal of Psychological Assessment* 9:57–68.
Hambleton, Ronald, and John Hal de Jong. 2003. "Advances in Translating and Adapting Educational and Psychological Tests." *Language Testing* 20(2):127–134.
Hambleton, Ronald, and Anil Kanjee. 1995. "Increasing the Validity of Cross-cultural Assessments: Use of Improved Methods for Test Adaptations." *European Journal of Psychological Assessment* 11:147–157.
Hambleton, Ronald, and Liane Patsula. 1999. "Increasing the Validity of Adapted Test: Myths to Be Avoided and Guidelines for Improving Test Adaptation Practices." *Applied Testing Technology* 1(1):1–16.
Hambleton, Ronald, Peter Merenda, and Charles Spielberger. 2005. *Adapting Educational and Psychological Tests for Cross-Cultural Assessment*. Mahwah, NJ: Lawrence Erlbaum Associates.
Harkness, Janet. 1998. *Cross-Cultural Equivalence*. Mannheim: Zuma.
International Test Commission. 2010. *International Test Commission Guidelines for Translating and Adapting Tests.* Accessed June 28, 2013: http://www.intestcom.org/
Kamin, Leon. 1995. "The Pioneers of IQ Testing." In *The Bell Curve Debate: History, Documents, Opinions,* edited by Russell Jacoby, and Naomi Glauberman, 476–509. New York: Times Books.
Khan, Rubina. 2006. "The IELTS Speaking Test: Analysing Culture Bias." *Malaysian Journal of ELT Research* 2:60–79.
Leplège, Alain, Emmanuel Ecosse, Angela Verdier, and Thomas Perneger. 1998. "The French SF-36 Health Survey: Translation, Cultural Adaptation, and Preliminary Psychometric Evaluation." *Journal of Clinical Epidemiology* 51(11):1013–1023.
Li, Lu, Huai Wang, and Yu-Cheng Shen. 2003. "Chinese SF-36 Health Survey: Translation, Cultural, Adaptation, Validation, and Normalization." *Journal of Epidemiology and Community Health* 57:259–263.
Lonner, Walter. 1990. "An Overview of Cross-cultural Testing and Assessment." In *Applied Cross-Cultural Psychology*, edited by Richard Brislin, 56–76. Newbury Park, CA: Sage.
Lowenberg, Peter. 2000. "Non-Native Varieties and Issues of Fairness in Testing English as a World Language." In *Fairness and Validation in Language Assessment*, edited by Anthony Kunnan, 43–59. Cambridge: Cambridge University Press.

Malgady, Robert, Lloyd Rogler, and Giuseppe Costantino. 1987. "Ethnocultural and Linguistic Bias in Mental Health Evaluation of Hispanics." *American Psychologist* 42(3):228–234.

Merenda, Peter. 2005. "Cross-cultural Adaptation of Educational and Psychological Testing." In *Adapting Educational and Psychological Tests for Cross-Cultural Assessment*, edited by Ronald Hambleton, Peter Merenda, and Charles Spielberger, 40–58. Mahwah, NJ: Lawrence Erlbaum Associates.

McGuire, Frederick. 1994. "Army Alpha and Beta Tests of Intelligence." In *Encyclopedia of Intelligence*, edited by Robert Sternberg. New York: Macmillan.

McNamara, Tim, and Carsten Roever. 2007. *Language Testing: The Social Dimension*. Malden, MA: Blackwell.

Muñiz, José, Ronald Hambleton, and Dehui Xing. 2001. "Small Sample Studies to Detect Flaws in Test Translation." *International Journal of Testing* 1:115–135.

Petersen Morten, Mogens Groenvold, Jakob Bjorner, Neil Aaronson, Thierry Conroy, Ann Cull, Peter Fayers, Marianne Hjermstad, Mirjam Sprangers, and Marianne Sullivan. 2003. "Use of Differential Item Functioning Analysis to Assess the Equivalence of Translations of a Questionnaire." *European Organisation for Research and Treatment of Cancer Quality of Life Group, Quality of Life Research* 12:373–385.

Romaine, Suzanne. 1994. *Language in Society: An Introduction to Sociolinguistics*. Oxford: Oxford University Press.

Shepard, Lorrie, Gregory Camilli, and Marilyn Averill. 1981. "Comparison of Six Procedures for Detecting Test Item Bias Using Both Internal and External Ability Criteria." *Journal of Educational Statistics* 6:317–375.

Siegler, Robert. 1992. "The Other Alfred Binet." *Developmental Psychology* 28:179–190.

Solano-Flores, Guillermo, Eduardo Backhoff, and Luis Contreras-Niño. 2009. "Theory of Test Translation Error." *International Journal of Testing* 9:78–91.

Stansfield, Charles. 2003. "Test Translation and Adaptation in Public Education in the USA." *Language Testing* 20(2):189–207.

Tanzer, Norbert. 2005. "Developing Tests for Use in Multiple Languages and Cultures: A Plea for Simultaneous Development." In *Adapting Educational and Psychological Tests for Cross-Cultural Assessment*, edited by Ronald Hambleton, Peter Merenda, and Charles Spielberger, 235–263. Mahwah, NJ: Lawrence Erlbaum Associates.

van de Vijver, Fons, and Ronald Hambleton. 1996. "Translating Tests: Some Practical Guidelines." *European Psychologist* 1:89–99.
van de Vijver, Fons, and Karey Leung. 1997. *Methods and Analysis for Cross-Cultural Research.* London: Sage.
van Haaften, E. Heleen, and Fons van de Vijver. 1996. "Psychological Consequences of Environmental Degradation." *Journal of Health Psychology* 1:411–429.
van Widenfelt, Brigit, Philip Treffers, Edwin de Beurs, Bart Siebelink, and Els Koudijs. 2005. "Translation and Cross-Cultural Adaptation of Assessment Instruments Used in Psychological Research with Children and Families." *Clinical Child and Family Psychology Review* 8(2):135–47.
Wolfram, Walt. 2008. "Language Diversity and the Public Interest." In *Sustaining Linguistic Diversity: Endangered and Minority Language and Language Varieties*, edited by Kendall King, Natalie Schilling-Estes, Lyn Fogle, Jia Lui, and Barbara Soukup, 187–202. Washington, DC: Georgetown University Press.
—. 1983. "Test Interpretation and Sociolinguistic Differences." *Topics in Language Disorders* 3(3):21–34.

# Appendix

**The 22 ITC Guidelines for Test Adaptation and Translation**
(International Test Commission 2012)

| Context | C.1 Effects of cultural differences which are not relevant or important to the main purposes of the study should be minimized to the extent possible. |
|---|---|
| | C.2 The amount of overlap in the construct measured by the test or instrument in the populations of interest should be assessed. |
| Test Development & Adaptation | D.1 Test developers/publishers should ensure that the adaptation process takes full account of linguistic and cultural differences among the populations for whom adapted versions of the test or instrument are intended. |
| | D.2 Test developers/publishers should provide evidence that the language use in the directions, rubrics, and items themselves as well as in the handbook are appropriate for all cultural and language populations for whom the test or instrument is intended. |

D.3 Test developers/publishers should provide evidence that the choice of testing techniques, item formats, test conventions, and procedures are familiar to all intended populations.

D.4 Test developers/publishers should provide evidence that item content and stimulus materials are familiar to all intended populations.

D.5 Test developers/publishers should implement systematic judgmental evidence, both linguistic and psychological, to improve the accuracy of the adaptation process and compile evidence on the equivalence of all language versions.

D.6 Test developers/publishers should ensure that the data collection design permits the use of appropriate statistical techniques to establish item equivalence between the different language versions of the test or instrument.

D.7 Test developers/publishers should apply appropriate statistical techniques to (1) establish the equivalence of the different versions of the test or instrument, and (2) identify problematic components or aspects of the test or instrument which may be inadequate to one or more of the intended populations.

D.8 Test developers/publishers should provide information on the evaluation of validity in all target populations for whom the adapted versions are intended.

D.9 Test developers/publishers should provide statistical evidence of the equivalence of questions for all intended populations.

D.10 Non-equivalent questions between versions intended for different populations should not be used in preparing a common scale or in comparing these populations. However, they may be useful in enhancing content validity of scores reported for each population separately.

| | |
|---|---|
| **Administration** | A.1 Test developers and administrators should try to anticipate the types of problems that can be expected, and take appropriate actions to remedy these problems through the preparation of appropriate materials and instructions.<br><br>A.2 Test administrators should be sensitive to a number of factors related to the stimulus materials, administration procedures, and response modes that can moderate the validity of the inferences drawn from the scores.<br><br>A.3 Those aspects of the environment that influence the administration of a test or instrument should be made as similar as possible across populations of interest.<br><br>A.4 Test administration instructions should be in the source and target languages to minimize the influence of unwanted sources of variation across populations.<br><br>A.5 The test manual should specify all aspects of the administration that require scrutiny in a new cultural context.<br><br>A.6 The administrator should be unobtrusive and the administrator-examinee interaction should be minimized. Explicit rules that are described in the manual for administration should be followed. |
| **Documentation & Score Interpretations** | I.1 When a test or instrument is adapted for use in another population, documentation of the changes should be provided, along with evidence of the equivalence.<br><br>I.2 Score differences among samples of populations administered the test or instrument should not be taken at face value. The researcher has the responsibility to substantiate the differences with other empirical evidence.<br><br>I.3 Comparisons across populations can only be made at the level of invariance that has been established for the scale on which scores are reported.<br><br>I.4 The test developer should provide specific information on the ways in which the socio-cultural and ecological contexts of the populations might affect performance, and should suggest procedures to account for these effects in the interpretation of results. |

# CHAPTER ELEVEN

## USING TRANSLATION AS A TEST ACCOMMODATION WITH CULTURALLY AND LINGUISTICALLY DIVERSE LEARNERS

## SULTAN TURKAN, MARIA ELENA OLIVERI AND JULIO CABRERA

### 1. Introduction

In this chapter, we discuss three main issues associated with using language translation[1] as a testing accommodation in content assessments administered to diverse learners. By *diverse learners* we refer to: a) English language learners (ELLs) schooled in the United States (US) and b) culturally and linguistically diverse students (CLDs) around the world. Although the two acronyms (i.e. ELLs and CLDs) might refer to diverse student populations with different characteristics, we use the broader term CLDs to refer to these two types of students. We use examples from the US to illustrate particular points associated with translation as an accommodation. However, we conjecture that these issues apply to other countries and contexts with large populations of CLD test-takers.

We highlight examples from the US because the heterogeneity of the CLDs taking standardized content assessments is remarkable, yet there are monolithic approaches to providing accommodations to these students. The "one size fits all" approaches may not be conducive to meeting the linguistic and cultural needs of CLDs. Heterogeneity is evidenced by the multitude of native languages, cultural backgrounds and diverse ways of

---

[1] We use the term *test translation* to align this chapter with the rest of the book, wherein this term is used. However, the term *adaptation* might be more suitable for the types of accommodations conducted at the state level, as they go beyond literal translation to include cultural and other adaptations.

schooling in the home countries of the students. During the course of their US schooling, CLDs display traits of heterogeneity in relation to their English language proficiency in four areas of language: listening, reading, speaking, and writing. There is also diversity in their English proficiency dependent on context (e.g. at school, at home, with friends, with relatives, etc.; see Solano-Flores 2008, 190). These factors lead to heterogeneity of CLDs and pose continuous challenges to test developers in relation to finding ways to accommodate diversty of CLDs in content assessments. Translation accommodation is promising for those CLDs who could benefit from demonstrating content knowledge in their native (or strongest) language.

Testing accommodations are changes made to an assessment without altering the underlying construct. Accommodations are intended to provide increased access to content by making the assessment tasks comprehensible to students with limited language proficiency. Factors precluding access to the assessed construct might be related to cultural and linguistic differences between the culture of the test takers and the culture of the test developers, or the mainstream culture of the students for whom the test is developed. Language can also introduce construct irrelevance or underrepresentation in assessments. Construct irrelevance happens when the test performance of an individual is influenced by factors other than the measured construct. Construct irrelevant variance might occur in translated assessments that were developed for one mainstream population and administered to another population. As language carries cultural beliefs, values, and practices, the group of linguistically and culturally diverse test takers may not have shared knowledge or experience with the mainstream culture, resulting in measurement issues that are not related to the test content. Moreover, when test items are translated across languages, sources of incomparability might arise when the standard dialect used in the test does not match the dialect used at home (cf. Solano-Flores 2008). Construct underrepresentation occurs when relevant content that makes up the targeted construct is not included in an assessment (cf. Messick 1994). Messick argues that the assessment should authentically represent the targeted construct. These two issues might constitute major threats to the validity of inferences made from the content assessment. The objective of translation accommodation is to reduce construct irrelevant variance that might arise from the linguistic and cultural difficulties CLDs face in demonstrating knowledge on standardized content assessments.

Difficulties with measurement comparability between multiple language versions of a test constitute another threat to test validity and fairness because this might introduce bias for or against certain groups of test takers. Translation committees need to provide evidence to demonstrate that the meaning intended for the targeted construct is equivalent between two language versions of the test and does not favor any group of test takers over another for whom the test structure is similar. An item or instrument that is biased will produce non-equivalent scores, and is a concern when tests are translated across languages (cf. Oliveri and Ercikan 2011). This may take place because particular words or terms may be used in one language version as compared to another, changing the meaning and differential difficulty of an item. For example, in a Swedish-English comparison (Ex. 1), English-speaking examinees were presented with the following item:

Ex. 1 Where is a bird with webbed feet most likely to live?
a. in the mountains
b. in the woods
c. in the sea
d. in the desert[2]

In the Swedish translation, *webbed feet* was translated to *swimming feet*, providing a clue to the correct choice and giving an advantage to the Swedish examinees. This illustration exemplifies the type of issues one needs to consider when translating items because a difference in test performance may be incorrectly attributed to differences in ability across examinee groups when the difference is related to test adaptation.

The main benefits of using translation accommodations are that they provide CLDs with increased access to tested content and equitable opportunity to demonstrate their content knowledge in the language over which they have most command. These benefits are particularly important for CLDs in the US due to their large representation in the student population. CLDs represent approximately 11 percent (above five million) of the total PK-12 US public school population (NCES 2012), with some states having at least 15 percent of CLDs (i.e. Texas, Arizona, California, and Nevada; see Batalova and McHugh 2010). These students often lag behind in many content areas compared to their English monolingual peers, as their English language literacy skills take longer to develop (cf. Lesaux and Geva 2006). Further, under the US *No Child Left Behind* (NCLB 2002) policy, schools and districts are accountable for the academic achievement of CLDs. After NCLB, the new era of American public schooling is being defined by *Common Core State Standards*

---

[2] Hambleton 1994, 235.

(CCSS), an effort being led by the *National Governors Association and the Council of Chief State School Officers.*

Adopted by 45 states, CCSS provides national standards for developing national assessments. Similar to the assessments administered under the NCLB era, the new common core standards-based assessments will hold all students to the same expectations as guided by the CCSS. To meet these expectations, states will need to adopt effective ways of providing CLDs with relevant testing accommodations, taking into account the effectiveness and relevance of different types of accommodations to the linguistic and cultural needs of the heterogeneous characteristics of CLDs. Unfortunately, there is little empirical research about the effectiveness of different types of accommodations on the performance of CLDs to guide the design of the new common core based tests. Despite the lack of empirical research, framework documents have been written to guide the design of certain accommodations. For instance, to guide the assessments to be developed by *Smarter Balanced Assessment Consortium*, Solano-Flores (2012) identifies challenges in developing effective translation accommodations for CLDs and discusses the limitations and potentials of four translation accommodations in relation to fairness and validity considerations. Still, there is no sufficient empirical research on the effectiveness of translation accommodation (Robinson 2010; Hoffstetter 2003). This could be due to the limited use of translation accommodations across the US In fact, findings from our review of the state test translation practices (Turkan and Oliveri, forthcoming), revealed that 12 of the 50 states provided adapted versions of content tests in languages other than English. One striking finding was the large variability in the measures taken to ensure comparability between multiple language versions of the tests.

In this chapter, we approach the fundamental issues of comparability between multiple language versions of the tests by discussing test design, administration, and validity of inferences made from results of assessments translated into a language other than English (i.e. translation accommodation). First, we discuss design and administration issues and provide recommendations to minimize translation error. Also, to increase comparability of items and the test, we offer particular examples of practices which can enhance test adaptation efforts, such as identifying the right expertise to translate assessments and consider the dialect of the target language of translation. We also provide strategies to improve the test review process in order to minimize inevitable translation errors. We emphasize the principle of assigning translation accommodations to CLDs by utilizing a mix of qualitative and quantitative methodologies to increase measurement comparability and minimize threats to test validity in translated assessments. In terms of validity-related considerations, we describe post-test administration strategies to eliminate threats to validity of translated tests.

## 2. Test translation design and administration issues

In this section, we provide suggestions about which approaches and methods to use when designing fair and valid test translation accommodations. These are important as the process of test translation involves more than just rewriting items in another language (cf. Solano-Flores and Gustafson 2013).

### 2.1 Finding the right expertise to do the translation job

The first step of translating a test into a targeted language involves determining who will be part of the translation committee. Test translators are selected from a pool of individuals who are content experts and bilinguals or have a native-like command of English (Stansfield 2003). The risk here is that bilingual or native-like test translators may not be good at translation, even if they may be experts on the content covered on the assessment. We argue that test translators with expertise in content matters and/or test development ought to do the test translation. Moreover, test translators, content specialists, and test developers ought to form the core of the test translation review committees. If the right expertise is not recruited to translate the test, principles of comparability and test validity might be compromised. We thus suggest dispelling the myth of inferring high quality translation capabilities of individuals with expertise in bilingual education and teaching English as a foreign language without additional training in translation (Solano-Flores 2008). Similarly, bilingual translators might not be qualified to translate tests in all four language skill areas (i.e. reading, speaking, listening, and writing).

Measures ought to be taken to ensure selecting the right expertise. There are exemplar cases reflecting selection of the right expertise. For instance, the *Trend in International Mathematics and Science Study*'s (TIMSS) guidelines require that there will be language experts, subject matter specialists, and external highly qualified reviewers on test translation committees that oversee the translation of a test (Martin *et al.* 1999; Yu and Ebbs 2011). More specifically, TIMSS employs a group of qualified translators for an initial translation of the international English version of the TIMSS. Following this translation, a panel of subject experts reviews the translation, identifies any translation and adaptation issues, and highlights adaptation needs. After the field test, the translated assessment is reviewed and updated again by the same teams of translators and reviewers. Then, an external review is completed by the *International Association for the Evaluation of Educational Achievement*.

In assembling this team, the qualifications and background knowledge of the translators should be considered. As highlighted in a study conducted by Roth *et al.* (forthcoming), translators may notice different issues in translations depending on their educational background and work experiences. In their study, three experts were asked to think out loud while reviewing adaptations of a science test administered to English- and French-speaking students. The experts differed in their knowledge (pedagogical, pedagogical and content, or linguistic). Study findings revealed that experts with content and pedagogical knowledge identified the type of differences potentially impacting responses to items by the students (e.g. the interaction between the item, its content, and the translation issues), whereas the language expert solely identified linguistic differences across test language versions. A committee of test translators, content specialists, and test developers should thus conduct reviews to ensure the comparability in structural, semantic, cultural and mechanical use of language between test versions. Instead, we suggest considering the proficiency of bilingual translators in the four skill areas of language and including linguistically qualified experts with pedagogical knowledge and pedagogical and specific knowledge in the content area of translation. These expert reviews are essential to ensuring fair and valid test translation. Once the right expertise is properly selected, another key issue to keep in mind when translating tests is the minimization of translation error.

## 2.2 Minimizing the inevitable translation error

To provide evidence for comparability between multiple language versions of a content test, sources of test translation error should be investigated and minimized at the item-level. When translating tests, errors in conveying the targeted meaning are inevitable. The investigation of cultural and linguistic factors underlying test translation error is important because it threatens comparable and valid measurement of students' skills. Lack of equivalence across multiple language versions of the test items is defined as "test translation error" (Solano-Flores *et al.* 2009). To minimize translation error, comprehensive item reviews should be conducted at the design and test piloting stages. To help with these reviews, Solano-Flores *et al.* (2009) discuss a theory of translation error and guide test translators to utilize the theory in their immediate context and for the particular purpose of test translation.

The theory of test translation error is based on the understanding that language is not a fixed category or aptitude, but a dynamic and probabilistic phenomenon (Solano-Flores and Trumbull 2003). According to this view, language encapsulates cultural norms and cognitive schemas. This view of language acknowledges that language proficiency is not deterministic but is influenced by multiple factors including levels of native- and English-language proficiency. Within this theory, the process of test translation is systematized in relation to quality control (Solano-Flores *et al.* 2009). For effective systematization of test translation, it is beneficial to bring all stakeholders to a level of understanding of the process of test translation, following a standard theory for translating tests.

Test translation theory identifies two main types of translation error: internal and external. Solano-Flores *et al.* (2009) identify ten dimensions of translation error: style, format, conventions, grammar and syntax, semantics, register, information, construct, curriculum, and origin. These dimensions are classified into *internal* or *external* dimensions. Internal dimensions (style, semantics, register, conventions, grammar and syntax, information, construct) are concerned with the work of the translators, while the external dimensions (format, origin, and curriculum) are outside the scope of translators' work. Translation error types are identified under the specific type of dimensions mentioned above. For instance, under the internal dimension of *conventions* there are error types such as: *grammatical inconsistency between stem and answer options in multiple-choice items*, among others. Within the external dimension, namely *format*, the following error types are identified: *change of size, font,* among others (see Solano-Flores *et al.* 2009 for more discussion). The theory does not universalize the set of test translation error dimensions and the error types included within each dimension. Rather, theory informs that these dimensions be modified according to the specific needs of each test translation project.

This theory sets an example for content reviews that every translation committee ought to complete during test translation design and piloting stages. If possible errors originating from the factors related to item sampling and content, which are somewhat outside the test translators' control, are recognized, then the focus could be more readily given to the language-related sources of translation error. Otherwise, reviews could be haphazardly random and may not capture the core sources of errors residing from internal language related dimensions of test translation.

## 2.3 Addressing dialect variation

Dialect variation, a cultural and linguistic factor, is another potential source of threat to the validity and fairness of a translated test. There may be inevitable differences in the meaning conveyed between the two language versions of the translated test using different dialects in the same language. Solano-Flores (2006) defines dialects as "a variation of a language that is characteristic of the users of that language". He argues that dialects *within* a language (e.g. Cantonese and Mandarin) might be more distant than those *across* languages (e.g. Danish and Norwegian).

A dialect does not merely encompass variation in the linguistic structure of a language but also in cultural expressions. Moreover, dialects spoken by the populations of CLDs might not always match the standard dialect used in test development; therefore, CLDs may be somewhat unfamiliar with words and expressions used in the test (Solano-Flores and Gustafson 2013). These types of dialect differences were identified in a study conducted by Oliveri and Ercikan (2011) wherein words that were more appropriate for a test developed for French speakers from France were used in a French version of a test used in Quebec, Canada. Moreover, an interaction among the dialect, items, and student were reported in a study conducted by Solano-Flores and Li (2008). Study findings imply that dialect of the translated test influences the way CLDs respond to the items which ultimately have an effect on their test performance. Failure to account for dialect variation in the target language of the test, might make the inclusion of CLDs in large-scale assessments invalid and unfair.

Consequently, Solano-Flores (2006) argues that different dialects should be represented in test translation review committees. Dialect variation might constitute a source of measurement error in tests administered in the US due to the diversity of Spanish speakers. Approximately 80 percent of ELLs are Spanish speakers (NCES 2004). They come from multiple countries including Cuba, Ecuador, Mexico, and Puerto Rico, all of whom speak different versions of Spanish. Dialect variation should thus be considered when translating tests for test takers from these various Spanish-speaking countries.

One of the ways to eliminate any threats to validity resulting from the dialect variation of the target language is to pilot test the translated items to a representative sample of the target student population and follow up with in-depth interviews. Doing so would introduce both quantitative and qualitative evidence for ensuring validity and fairness of the translated test. Moreover, ensuring that items do not contain words that are particularly associated with one dialect (e.g. *chaval* in Spain to indicate *boy*, since *chico* might be more readily understood by all or most Spanish speakers) should also be considered in pilot testing. Another way is to conduct extensive reviews. For instance, PISA translation guidelines recommend forming a committee of two independent translators and a third individual who develop the test through a "double-translation and reconciliation" procedure. This procedure involves translating the source material into the target language and reconciling the source languages into one single national version.

Dialect variation in the target language remains a source of threat to the validity of the test scores. We have recommended that the translated version of the test be piloted with students representing diverse linguistic backgrounds to ensure that the dialect the test was constructed in applies to a majority of the target test takers. The process of piloting and revising the test translation calls for time and resources. If the essential time and resources are not invested, the design of translated tests might compromise from the value of piloting and revising the translated versions of the tests (Solano-Flores and Gustafson 2013), which could, in turn, threaten the validity of the translated tests.

## 2.4 Assigning translation accommodation to diverse learners

Test translation accommodation is important to be assigned to students with the relevant linguistic and cultural needs (Pennock-Roman and Rivera 2011). The first question in relation to assigning relevant test accommodation in the form of a translated version of the test is: What makes a student eligible to take the translated version? One of the main criteria for assigning translation accommodation is that CLDs have received instruction in their native language or the target language of the translated test. If not, written translated tests should not be administered to CLDs, but individual student cases could be evaluated to determine if oral test translation might be appropriate and relevant to administration (Stansfield 2011). In the US, oral translation is provided as an accommodation, usually by bilingual teachers, for those ELLs who cannot read the translated script of a test in their native language. Therefore, test translation accommodation might be irrelevant to those who do not have literacy skills.

Blanket approaches to assigning translation accommodation to CLDs should be avoided. In assigning testing accommodations, it is important to consider not only the educational backgrounds of CLDs, but also their linguistic and cultural needs in their native language as well as in English. In other words, the decisions made about whether to assign translation accommodation should be based on a range of variables such as a student's literacy levels in the native language and English, the predominant language of instruction, length and degree of formal schooling in the native language and so on.

Unfortunately, the vast literature in misclassification/misassignment continues to suggest that identification of CLDs remains a challenge not only due to the linguistic and cultural differences of students but also to the arduous differentiation between learning disabilities and second language acquisition (Klingner *et al.* 2006). Cultural differences between school personnel and CLDs increase inappropriate CLD referrals to special/remedial classes (Brown 2004), and are further compounded by unconscious stereotypes (i.e. racial biases). These inappropriate referrals are further increased because of the similarities between the characteristics of second language acquisition and learning disabilities and difficulties (Lesaux 2006). Poor assignment practices (e.g. lack of proper teacher preparation to identify ELLs) may result in being more harmful than beneficial (Artiles *et al.* 2005; Brown 2004). For instance, Brown (2004) highlights the over-representation of CLD students in special education compared to their representation in the general population (14.2% as opposed to 5%), and compared to their non-CLD counterparts (62.5% as opposed to 63.1%). Misdiagnosis and misclassification of CLDs may result in misassignment of translation accommodation because CLDs may not have the literacy skills and/or may not have received instruction in the language of the translated test.

One way to address the issue of misassignment is to identify CLDs' needs. Based on a meta-analysis on accommodation effects, Pennock-Roman and Rivera (2011) found that CLDs with high native language proficiency and low English language proficiency benefit from a translated test more than CLDs with low native language proficiency and intermediate levels of English proficiency, because they can process the items translated in their native language. Alternatively, newly arrived CLDs who have received content and literacy instruction in their native languages may still face challenges with test content in their native language because of possible curricular differences in the way content was presented in their home countries. In other words, the curricular differences, or methods of learning a particular subject (e.g. the use of calculators), may be different from the mainstream approach.

It is important to translate a test in a target language the students have been exposed to during instruction of the tested content (Liu *et al.* 1999) and to minimize misclassifications. One key difference between the US-based tests and international tests is that students who take the international tests, like the ones listed above, receive instruction in the language in which the test is administered; however, in the US, the language in which CLDs receive instruction is predominantly English. Hence, it is more important that those who assign translation accommodations to CLDs in the US follow these criteria than their international counterparts.

## 3. Identification of sources of threats to validity of translated tests

Due to the manifold sources of errors, there ought to be evidence indicating that a translated test as an accommodation is valid in terms of its comparability with the language of the original test. The evidence should demonstrate that the meaning intended, as part of the construct assessed, is equivalent between two or multiple versions of the test in any language. If the evidence is not collected, there may be threats to test validity.

Specifically, in review of the practices followed across the US, the issue of comparability was not taken seriously. Most states do not have procedures to systematically ensure comparability and measurement equivalence between multiple language versions of a test. Common practice is to check the translated version of the test against a few criteria: a) minimize cultural differences, b) confirm that the essential meaning has not changed after translation, and c) confirm that the words and phrases are equivalent. To illustrate a more specific case, the Oregon State Department of Education takes three measures to ensure the comparability of test scores driven from the translated versions (see, for an extensive discussion, Turkan and Oliveri, forthcoming). First, they ensure the accuracy of the translation according to four dimensions: *syntactical accuracy*, *cognitive complexity*, *cultural relevance*, and *back translation*. In addition to the review of every item translated by Oregon teachers, an independent reviewer is contracted to troubleshoot any translation problems that potentially influence the meaning of the language used in each item. The third step is to periodically conduct statistical tests such as DIF and multi-group confirmatory factor analyses to evaluate whether construct invariance can be established between the English only and dual language (English-Spanish) versions. Examples as such indicate how different measures could be taken to conduct investigations of comparability during and after test administration.

In this section, we identify sources of threat to test validity and discuss three strategies that could be taken in the post-test administration to minimize or eliminate the threats (see Ercikan *et al.* 2012, for a more comprehensive review). The strategies are: a) psychometric (e.g. DIF, classical test theory and dimensionality) analyses, b) expert review of test items, and c) monitoring student cognitive processes using think aloud protocols.

## 4. Strategies for eliminating threats to test validity in the post-test administration.

To detect potential differences in performance across examinees on an item, DIF analyses are conducted. It is recognized that DIF might help identify the sources of translation error across multiple language versions of the test (e.g. Ercikan *et al.* 2004). In DIF analyses, examinees of the same ability are matched; DIF is identified if matched examinees have differential probabilities of responding to a test item. There may be different ways and methods of detecting DIF, such as contingency tables (e.g. Mantel-Haenszel), regression equations (e.g. logistic regression), or unidimensional item response theory (IRT) (for a review of these and other methods, see Roussos and Stout 2004). Once DIF is detected, further analyses (e.g. linguistic reviews of items) are typically conducted by panels of experts to identify bias and sources of DIF (Oliveri and Ercikan 2011). These reviews often focus on examining comparability of a) test item content, b) cognitive complexity, c) cultural load, and d) linguistic differences across test versions. These reviews are conducted to examine whether responses not only reflect ability on the measured construct but also signal construct irrelevant variance. Reviews are important because bias threatens score comparability and reduces the validity of inferences made based upon test scores.

To illustrate, previous studies conducted to investigate differences in adapted versions of tests reveal difficulties associated with this process and highlight difficulties encountered in cross-cultural studies involving translated tests. For example, a study conducted by Angoff and Cook (1988) using verbal and mathematical items from the *Scholastic Aptitude Test* (SAT) and the *Prueba de Aptitud Academica* (the Spanish language equivalent of the SAT) revealed low correlations for the difficulties in verbal items between the two language versions. Moreover, Solano-Flores *et al.* (2006), using data from the 1995 Spanish version of TIMSS administration in Mexico, also found high percentages of items with translation errors and a high correlation between the severity of translation errors and item difficulty for the Spanish-speaking students, suggesting the test items were more difficult for Spanish-speaking students. Furthermore, results of a study conducted by Sandilands *et al.* (forthcoming), using data from the 2006 PIRLS administration to English and Spanish speakers from the US and Colombia, revealed the following differences across the Spanish and English versions of tests: a) item instructions and phrasing of the questions, b) grammatical structure, c) sentence length, d) vocabulary complexity, and e) word usage in 8 out of 24 items.

One of the constraints described above in providing translation as an accommodation is related to limited financial resources and qualified translators. Conducting analyses of DIF (particularly with small sample sizes) might be costly and require psychometric expertise (Ercikan et al. 2012). The use of expert reviews on test translations, which could be cost effective, might be useful in such cases to minimize DIF.

Other psychometric analyses can also be conducted to investigate potential differences across different language versions of a test. For example, classical test theory based analyses of test data involve examining item discrimination indices such as point-biserial correlations, and internal consistency reliability indices (Bowles and Stansfield 2008). Item difficulty values (or $p$-values) and conditional $p$-values (Muñiz et al. 2001) analyses might be conducted with relatively small sample sizes, particularly, for low to medium stakes tests. For example, item statistics (difficulty and discrimination indices) can be compared and correlations of these indices can be calculated to obtain evidence of the degree to which items are ordered similarly for the comparison groups. If differences occur for particular items, those items are flagged and can be further examined by panels of experts. Dimensionality analyses can also be conducted to investigate similarity of factor structure at the test-level (Ercikan and Koh 2005, 25) and can be conducted at exploratory (Oliveri and Ercikan 2011) or confirmatory levels. Using these analyses (as well as those at the item-level) to investigate DIF require large sample sizes, which may not be feasible in states with small numbers of ELL students.

A third approach is based on utilizing think aloud protocols to investigate student cognitive processes. These analyses are conducted to examine whether differences in particular item attributes (response format, item type) and item content lead to differences in item responding across examinee groups. A study conducted by Ercikan et al. (2010) suggests the usefulness of think aloud protocols to examine measurement comparability of test items. In the study, think aloud protocols were used to investigate students' thought processes as they responded to test items using two language versions of tests (English and French) and to confirm whether results from think aloud protocols confirmed differences identified by expert reviews. Results indicated that the think aloud study confirmed differences identified by expert reviews for 10 out of 20 DIF items.

Findings suggest item attributes identified in expert reviews may not be the actual sources of DIF and expert reviews should not be used in isolation to detect bias. Results from the Ercikan *et al.* (2010) study suggest combining what students verbalize, observations from the test administrator while students are problem solving before and after task completion, and students' (correct and incorrect) responses as evidence of students' thought processes. Thus, the use of these methods might serve to complement expert reviews and be viable even in cases of small sample sizes (Ercikan *et al.* 2012).

## 5. Conclusion

In this chapter, we discussed test translation as an accommodation along with the design, administration, and validity issues in using translation as an accommodation with culturally and linguistically diverse learners. We first presented issues related to designing and administering translated tests, in which four issues were discussed. First, it is essential that test translation is conducted by individuals with the right expertise, including bilingual, content and pedagogical experts. Unless the right expertise is selected for test translation, multiple language versions of the test might render incomparable, which constitutes a threat to the validity of the test. Second, the design of the test translation is inevitably error prone but could be minimized through extensive reviews against a common set of error dimensions. Third, the target language of translation might not represent the dialect that students learn and speak at home, and unless the language of the test is familiar to the students, the results of the test and score interpretations might render invalid and unfair. Lastly, we discussed the importance of assigning the translation accommodation to the relevant groups of diverse learners. The testing accommodation would not be of any use if the students did not have the literacy skills of the targeted language or did not receive instruction in that language.

Test translation is a promising type of test accommodation allowing diverse learners to demonstrate content knowledge in their native language. However, CLDs are heterogeneous groups coming from varied ethnic backgrounds, first languages, socioeconomic statuses, quality of prior schooling, literacy skills, and levels of English language proficiency, which brings along complexities in designing, administering, and ensuring validity of test translation. In terms of design, the first and foremost measure to take is to form an expert group of translators with expertise both in the language and content. Test translations should be designed by a multidisciplinary team composed of

[...] curriculum experts, teachers who taught the corresponding grades and subjects, a linguist, an American Translators Association-certified translator, a test developer, and a psychometrician.[3]

It is highly recommended that a multidisciplinary team of differing expertise be formed to identify and resolve multiple dimensions of test translation errors. As the inevitable test translation errors are minimized, results and score interpretations of the test translation accommodation become more valid and fair.

Another major consideration related to test administration is that translation accommodations should be assigned to those culturally and linguistically diverse test takers who have content knowledge but not the language proficiency to take the test in its original language version. However, it should be required that these diverse test takers receive instruction in the language of translation. Otherwise, administering the translation accommodation would not serve its intended purpose. A systematic classification program that identifies the linguistic, cultural, and educational backgrounds of CLDs would help to detect which groups of CLDs would be most eligible to qualify for test translation accommodation.

Moreover, in terms of ensuring test validity, it is absolutely essential that test translation accommodation not favor any group of test takers over others who fall under the same underlying trait structure and manifest similar probabilities of correctly responding to an item. Furthermore, multiple versions of the test must be comparable in terms of construct representation. To ensure construct equivalence, stakeholders should utilize a combination of qualitative and quantitative methods either before the two versions of the test are operationally administered or after administration, at periodic intervals. For instance, it is recognized that DIF analyses might reveal the inaccurate translation of terms across languages (e.g. Ercikan *et al.* 2004; Ercikan 2002). To ensure comparability at the development and design stage, simultaneous test development approaches should be followed, as Ercikan *et al.* (2012) argue, as it enables formulation and conceptualization of the underlying construct and its measurement to the target languages at early stages of test development. By using a simultaneous test development approach, decentralized views of test development can be resorted to. These views are important because when adapting tests across languages there might be linguistic and cultural features that cannot be directly translated. This might lead to modifications of the test version in the source language to include references that are not

---

[3] Solano-Flores *et al.* 2009, 83.

centered within one particular (dominant) culture, but instead, are more amenable to transadaptation.

The discussion presented in this chapter is timely, especially when the US faces the challenge of developing the next generation of standardized assessments that measure higher order cognitive skills of *all* students. With large percentages of ELLs in the US and linguistically diverse learners across the world, addressing ways to enable learners to accurately express their content knowledge is imperative. Further, this discussion contributes to understanding the mechanisms of test translation as an accommodation, as the available literature mostly focuses on the effects of translation accommodations on ELL performance (Hofstetter 2003; Kieffer *et al.* 2009). Very few conceptual framework papers (Solano-Flores 2012) exist that discuss major design, administration, and validity issues in translation accommodations for both US-based and international tests. Discussion, as such, would enhance understanding of translation as test accommodation, which could then lead to increased fairness and validity of inferences made based upon results of the next generation assessments administered to linguistically diverse learners. Also, the review presented in this paper about issues and opportunities in administering translation accommodation is intended to serve next generation student assessments that are administered to diverse groups of students in the US and around the world.

To further our understanding of translation accommodation, future empirical research directions might include investigating which content tests are most conducive to providing this accommodation with minimal test translation error. Also, future investigations could be pursued to understand what types of CLDs with interrupted formal schooling would best benefit from translation accommodations. Some might migrate to a new country with a solid background in content knowledge, while others might arrive with neither native language literacy nor any content knowledge. This type of research could be replicated with different groups of CLDs representing various native languages.

## Works cited

Angoff, William H., and Linda Cook. 1988. *Equating the Scores of the College Board Prueba de Aptitud Academica and the College Board Scholastic Aptitude Test. (College Board Report No. 88-2).* New York: College Entrance Examination Board.

Artiles, Alfredo J., Robert Rueda, Jesus J. Salazar, and Ignacio Higareda. 2005. "Within-group Diversity in Minority Disproportionate

Representation: English Language Learners in Urban School Districts." *Exceptional Children* 71(3):283–300.

Batalova, Jeanne, and Margie McHugh. 2010. *Number and Growth of Students in US Schools in Need of English Instruction.* Washington, DC: Migration Policy Institute.

Bowles, Melissa, and Charles W. Stansfield. 2008. *A Practical Guide to Standards-based Assessment in the Native Language.* Illinois: NLA–LEP Partnership.

Brown, Clara L. 2004. "Reducing the Over-referral of Culturally and Linguistically Diverse Students (CLD) for Language Disabilities." *NABE Journal of Research and Practice* 2(1):225–243.

Ercikan, Kadriye, and Kim Koh. 2005. "Examining the Construct Comparability of the English and French Versions of TIMSS." *International Journal of Testing* 5(1):23–35.

Ercikan, Kadriye, Marielle Simon, and Maria E. Oliveri. 2012. "Score Comparability of Multiple Language Versions of Assessments within Jurisdictions." In *Improving Large-scale Assessment in Education: Theory, Issues and Practice,* edited by Marielle Simon, Kadriye Ercikan, and Michael Rousseau, 110–124. New York: Routledge & Taylor and Francis.

Ercikan, Kadriye, Mark J. Gierl, Tanya McCreith, Gautam Puhan, and Kim Koh. 2004. "Comparability of Bilingual Versions of Assessments: Sources of Incomparability of English and French versions of Canada's National Achievement Tests." *Applied Measurement in Education* 17:301–321.

Ercikan, Kadriye, Rubab G. Arim, Danielle M. Law, Jose. F. Domene, France Gagnon, and Serge Lacroix. 2010. "Application of Think-aloud Protocols in Examining Sources of Differential Item Functioning." *Educational Measurement: Issues and Practice* 29(2):24–35.

Ercikan, Kadriye. 2002. "Disentangling Sources of Differential Item Functioning in Multi-language Assessments." *International Journal of Testing* 2:199–215.

Hambleton, Ronald K. 1994. "Guidelines for Adapting Educational and Psychological Tests: A Progress Report." *European Journal of Psychological Assessment* 10:229–244.

Hofstetter, Carolyn H. 2003. "Contextual and Mathematics Accommodation Test Effects for English-Language Learners." *Applied Measurement in Education* 16(2):159–188.

Kieffer, Michael J., Nonie K. Lesaux, Mabel Rivera, and David J. Francis. 2009. "Accommodations for English Language Learners Taking

Large-scale Assessments: A Meta-analysis on Effectiveness and Validity." *Review of Educational Research* 79(3):1168–1201.
Klingner, Janette K., Alfredo J. Artiles, and Laura Méndez Barletta. (2006). "English Language Learners who Struggle with Reading: Language Acquisition or Learning Disabilities?" *Journal of Learning Disabilities* 39:108–128.
Lesaux, Nonie K. 2006. "Building a Consensus: Future Directions for Research on English Language Learners at Risk for Learning Difficulties." *Teachers College Record* 108:2406–2438.
Lesaux, Nonie K., and Esther Geva. 2006. "Development of Literacy in Language-minority Students." In *Developing Literacy in Second-language Learners: Report of the National Literacy Panel on Language-Minority Children and Youth,* edited by Diane August and Timothy Shahan, 53–74. Mahwah, NJ: Lawrence Erlbaum Associates.
Liu, Kristin K., Michael E. Anderson, Bonnie Swierzbin, and Martha L. Thurlow. 1999. *Bilingual Accommodations for Limited English Proficient Students on Statewide Reading Tests: Phase 1.* (*State Assessment Series, Minnesota Report 20.*) Minneapolis, MN: National Center on Educational Outcomes, University of Minnesota.
Martin, Michael O, Keith Rust, Raymond J. Adams. 1999. "Technical Standards for IEA Studies." International Association for the Evaluation of Educational Achievement.
Messick, Samuel. 1994. "The Interplay of Evidence and Consequences in the Validation of Performance Assessments." *Educational Research* 23(2):13–23.
Muniz, Jose, Ronald K. Hambleton, and Dehui Xing. 2001. "Small Sample Studies to Detect Flaws in Item Translations." *International Journal of Testing* 1(2):115–135.
National Center for Education Statistics (NCES). 2004. "English Language Learner Students in US Public Schools: 1994 and 2000." *Issue Brief,* http://nces.ed.gov/pubs2004/2004035.pdf/
—. 2012. "English Language Learners in Public Schools. (Indicator 8-2012)" *The Condition of Education,* http://nces.ed.gov/programs/coe/indicator_ell.asp/
No Child Left Behind (NCLB) Act of 2001. 2002. 20 USC. 70 § 6301 *et seq.*
Oliveri, Maria. E., and Kadriye Ercikan. 2011. "Do Different Approaches to Examining Construct Comparability Lead to Similar Conclusions?" *Applied Measurement in Education* 24:1–18.
Pennock-Roman, Maria, and Charlene Rivera. 2011. "Mean Effects of Test Accommodations for ELLs and non-ELLs: A Meta-analysis of

Experimental Studies." *Educational Measurement: Issues and Practice* 30: 10–28.

Robinson, Joseph P. 2010. "The Effects of Test Translation on Young English Learners' Mathematics Performance." *Educational Researcher* 39(8):582–590.

Roth, Wolff-Michael, Maria E. Oliveri, Debra Sandilands, and Juliette Lyons-Thomas. Forthcoming. "Tracking Sources of DIF Using Expert Think-aloud Protocols." *International Journal of Science Education.*

Roussos, Louis A., and William Stout. 2004. "Differential Item Functioning Analysis." In *The Sage Handbook of Quantitative Methodology for the Social Sciences*, edited by David W. Kaplan, 107–116. Thousand Oaks, CA: Sage.

Sandilands, Debra, Maria E. Oliveri, Bruno D. Zumbo, and Kadriye Ercikan. Forthcoming. "Investigating Sources of Differential Item Functioning in International Large-scale Assessments Using a Confirmatory Approach." *International Journal of Testing.*

Solano-Flores, Guillermo. 2006. "Language, Dialect, and Register: Sociolinguistics and the Estimation of Measurement Error in the Testing of English Language Learners." *Teachers College Record* 108(11):2354–2379.

—. 2008. "Who Is Given Tests in What Language by Whom, When, and Where? The Need for Probabilistic Views of Language in the Testing of English Language Learners." *Educational Researcher* 37(4):189–199.

—. 2012. "Smarter Balanced Assessment Consortium: Translation Accommodations Framework for Testing English Language Learners in Mathematics." *Smarter Balanced Assessment Consortium (SBAC).* September 18, 2012.

Solano-Flores, Guillermo, Eduardo Backhoff, Luis A. Contreras-Niño. 2009. "Theory of Test Translation Error." *International Journal of Testing* 9:78–91.

Solano-Flores, Guillermo, Luis A. Contreras-Niño, and Eduardo Backhoff-Escudero. 2005. "The Mexican Translation of TIMSS-95: Test Translation Lessons from a Postmortem Study." Paper presented at the annual meeting of the National Council on Measurement in Education, Montreal, Quebec, Canada.

Solano-Flores, Guillermo, and Martha Gustafson. 2013. "Academic Assessment of English Language Learners: A Critical, Probabilistic, Systemic View." In *Improving Large Scale Education Assessment in Education: Theory, Issues, and Practice,* edited by Marielle Simon,

Kadriye Ercikan, and Michael Rousseau, 87–109. New York: Routledge & Taylor and Francis.

Solano-Flores, Guillermo, and Min Li. 2008. "Examining the Dependability of Academic Achievement Measures for English-Language Learners." *Assessment for Effective Intervention* 33(3):135–144.

Solano-Flores, Guillermo, and Elise Trumbull. 2003. "Examining Language in Context: The Need for New Research and Practice Paradigms in the Testing of English-language Learners." *Educational Researcher* 32(2):3–13.

Stansfield, Charles W. 2003. "Test Translation and Adaptation in Public Education in the USA." *Language Testing* 20(2):189–207.

—. 2011. "Oral Translation as a Test Accommodation for ELLs." *Language Testing* 28(3):401–416.

Turkan, Sultan, and Maria E. Oliveri. Forthcoming. "Considerations for Providing Test Translation Accommodations on Common Core Standards-Based Assessments." *International Multilingual Research Journal*.

Yu, Alana, and David Ebbs. 2011. "Translation and Translation Verification." In *Methods and Procedures,* edited by Michael O. Martin and Ina V.S. Mullis, 1–13. Chestnut Hill, MA: TIMSS and PIRLS International Study Center, Boston College.

# Chapter Twelve

# Assessing Second/Foreign Language Competence Using Translation: The Case of the College English Test in China

## Youyi Sun and Liying Cheng

### 1. Introduction

Translation as a teaching and learning activity has long been used in the second/foreign language classroom. However, a limited number of empirical studies have investigated the role of translation in second/foreign language teaching and learning, and even less in assessment. Recently, along the development of Translation Studies there has been growing interest in the objects, types, functions, aims and means of translation assessment (Martínez Melis and Hurtado Albir 2001) among researchers from different fields, such as applied linguistics, pragmatics, and cultural studies (Angelelli and Jacobson 2009; Ghanooni 2012; Schäffner 1998). However, there is a lack in empirical studies that investigate the usefulness of translation as a means to assess students' second/foreign language competence.

This study addresses the aforementioned issue by investigating the relationship between students' performance on the translation task of the College English Test (CET) in China and their performance on other tasks of the test, such as listening comprehension, reading comprehension and writing. It also investigates students' perceptions of the translation task in terms of task demand, task difficulty and the validity of the translation test score as a measure of their actual translation ability. Findings of this study not only shed light on the understanding of the validity of translation as a test format in second/foreign language assessment, but also highlight the useful role translation could play in second/foreign language teaching, learning and assessment.

## 2. Translation in second/foreign language teaching/learning and translation ability

Translation has a long tradition as a classroom activity and a test format of students' second/foreign language competence. Up to the end of the 19th century, it was the dominant method to teach the second or foreign language with a focus on learning grammatical rules and vocabulary (Bowen, Madsen and Hilferty 1985). The emergence of the Natural Method Movement, however, challenged the value of translation in second/foreign language teaching and learning (Cook 2007). The criticism of grammar-translation pedagogy has focused on its overemphasis on the learning of written language, i.e. tedious grammar rules and long lists of vocabulary without providing opportunities for students to prepare to communicate in real-world situations (Brown 1994). Thus, since the 1960s, there has been an interest in communicative approaches in second/foreign language teaching with emphasis on meaningful input, i.e. exposing students to the target language in real situations. Innovative approaches such as the Natural Approach (e.g. Krashen and Terrell 1983), the Total Physical Response (TPR) Approach (Asher 1982), and the Suggestopedia Method (Lozanov 1982) were introduced, where the teaching of explicit linguistic forms and the use of the first language were avoided in teaching second/foreign language.

Despite the influences of the Natural Method Movement and the communicative approaches on second/foreign language teaching, translation has never been completely banned in the classroom as a teaching technique and for testing purposes (House 2008) due to its uniqueness in scaffolding students' learning via the first language. Over the past three decades there have been influences of cognitive and constructivist approaches on second language acquisition (SLA) research (e.g. Achard and Niemeier 2004; Robinson 2001). Critics of the approach known as Communicative Language Teaching argue that it is an inappropriate methodology in contexts where accuracy of language use is valued more highly than fluency (Thornbury 2003). There has been an ongoing argument for the integration of explicit instruction of linguistic forms into communicative approaches to second/foreign language teaching in the field of applied linguistics. For example, Ellis (1996) argued that teaching grammar can enhance learner proficiency and accuracy, and assist learners to acquire the syntactic system of the language. Brown (1994) and Larsen-Freeman

(1991) discussed the need for teaching grammar along with communicative tasks. Doughty and Williams (1998) suggested that the *focus-on-form-*instruction should be integrated into language teaching.

Meanwhile, the use of translation in second/foreign language instruction and the role of the first language in SLA have been re-evaluated. For example, Stern (1983) argues that translation can be used with second/foreign language learners to develop an awareness of contrast between native and foreign language items and structures. Machida (2011) lists many of the roles that translation can play in the second/foreign language classroom. These include promoting positive use of learners' first language, assisting higher cognitive development in second/foreign language learners, providing ideal opportunities to focus on form, and increasing *intake* of available input.

House (2008) argues that one important reason for the controversy about translation in the language classroom is the lack of a thorough theoretical understanding of the nature of translation. Translation Studies started as a discipline in the 1970's (Bassnett 2002; Ghanooni 2012; Holmes 2000). The discipline is concerned with complex problems clustered around the phenomenon of translating and translations (Holmes 2000). Since its emergence, research in this area has focused among others on addressing the problem of the actual process involved in translation. Schäffner (1998) points out that given the complexity of translation as both a cognitive and a social activity, it cannot be fully explained by reference to concepts derived from linguistics only, and Translation Studies can be characterized as interdisciplinary.

The notion of translation ability has been expanded from a bilingual perspective, i.e. from adding a source language text-analytical competence and a corresponding target language text-reproductive competence (Wilss 1982) to a multi-component model. For example, Hatim and Mason (1997), drawing on Bachman's (1990) model of communicative language ability, presented a model of the translation process consisting of three phases (source text processing, transfer, target text processing) and named a number of skills for each of those component phases. Hewson (1995) added cultural and professional elements to the notion of translation ability. Angelelli (2009) points out that translation is a multi-dimensional and highly complex activity that involves diverse knowledge, skills and strategies.

The complexity of translation presents challenges for its assessment and evaluation. In recent years, assessment issues in translation have received increasing attention in the field of Translation Studies (e.g. Angelelli and Jacobson 2009; Eyckmans, Anckaert and Segers 2012).

Research into assessment and evaluation in the field of translation has generally focused on three areas: evaluation of translations of literary and sacred texts, assessment of translation professionals at work, and assessment of trainee translators (Martínez Melis and Hurtado Albir 2001). Despite the long history of translation in second/foreign language education, research on translation in second/foreign language assessment has been neglected. Thus, there is a lack of empirical studies investigating the validity of using translation tasks to assess second/foreign language competence.

This study aims to examine the relationship between students' performance on the translation task in the College English Test (CET) in China and their performance on other tasks of the test, such as listening, reading, cloze and writing. It also aims to investigate students' perceptions of the translation task in terms of task demand, task difficulty, their self-efficacy for the task, and of the translation test score as a measure of their actual translation ability.

## 3. The design of the study: Overview and methodology

### 3.1 The College English Test in China[1]

The CET in China was launched in 1987 to promote the implementation of the national College English Teaching Syllabus (now called the College English Curriculum Requirements). The syllabus was developed based on the social and professional needs of college and university students with respect to their language proficiency in English in the context of China's reform and opening-up policy since the late 1970s. College English is a required course for all non-English major undergraduate students in Chinese universities and colleges. Students usually take the CET in their second year when they have completed the College English course. Over the past 20 years or so, the number of CET test-takers has increased dramatically. Currently it has an annual test-taking population of over 18 million (Jin 2011).

Translation was added, together with other task types (*Long Conversations* in *Listening Comprehension*, and *Skimming and Scanning* and *Banked Cloze* in *Reading comprehension*), to the CET in 2006. The purpose of this addition was to align the test with the changing teaching syllabi or curriculum requirements, and promote its positive washback effect on

---

[1] For further and detailed information about the CET see Jin 2009; National College English Testing Committee 2006; Zheng and Cheng 2008.

teaching and learning. This was realized by increasing the weighting of constructed response items, and giving more emphasis to contextualized language use instead of context-free knowledge of language. In order to promote the importance of the CET score, another significant change made by the CET developer in 2006 was to replace the pass/fail rating of the CET certificate with a CET Score Report Form including the overall total score as well as the profile subscore (Jin 2008). Table 1 presents the structure of the latest CET version.

| Test Component | Weighting | Time (minutes) |
| --- | --- | --- |
| **Part I**: Writing | 15 | 30 |
| **Part II**: Skimming and Scanning | 10 | 15 |
| **Part III**: Listening Comprehension<br>Section A: Short Conversations<br>Long Conversations<br>Section B: Listening Passages<br>Section C: Compound Dictation | 35 | 35 |
| **Part IV**: Reading in Depth<br>Section A: Banked Cloze<br>Section B: Passage Reading | 25 | 25 |
| **Part V**: Cloze | 10 | 15 |
| **Part VI**: Translation | 5 | 5 |

**Table 1. CET Test Structure**

Four subscores are reported in the CET Score Report Form in addition to the total score: (A) *Listening Comprehension*, (B) *Reading Comprehension*, (C) *Cloze*, and (D) *Writing and Translation*:

A. *Listening Comprehension* is a measure of students' abilities to understand oral conversations or passages based on standard American or British English. This part includes:
   a. eight *Short Conversations* (one round of conversation and a multiple choice question following each conversation),
   b. two *Long Conversations* (5–8 rounds of conversational exchanges and 3–4 multiple choice questions following each conversation),
   c. three Listening Passages, each followed by 3–4 multiple choice questions,
   d. one Compound Dictation passage, where students are required to fill in the blanks with the exact words they hear (7 items),

and fill in the missing information by using the exact words they hear, or the main points in their own words (3 items).
B. *Reading Comprehension* is a measure of students' ability to understand written English. It includes:
   a. Skimming and Scanning (one long article of approximately 1,000 words, followed by 7 multiple choice questions and 3 sentence completion items. Students have 15 minutes to go over the passage quickly, find the main idea of the passage, locate important information and complete the questions.
   b. Reading in Depth includes two sections:
      1) Banked Cloze (one short passage of 300–350 words with 10 blanks). Students are asked to select one word for each blank from a list of 15 choices given in a word bank following the passage.
      2) Passage Reading (two short passages of 360–380 words, each followed by 5 multiple choice questions).
C. *Cloze* tests students' abilities to understand and infer meanings from vocabulary, sentences, and paragraphs. Students are asked to choose correct answers from four choices for the 20 blanks in a short passage (220–250 words).
D. *Writing and Translation* is a measure of students' ability to communicate ideas using written English.
   a. *Writing*: Students are asked to write a composition of no less than 120 words based on the information provided (e.g. title of the topic, outline, situation, pictures, or graphs etc.).
   b. *Translation*: Students are asked to complete five incomplete English sentences by translating content from Chinese into English provided for each incomplete English sentence. Students have 5 minutes to complete the translation task.

### 3.2 Participants

The participants of this study were 524 (52.5% females, 47.5% males) second-year undergraduate students from two Chinese universities. These students had completed their College English course and were preparing for the CET exam when the data were collected. Their majors included mechanical engineering, finance, accounting, business management and biological engineering. On average, they had learned English for 9.5 years. 86.4% of the participants reported that they were familiar or very familiar with the CET structure, task types and score report.

## 3.3 Instruments and Data Collection

A CET test paper was created by combining different sections of the CET papers from 2006 onwards, and was reviewed by a test developer's representative for accuracy and validity purposes. The test paper was administered to the participants two weeks before they took the official CET. Procedures of the test administration were essentially the same as those of the standard CET test as shown in Table 1 above. To obtain the item-level test score data, responses to the multiple choice items were scored by a scoring machine and responses to the writing and translation items were scored by two experienced CET raters using the CET official scoring rubrics. When there was a disagreement of more than three points between the two raters for the *Writing* section, the discrepancy was adjudicated by a third rater. The other constructed responses such as the *Compound Dictation* and the sentence completion items in *Skimming and Scanning* were scored by the researcher. The item-level test scores within each section of the CET were combined to obtain the section-level test score data. The section-level test score data were used for data analyses in this study. The following are the translation items[2] on the CET test paper used for this study:

*Complete the sentences by translating into English the Chinese given in brackets.*

1. *To make sure that he attends the meeting* (为了确保他参加会议), I called him up in advance.

2. The magnificent museum *is said to have been built* (据说建成于) about a hundred years ago.

3. There would be no life on earth *without the earth's unique environment* (没有地球独特的环境).

4. *What impressed the tourists most (deeply)/What left the deepest impression on the tourists* (给游客印象最深的) was the friendliness and warmth of the local people.

5. They requested that *the books I borrowed be returned to the library* (我借的书还回图书馆) by next Friday.

---

[2] The underlined part in each item is the translation of the Chinese in brackets.

Immediately after the test, the participants were asked to answer a questionnaire[3]. The questionnaire was on the CET test. With regard to translation, it included three 7-point Likert items (1=strongly disagree; 7=strongly agree) and one open-ended question about the knowledge, skills and strategies that are required to answer the CET *Translation* questions. The questionnaire also included an open-ended question about the students' preparation for the CET translation task. There were five 7-point Likert items (1=strongly disagree; 7=strongly agree) in the questionnaire asking the students about their perceptions of the values of the different CET sections in terms of measuring their language use abilities. Eighteen 7-point Likert items (1=strongly disagree; 7=strongly agree) measured students' perceptions of the difficulties of the different sections of the CET and their self-efficacy in English proficiency in relation to test difficulty.

## 3.4 Data Analysis

First, inter-rater reliability for the writing and translation scores assigned by the two raters was calculated. Then, these scores were averaged. The average score was used for the following analyses. Descriptive statistics analyses were performed to test the normality of the distributions of the section-level test scores before conducting the correlation analyses.

To answer the first research question, Pearson correlation analyses were conducted to examine the relationship between students' performance on the CET *Translation* task and their performance on the other tasks of the test, i.e. *Listening Comprehension*, *Reading Comprehension*, *Cloze* and *Writing*. To answer the second research question, descriptive statistics were performed to analyze the questionnaire data. SPSS 17.0 was used for data analysis in this study. For all analyses, a critical value of $\alpha=.05$ was used as statistical significance.

---

[3] This study is part of a larger research project. The questionnaire was developed for this project based on previous research (Green 2007; Hawkey 2006; Xie 2010). It is written in Chinese to ensure the participants' accurate understanding of the items. The questionnaire measures students' perceptions of the CET design, usefulness and values of the test score, as well as their expected demands of the CET and their self-efficacy in English proficiency in relation to the test demands. It also collected data concerning students' learning processes and the demographic data of the participants. Only results about the students' perceptions of the translation section of the CET are reported here.

## 4. Results

Results of the inter-rater reliability analysis showed that the scores assigned by the two raters for the writing and translation sections were highly consistent ($r=.76$, $p$ (one-tailed) <.01 for *Writing*; $r=.87$, $p$ (one-tailed) <.01 for *Translation*.). Descriptive statistics of the section-level test score data are presented in Table 2 below. These statistics provide a description of the students' performance on the CET in general.

| Sections | | N | M | SD | Skewness | Kurtosis |
|---|---|---|---|---|---|---|
| Listening Comprehension | Short Conversations | 524 | 4.91 | 1.96 | -.24 | -.73 |
| | Long Conversations | 524 | 4.58 | 1.69 | -.46 | -.32 |
| | Listening Passages | 524 | 5.20 | 2.24 | .24 | -.26 |
| | Compound Dictation | 524 | 5.17 | 2.34 | -.14 | -.78 |
| Reading Comprehension | Skimming and Scanning | 524 | 7.68 | 1.90 | -1.30 | 1.03 |
| | Banked Cloze | 524 | 2.56 | 1.22 | -.08 | -.39 |
| | Passage Reading | 524 | 12.66 | 3.99 | -.53 | -.14 |
| Cloze | | 524 | 5.65 | 1.66 | -.63 | .69 |
| Writing and Translation | Writing | 524 | 8.13 | 1.75 | -.01 | .74 |
| | Translation | 524 | 2.85 | 1.14 | -.78 | .06 |

**Table 2. Descriptive Statistics of the Section-Level Test Score Data**

Results of the Pearson correlation analyses showed that students' performance on the CET *Translation* task was significantly correlated with their performance on *Writing* [$r=.40$, $p$ (one-tailed) <.01], *Reading Comprehension* [$r=.40$, $p$ (one-tailed) <.01], *Listening Comprehension* [$r=.45$, $p$ (one-tailed) <.01], and *Cloze* [$r=.37$, $p$ (one-tailed) <.01]. Further Pearson correlation analyses indicated that the CET *Translation* score was significantly correlated with the *Compound Dictation* score in *Listening Comprehension* [$r=.42$, $p$ (one-tailed) $<.01$], and the *Banked Cloze* score in *Reading Comprehension* [$r=.36$, $p$ (one-tailed) $<.01$].

| Items in the Questionnaire | N* | M | SD |
|---|---|---|---|
| 1. In order to do the translation section well, knowledge of English grammar and syntax is crucial | 503 | 5.56 | 1.41 |
| 2. In order to do the translation section well, knowledge of English phrases and vocabulary is very important | 503 | 5.98 | 1.38 |
| 3. In order to do the translation section well, translation skills and strategies are necessary | 503 | 4.02 | 1.59 |
| 4. The CET total score provides an accurate measure of my English proficiency in general | 501 | 4.70 | 1.59 |
| 5. The CET Listening Comprehension score provides an accurate measure of my English listening ability | 501 | 4.92 | 1.60 |
| 6. The CET Reading Comprehension score provides an accurate measure of my English reading ability | 501 | 4.94 | 1.58 |
| 7. The CET Writing score provides an accurate measure of my English writing ability | 501 | 4.81 | 1.56 |
| 8. The CET Translation score provides an accurate measure of my English translation ability | 501 | 4.68 | 1.51 |

*15 of the participants did not complete the questionnaire.

**Table 3. Statistics of Students' Perceptions of the CET Translation Task and the Values of Different Sections of the CET**

Descriptive statistics of the questionnaire data concerning students' perceptions of the demand of the CET *Translation* questions (Items 1–3) and their perceptions of the scores on the different CET sections in terms of measuring different aspects of their English language use abilities (Items 4–8) are presented in Table 3 above. These results show that among the knowledge, skills and strategies required to answer the CET *Translation* questions, English lexical knowledge (*M*=5.98; *SD*=1.41) was rated highest by the students, and translation skills and strategies were rated lowest (*M*=4.02; *SD*=1.59). Regarding the students' perceptions of the values of the CET scores as measures of different aspects of their English language use abilities, the students' rating of the CET total score as a measure of their general English language proficiency was low (*M*=4.70; *SD*=1.59) compared with their ratings of the different CET subscores. Among the subscores, *Listening Comprehension* was rated highest (*M*=4.94; *SD*=1.58), and Translation was rated lowest (*M*=4.68; *SD*=1.51).

In responding to the open-ended question *What other skills or knowledge do you think are necessary to do the translation section well in the CET?*, the students highlighted the skills of using English lexical and grammatical knowledge in relation to the context. The students' responses mainly focused on the importance of interpreting the linguistic information in English given in each sentence. For the students, this information provides the context that is crucial to the translation task. By virtue of this information, they can decide, for example, what verbs collocate with what nouns, what tense to use, whether a singular or plural should be used, and other important lexical and grammatical aspects of their translation.

The students' responses also stressed the importance of collocation and idiomaticity in translation. It is important for the students to produce idiomatic expressions in English based on their knowledge of English collocations, and avoid odd expressions in translation due to interference from the Chinese (source) language.

In responding to the open-ended question *How do you prepare for the translation task on the CET?*, the students listed a wide range of English language learning and test preparation activities. The activities that were mentioned most frequently are: a) *paying attention to and memorizing useful collocations from the textbook*, b) *doing translation exercises in the textbook*, c) *paying special attention to the usage of words and expressions*, and d) *reading extensively to get familiar with English expressions*.

Descriptive statistics of the data on students' perceptions of the difficulties in the different CET sections (Items 9–18), and their self-efficacy in English proficiency in relation to different CET tasks (Items 19–28) are presented in Table 4 below. With respect to task difficulty, *Cloze* was perceived as the most difficult by the students (*M*=5.16; *SD*=1.68). Among all the CET task types, the students' rating of the difficulty of *Translation* (*M*=4.55; *SD*=1.71) was relatively low, but higher than that of *Skimming and Scanning* (*M*=4.27; *SD*=1.85) in *Reading Comprehension* and of *Short Conversations* (*M*=4.01; *SD*=2.04) in *Listening Comprehension*. With regard to the students' perceived self-efficacy in the various CET task types, in general, the results showed a higher level of student confidence in tasks with lower level of perceived difficulty such as *Short Conversations* ($M$=5.57; $SD$=1.56) in *Listening Comprehension,* and *Skimming and Scanning* ($M$=5.47; $SD$=1.48), and *Passage Reading* ($M$=5.45; $SD$=1.45) in *Reading Comprehension,* and *Translation* ($M$=5.42; $SD$=1.52).

| Items in the Questionnaire | $N^*$ | $M$ | $SD$ |
|---|---|---|---|
| 9. To me the Short Conversations Section in *Listening Comprehension* of the CET is difficult | 504 | 4.01 | 2.04 |
| 10. To me the Long Conversations Section in *Listening Comprehension* of the CET is difficult | 504 | 4.90 | 1.90 |
| 11. To me the Listening Passages Section in *Listening Comprehension* of the CET is difficult | 504 | 4.93 | 1.81 |
| 12. To me the Compound Dictation Section in *Listening Comprehension* of the CET is difficult | 504 | 4.92 | 1.78 |
| 13. To me the Skimming and Scanning Section in *Reading Comprehension* of the CET is difficult | 504 | 4.27 | 1.85 |
| 14. To me the Banked Cloze Section in *Reading Comprehension* of the CET is difficult | 504 | 4.86 | 1.63 |
| 15. To me the Passage Reading Section in *Reading Comprehension* of the CET is difficult | 504 | 4.47 | 1.72 |
| 16. To me the Translation Section of the CET is difficult | 504 | 4.55 | 1.71 |
| 17. To me the Cloze section of the CET is difficult | 504 | 5.16 | 1.68 |
| 18. To me the Writing Section of the CET is difficult | 504 | 4.77 | 1.69 |
| 19. I have confidence in doing well in the Short Conversations Section in *Listening Comprehension* | 499 | 5.57 | 1.56 |

| | | | |
|---|---|---|---|
| 20. I have confidence in doing well in the Long Conversations Section in *Listening Comprehension* | 499 | 5.19 | 1.58 |
| 21. I have confidence in doing well in the Listening Passages Section in *Listening Comprehension* | 499 | 5.20 | 1.65 |
| 22. I have confidence in doing well in the Compound Dictation Section in *Listening Comprehension* | 499 | 5.17 | 1.59 |
| 23. I have confidence in doing well in the Skimming and Scanning Section in *Reading Comprehension* | 499 | 5.47 | 1.48 |
| 24. I have confidence in doing well in the Banked Cloze Section in *Reading Comprehension* | 499 | 5.18 | 1.55 |
| 25. I have confidence in doing well in the Passage Reading Section in *Reading Comprehension* | 499 | 5.45 | 1.45 |
| 26. I have confidence in doing well in the Translation Section | 499 | 5.42 | 1.52 |
| 27. I have confidence in doing well in the Cloze section | 499 | 5.19 | 1.54 |
| 28. I have confidence in doing well in the Writing Section | 499 | 5.28 | 1.48 |

*15 of the participants did not complete the questionnaire.

**Table 4. Statistics of Students' perceptions of CET *difficulty* and *self-efficacy***

## 5. Discussion

This study examines the relationship between students' performance on the *Translation* task of the CET in China and their performance on the other tasks of the test such as *Listening Comprehension, Reading Comprehension, Writing* and *Cloze*. It also investigates students' perceptions of the difficulty of the *Translation* task, their perceptions of the value of the Translation score as a measure of their translation abilities, as well as their perceptions of their self-efficacy in performing the *Translation* task.

With regard to the relationship between students' performance on the

*Translation* task and their performance on the other CET tasks, results from the correlational analyses suggest significant associations between the *Translation* score and scores for *Listening Comprehension, Reading Comprehension, Writing* and *Cloze* despite task differences in content, mode and format. Given that these subscores are measures of the different but interrelated components of the same construct of English language proficiency, the moderate correlation coefficient between the subscores is not surprising. Considering that a CET subscore of *Writing and Translation* is reported, what is surprising is that the correlation coefficient between the *Translation* score and the *Writing* score is not as high as that between the *Translation* score and the *Listening Comprehension* score. To better understand this issue, further correlations were calculated between the *Translation* score and the scores for all the sections that are included in the *Listening Comprehension* composite score and the *Reading Comprehension* composite score.

Results from these further Pearson correlation analyses indicated that the correlation between the *Translation* score and the *Listening Comprehension* score could be accounted for mainly by the significant correlation between the *Translation* score and the *Compound Dictation* score within *Listening Comprehension*. Furthermore, the results also indicated that the correlation between the *Translation* score and the Reading Comprehension score was mainly accounted for by the significant correlation between the *Translation* score and the *Banked Cloze* score within *Reading Comprehension*. To explain these findings, it is necessary to closely compare these three CET task types—*Translation, Compound Dictation* and *Banked Cloze.*

All these three tasks of the CET provide contextual information in written English. The students are required to use accurate lexical and grammatical forms to complete the tasks in relation to the contextual information provided. These task types are different in some respects. For example, while the *Translation* task requires the students to construct their responses based on the content information provided in written Chinese, the *Compound Dictation* task requires the students to do so based on the English input they hear. The *Banked Cloze* task, on the other hand, requires the students to make choices among words given. These differences imply that different cognitive processes and different student's strategies may be involved in completing these different tasks.

Results from analysis of the questionnaire data on students' perceptions of the *Translation* task demand and the values of the Translation score suggest that this CET task measures students' English lexical and grammatical knowledge and their skills in using this knowledge in relation to context, rather than their translation ability. This finding is consistent with the results from the correlation analysis discussed above. It presents a challenge to the validity of the CET in terms of the interpretation and use of its *Writing and Translation* subscore, although the score for *Translation* only accounts for 5% of the CET total score. Translation ability, as it is defined and discussed in the literature of translation studies (e.g. Angelelli 2009; Hatim and Mason 1997; Hewson 1995), is a complex and multi-componential construct, in which accurate use of the lexical and grammatical forms of the target language (English in this case) is a necessary but not sufficient condition.

Based on the results from analysis of the questionnaire data on students' perceptions of task difficulty and perceptions of self-efficacy, the level of perceived difficulty of the *Translation* task is relatively low and the level of perceived self-efficacy for it is relatively high, compared, in particular, with the *Compound Dictation* task and the *Banked Cloze* task. One possible explanation for this is that, for translation, the input in the first language induces lower cognitive load on the students, and consequently a lower level of difficulty. Thus, they have more flexibility in translation compared with Compound Dictation. Results of the questionnaire data on students' learning activities for the preparation for the CET *Translation* task suggest that this type of task may induce positive washback on students' second/foreign language learning in terms of *focus on form* (Doughty and Williams, 1998). For this, further research should be conducted.

## 6. Conclusions

The findings of this study indicate that the CET translation task has moderate correlation with other tasks, and thus the translation task can be used to measure second/foreign language competency in large-scale second/foreign language testing such as the CET. Pedagogically, the use of the first language in this CET translation task helps reduce the cognitive load on students and thus allows them to direct more attention to the accurate use of the target language form in context. To better understand this benefit of translation for second/foreign language learning, further research should be conducted. More particularly, future research can further investigate students' perceptions of the translation task in comparison with their perceptions of other task types, and the cognitive processes and strategies involved in completing different types of tasks.

It is not clear whether translation can be treated as a separate construct in the CET based on the data collected from this study. Reporting the CET score for translation as a measure of students' translation ability may threaten the validity of the test in terms of construct underrepresentation, given the complexity of the translation construct. Considering the moderate correlation between translation and writing, the CET may not have a valid case to combine writing and translation scores and report a subscore of *Writing and Translation*. To better understand the construct validity of the CET, it is necessary for future research to examine the factor structure of the test, using, for example, confirmatory factor analysis.

## Works cited

Achard, Michel, and Susanne Niemeier. 2004. *Cognitive Linguistics, Second Language Acquisition, and Foreign Language Teaching*. Berlin: Mouton de Gruyter.
Angelelli, Claudia. 2009. "Using a Rubric to Assess Translation Ability: Defining the Construct." In *Testing and Assessment in Translation and Interpreting*, edited by Claudia Angelelli, and Holly Jacobson, 13–49. Amsterdam: Benjamins.
Angelelli, Claudia, and Holly Jacobson, eds. 2009. *Testing and Assessment in Translation and Interpreting*. Amsterdam: Benjamins.
Asher, James J. 1982. *Learning Another Language through Actions: The Complete Teacher's Guidebook*, Second edition. Los Gatos, CA: Sky Oaks Productions.
Bachman, Lyle F. 1990. *Fundamental Considerations in Language Testing*. Oxford: Oxford University Press.
Bassnett, Susan. 2002. *Translation Studies,* Third Edition. New York: Routledge.
Bowen, Donald, Harold Madsen, and Ann Hilferty. 1985. *TESOL: Techniques and Procedures*. Rowley, MA: Newbury House Publishers.
Brown, Douglas H. 1994. *Principles of Language Learning and Teaching*. Englewood Cliffs, NJ: Prentice Hall Regents.
Cook, Guy. (2007). "A Thing of the Future: Translation in Language Learning." *International Journal of Applied Linguistics* 17(3):396–401.
Doughty, Catherine, and Jessica Williams, eds. 1998. *Focus on Form in Classroom Second Language Acquisition.* Cambridge: Cambridge University Press.
Ellis, Nick. 1996. "Sequencing in SLA: Phonological Memory, Chunking and Points of Order." *Studies in Second Language Acquisition* 18:91–126.
Eyckmans, June, Philippe Anckaert, and Winibert Segers. 2012. "Translation Assessment within a Common European Framework." In *Collaboration*

in *Language Testing and Assessment*, edited by Dina Tsagari and Ildiko Csepes, 171–184. Frankfurt: Peter Lang.
Ghanooni, Ali Reza. 2012. "A Review of the History of Translation Studies." *Theory and Practice in Language Studies* 2(1):77–85.
Green, Anthony. 2007. *IELTS Washback in Context: Preparation for Academic Writing in Higher Education, Studies in Language Testing* 25. Cambridge: Cambridge University Press and Cambridge ESOL.
Hatim, Basil, and Ian Mason. 1997. *The Translator as Communicator*. London & New York: Routledge.
Hawkey, Roger. 2006. *Impact Theory and Practice: Studies of the IELTS Test and Progetto Lingue 2000*. Cambridge: Cambridge University Press.
Hewson, Lance. 1995. "Detecting Cultural Shifts: Some Notes on Translation Assessment." In *Cross-words. Issues and Debates in Literary and Non-literary Translating*, edited by Ian Mason and Christine Pagnoulle, 101–108. Liège: L3–Liège Language and Literature.
Holmes, James S. 2000. "The Name and Nature of Translation Studies." In *The Translation Studies Reader*, edited by Lawrence Venuti, 172–185. New York: Routledge.
House, Juliane. 2008. "Using Translation to Improve Pragmatic Competence." In *Investigating Pragmatics in Foreign Language Learning, Teaching and Testing*, edited by Eva Alcon Soler, and Alicia Martinez-Flor, 135–152. Bristol: Multilingual Matters.
Jin, Yan. 2008. "Powerful Test, Powerless Test Designers: Challenges Facing the College English Test." *Teaching English in China* 31(5):3–11.
—. 2009. "The National College English Testing Committee." In *English Language Assessment and the Chinese Learner*, edited by Liying Cheng, and Andy Curtis, 44–59. New York: Routledge.
—. 2011. "Fundamental Concerns in High-stakes Language Testing: The Case of the College English Test." Paper presented at the 16th Conference of Pan-Pacific Association of Applied Linguistics Conference, Hong Kong.
Krashen, Stephen D., and Tracy D Terrell. 1983. *The Natural Approach: Language Acquisition in the Classroom*. Oxford: Pergamon/Alemany.
Larsen-Freeman, Diane. 1991. "Teaching Grammar." In *Teaching English as a Second or Foreign Language,* edited by Marianne Celce-Murcia, 279–295. Boston: Heinle & Heinle.
Lozanov, Georgi. 1982. "Suggestology and Suggestopedia." In *Innovative Approaches to Language Teaching,* edited by Robert W. Blair, 146–159. Rowley, MA: Newbury House Publishers.

Machida, Sayuki. 2011. "Translation in Teaching a Foreign (Second) Language: A Methodological Perspective." *Journal of Language Teaching and Research* 2(4):740–746.

Martínez Melis, Nicole, and Amparo Hurtado Albir. 2001. "Assessment in Translation Studies: Research Needs." *Meta* 46(2):272–287.

National College English Testing Committee. 2006. *CET-4 Test Syllabus and Sample Test Paper (Revised Version)*. Shanghai: Shanghai Foreign Language Education Press.

Robinson, Peter, ed. 2001. *Cognition and Second Language Instruction*. Cambridge: Cambridge University Press.

Schäffner, Christina. 1998. "Qualification for Professional Translators: Translation in Language Teaching versus Teaching Translation." In *Translation and Language Teaching*, edited by Kirsten Malmkjaer, 117–134. Manchester: St. Jerome.

Stern, Hans H. 1983. *Fundamental Concepts of Language Teaching*. Oxford: Oxford University Press.

Thornbury, Scott. 2003. *How to Teach Grammar*. Beijing: World Affairs Press.

Wilss, Wolfram. 1982. *The Science of Translation: Problems and Methods*. Tübingen: Narr.

Xie, Qin. 2010. "Test Design and Use, Preparation, and Performance: A Structural Equation Modeling Study of Consequential Validity." PhD diss., The University of Hong Kong.

Zheng, Ying, and Liying Cheng. 2008. "Test Review: College English Test (CET) in China." *Language Testing* 25:408–417.

# CONTRIBUTORS

*(in alphabetical order)*

**Beecroft, Raphaëlle** (*beecroft@ph-heidelberg.de*) is a researcher and Lecturer in foreign language teaching at the Heidelberg University, Germany. She specializes in the didactics of English for young learners as well as in teacher education in the same field. As an academically trained translator, she is interested in creating an interface between Translation Studies and Foreign Language Teaching. She is currently completing PhD research on improvisational theatre in foreign language teaching to promote speaking skills. Further research interests include the development of ICC, classroom-based language assessment and cultural studies.

**Belpoliti, Flavia** (*flbelpol@Central.UH.EDU*) is Assistant Professor at the Hispanic Studies Department of the University of Houston, USA. She teaches Hispanic linguistics and leads the Spanish Language Program. Her research interests include second- and heritage language acquisition, language teaching, discourse analysis and Spanish sociolinguistics. She has participated in a number of research projects developing assessments and materials for L2, and currently co-coordinates the Spanish-to-English Translation Certificate at the University of Houston.

**Bratož, Silva** (*Silva.Bratoz@pef.upr.si*) is Assistant Professor of English at the Faculty of Education of the University of Primorska, Slovenia, where she teaches several courses in the area of English language teaching. She has researched and published in the field of second language teaching and acquisition, cognitive linguistics, discourse studies and metaphor theory. Her current research focuses on exploring the potential of classroom interaction in English and applying cognitive linguistics principles in second language teaching.

**Cabrera, Julio** (*jcabrera@ets.org*) is Research fellow at the Foundational and Validity Research Division of the Educational Testing Service in Princeton, New Jersey, USA. He has researched, published, and presented in the fields of measurement, statistics, and psychometrics, with an emphasis in English language learning. He has worked on research projects funded by the National Science Foundation of the USA, and the Robert Wood Johnson Foundation, among others.

**Calfoglou, Christine** (*xkalfog@yahoo.gr*) is a linguist and has also specialized in translation and translation theory. She has taught general translation and linguistics courses as well as specialized and literary translation at the University of Athens, Greece. Her research and published work includes poetry translation, translation theory and linguistics, translation and teaching, semiotics, applied linguistics and distance education methodology. She is currently teaching on the MEd Program of the Hellenic Open University in Greece and is assistant editor of *RPLTL*, an online scientific journal.

**Cheng, Liying** (*liying.cheng@queensu.ca*) is Professor at the Faculty of Education, Queen's University in Kingston, Canada. She is also Director of the Assessment and Evaluation Group (AEG). Her primary research interests are the impact of large-scale testing on instruction, and the relationships between assessment and instruction. Her work has appeared in *Language Testing*, *Language Assessment Quarterly*, *Assessment in Education*, and *Assessment & Evaluation in Higher Education*. Her recent single-authored book, published under *TESOL English Language Teacher Development Series*, is entitled *Language Classroom Assessment* (2013).

**ElAtia, Samira** (*selatia@ualberta.ca*) is Associate Professor of Education and Languages at the University of Alberta, Canada. She has researched and published in the fields of language assessment and language acquisition, French language learning and teaching, sociolinguistic factors in educational tests and the interface between language policy and language assessment. She is the coordinator of language assessment services at Campus Saint-Jean of the University of Alberta and founding member of the Canadian Association of Language Assessment.

**Ibáñez Moreno, Ana** (*ana.ibanezmoreno2@hogent.be*) is Lecturer in English Language and Linguistics at the Faculty of Philology of the Spanish National University of Distance Education. She is also a researcher at the Faculty of Applied Language Studies of the University College of Ghent, Belgium. Her recent work deals with Flemish students' errors and communicative strategies when learning Spanish as a foreign language, as well as with the application of different didactic techniques in computer-assisted English language learning by Spanish students.

**Källkvist, Marie** (*marie.kallkvist@englund.lu.se*) is Associate Professor of English Linguistics at Lund University, Sweden. Her research and publications are in the fields of instructed second language acquisition, the acquisition of L2 grammar and vocabulary, language policy in education, and teaching and learning in higher education. She has carried out longitudinal research on the effect of translation on the learning of L2 grammar and on classroom interaction. She is currently conducting ethnographic research on the formation of language policy in higher education.

**Kocbek, Alenka** (*alenka.kocbek@fm-kp.si*) is Assistant Professor of English and German at the Faculty of Education, University of Primorska in Koper, Slovenia. She earned her BA in English and German and her PhD in linguistics from the Faculty of Arts in Ljubljana. She is member of the Association of Scientific and Technical Translators of Slovenia and of the European Society for Translation Studies. Her research interests include translation studies with a special focus on the cultural embeddedness of non-literary texts, legal translation and interpreting, and the role of translation in language teaching.

**Kokkinidou, Anna** (*annoukared@gmail.com*) is a lawyer, translator and foreign language teacher, currently working as a research associate at the Centre for the Greek Language in Athens (Hellenic Ministry of Education and Religious Affairs, Culture and Sports). Her research interests include legal translation as well as translation and foreign language teaching and assessment. She is equally involved in distance learning and the testing of Greek as a second/foreign language as well as to legal consulting relating to language certification. She has participated in various research projects either as researcher or as project coordinator.

**Koletnik Korošec, Melita** (*melitakk@gmail.com*) is Teaching Assistant at the Faculty of Arts of the University of Maribor in Slovenia, where she teaches students of English translation at the Department for Translation Studies. She holds an MA from the University of Graz, Austria, and is currently studying towards a PhD in translation studies at the University of Ljubljana. Her research interests include specialised translation (legal, financial, humanities) as well as intercultural communication and translator education, which is also the topic of her PhD thesis.

**Lee, Tzu-yi** (*t.y.lee@cycu.edu.tw*) received her PhD degree in Translating and Interpreting from Newcastle University, UK, in 2010. She currently works as Assistant Professor in the Department of Applied Linguistics and Language Study at Chung Yuan Christian University, Taiwan. Her research interests include literary translation, gender and translation, culture and translation, translation pedagogy, translation and ideologies.

**Oliveri, Maria Elena** (*moliveri@ets.org*) is Associate Research Scientist at the Foundational and Validity Research Division of the Educational Testing Service in Princeton, New Jersey, USA. Her research focuses on validity research and advances in psychometric modeling in relation to assessing culturally and linguistically diverse populations. She received an MA and a PhD in measurement, evaluation and research methodology from the University of British Columbia, Canada. She has over 15 years experience in instructing students from diverse cultural and linguistic backgrounds in the public school system.

**Plascencia-Vela, Amira** (*aplascen@Central.UH.EDU*) currently teaches Translation and Spanish as a Heritage Language at the Hispanic Studies Department of the University of Houston. She received her PhD in Spanish from the University of Houston in 2010. Her main research areas include US-Hispanic literature, Spanish as a heritage language in the US, translation studies and translation pedagogy.

**Spanou, Kyriaki** (*kirspanou@yahoo.com*) holds a BA in English Language and Literature from the University of Athens, a MEd in Educational Technology from the University of Manchester, and a Diploma in Translation from the Chartered Institute of Linguists in UK. She has worked as a teacher of English in private and public schools and as a researcher for the Centre for the Greek Language, where she was mostly involved in research programs in the area of teaching and testing Greek as a foreign/second language. She has also worked extensively as a translator and proofreader on a freelance basis both in Greece and abroad.

**Sun, Youyi** (*youyi.sun@queensu.ca*) is Assessment Consultant in Manitoba Education and PhD candidate in the Assessment and Evaluation Group (AEG) at the Faculty of Education, Queen's University in Kingston, Canada. His primary research interests include the interactions between assessment, teaching and learning, and the consequences and validation of large-scale testing. His recent publications include papers in

*Assessment in Education: Principles, Policy & Practice*, the *Canadian Journal of Applied Linguistics* and *Assessment Matters*.

**Turkan, Sultan** (*sturkan@ets.org*) is Associate Research Scientist at the Foundational and Validity Research Division of the Educational Testing Service in Princeton, New Jersey, USA. She received her PhD in teaching and teacher education with a focus on English language teaching and testing from the University of Arizona. She has researched and published in the areas of test fairness and valid accommodations for linguistically and culturally diverse learners, and measurement of effective content teaching to English language learners. She has experience in teaching English as a second language and diversity classes to pre-service content teachers in the USA.

**Vermeulen, Anna** (*anna.vermeulen@hogent.be*) is Senior Lecturer at the Faculty of Applied Language Studies of the University College of Ghent, Belgium. She teaches Spanish as a foreign language, translation from Spanish into Dutch and audiovisual translation (AVT). Her research interests and publications focus on linguistic variation in audiovisual translation, as well as the possibilities of using AVT as a didactic tool for FLA. She has held conferences and workshops at many universities in Spain and Latin America as a visiting professor.